Ragtime TO WARTIME

THE BEST OF
GOOD HOUSEKEEPING
1922 · 1939

Good Housekeeping

ONE SHILLING NETT · FEBRUARY 1932

Why are we failing the dead? *by* Godfrey Winn

Lorna Rea ~ O.Douglas ~ Mabel Constanduros
L.A.G.Strong ~ A.Duff Cooper ~ Clemence Dane

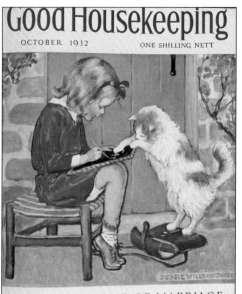

Good Housekeeping

OCTOBER 1932 · ONE SHILLING NETT

THE TECHNIQUE OF MARRIAGE
A New Series by Mary Borden

Martin Armstrong ~ Dame Ethel Smyth ~ Virginia Woolf
A.S.M Hutchinson ~ Lady Violet Bonham Carter

Good Housekeeping

December 1932

CHRISTMAS NUMBER

D.K.Broster ~ Vicki Baum ~ Francis Brett Young
I.A.R.Wylie ~ Kate O'Brien ~ Walter de la Mare

Good Housekeeping

DECEMBER 1934

Christmas Number

New Novel by Joanna Cannan

Beverley Nichols ~ Susan Ertz ~ Warwick Deeping
Maude Royden ~ Kathleen Norris ~ Temple Bailey

Good Housekeeping

JANUARY 1935 · ONE SHILLING NETT

Complete Story by
MARY PICKFORD

Doreen Wallace ~ Sylvia Thompson
Mary Roberts Rinehart ~ Naomi Mitchison
Articles of Special Appeal to All Who Love Children

Good Housekeeping

FEBRUARY 1935 · ONE SHILLING NETT

Special Illustrated Supplement :
SUGGESTIONS FOR GARDEN PLANNING
New Complete Story by Dorothy Whipple
Clare Sheridan : Joanna Cannan : Virginia Pye
Ursula Parrott : Emma Lindsay Squier

Good Housekeeping

JULY 1935 · ONE SHILLING NETT

NEW SHORT SERIAL by DOROTHY WHIPPLE
Sinclair Lewis : This Golden Half Century
Robert Bernays — Phyllis Duganne
Dr. W. Howard Hay — Sewell Stokes — Neil Bell

Good Housekeeping

SEPTEMBER. 1935 — ONE SHILLING

The Institute's Eleventh Birthday

Mary Roberts Rinehart ~ Naomi Mitchison
Noel Streatfeild ~ Countess of Oxford and Asquith
Christine Jope-Slade ~ Beverley Nichols

Good Housekeeping

NOVEMBER · 1935 · ONE SHILLING ·

WHAT IS THE MAIN BUSINESS OF LIFE ?
by Beatrice Kean Seymour *and* Vera Brittain

Mazo de la Roche ~ R.C.Sherriff
Michael Harrison ~ Eric Linklater

Ragtime TO WARTIME

THE BEST OF
GOOD HOUSEKEEPING
1922 · 1939

COMPILED BY

BRIAN BRAITHWAITE

NOËLLE WALSH

GLYN DAVIES

LEOPARD

This edition published in 1995 by Leopard Books
Random House, 20 Vauxhall Bridge Road, London SW1V 2SA

Copyright © 1986 by The National Magazine Company Limited

ISBN 0 7529 0045 5

Designer: Glyn Davies
Art Director: Frank Phillips
Editor: Suzanne Webber

Printed and bound in Great Britain by
Butler and Tanner, Frome and London

CONTENTS

The 1920's

The 1930's

FOREWORD

Good Housekeeping has been a leading magazine for 64 years, one-third of which I have had the privilege of sharing. As Deputy Editor since 1964 and Editor since 1973 I can hardly remember life before. For *Good Housekeeping* is not just a magazine, it's more a way of life – and the people who work on it (many of whom stay for years), all feel totally committed.

Our readers are loyal, too. Though they may originally have turned to *Good Housekeeping* for advice on setting up home, they stay with us because of the breadth of subjects that reflect the important issues in their lives at different stages. At our Diamond Anniversary celebrations in 1982 we met one family of three generations of readers: granny aged 84 having never missed a single issue.

I wasn't born in 1922 when the magazine was created and I was a schoolgirl at the start of the war where this book ends. I got married in 1948 when there was still food rationing and I needed the help of *Good Housekeeping* and its step-by-step cookery books.

It was to help people like myself that the magazine was conceived: to teach middle-class women how to run their homes, especially after the First World War, when the days of domestic help suddenly came to an end. Now, over 60 years later, women still need help and information – not only on the art of domestic

management and entertainment – but on the problems of family life and often, too, on the balancing act between home and career.

Good Housekeeping was the first consumer protection organisation in this country. Today, with legislation and 'fair trading', Britain leads the European community in consumer matters. Although the famous Seal of Guarantee no longer exists, its influence still lives on – as household equipment becomes even more sophisticated and complicated, *Good Housekeeping* continues to give guidance, explanation and words of caution.

Modern technology has helped us all to get out of the kitchen and the wide variety of subjects in the magazine of the Eighties reflects the fact that our choices are greater. In the year 2000 our readers will probably think we were all obsessed with home computers, microwaves and problems of the environment. Who knows what their major concerns will be?

Today, we can laugh at some of the problems and worries of the Twenties and Thirties shown in the following pages. But whatever the issues of the day – in the kitchen, boardroom or space shuttle – *Good Housekeeping* will always be there to help and advise with humour and understanding, I hope. Be sure to read this book and share our happy nostalgia for the way we were.

CHARLOTTE LESSING
FORMER EDITOR-IN-CHIEF, *GOOD HOUSEKEEPING*

Charlotte Lessing

The 1920's

In 1922, the first issue of *Good Housekeeping* appeared on the newsagents' shelves. It offered a new and exciting mixture of practical information, outspoken opinions, great contemporary fiction and fashion and beauty news to an audience who were themselves going through a challenging and stimulating time.

The end of the First World War, four years earlier, had brought about widespread social and economic changes which had an irrevocable effect on women's role in society: more women in the workplace, fewer domestic servants, new questioning attitudes towards marriage, technological advances in the home, and last, but not least, the first woman MP, Nancy Astor, to take her seat in the House of Commons.

Across the Atlantic, the Twenties boom was reflected in the era of the Flapper girls, the Jazz Age, and the birth of the Hollywood legend, while here the middle classes enjoyed a comfortable lifestyle which is reflected in the following pages.

The opening of the *Good Housekeeping* Institute in 1924 and the introduction of the *Good Housekeeping* Seal of Approval gave women easy access to expert consumer advice for the first time, while the *Good Housekeeping* Restaurant, opened in Oxford Street in 1927, was an extension of the invaluable service provided by the cookery team at *Good Housekeeping*. Whether you wanted to know how to bring up your child, what career to take up, how to keep skin young and beautiful, what length to wear your skirt that year, how to store vegetables so they would keep, what to do to save a rocky marriage – or if you simply wanted a good read – *Good Housekeeping* could provide the key.

But side by side with this recognition of the role of woman as homemaker (the good housekeeper is 'the keystone of the arch', and 'the pillar of the house', according to the first editorial), was a strong determination to air the burning issues of the day, discuss politics as it affected women and educate its readers in the fine arts.

That the Great War had caused the birth of a new attitude to women was evidenced by so many articles of the time. As W L George wrote in *Woman of the World* (page 12) '. . . great movements of mankind, like a European war, which tend to remake the face of the world, can affect women more than they do men, because they leave men where they are, while they make for women a new world with which they must cope.'

But the new role also created new problems. Women didn't want to give up their revered position as wives and mothers; nor did they want to choose between the traditional role and the pleasures and delights of newly-discovered independence. The stresses and strains of trying to cope with both were issues which then – as now – were discussed again and again in the pages of *Good Housekeeping*.

In *Should Married Women Work?* (page 29) Mrs Alfred Sidgwick tried to find an answer to the perennial problem of coping with the dual role. 'Everyone who takes an interest in the welfare of women knows that happiness and freedom hang on their economic independence. A woman should either own money or earn it.' And 'No one minds, as a rule, how much a woman drudges for her husband and children, but if she earns money in order to pay others to drudge, she is a shirker and her employees are slaves. What nonsense. The best thing for a nation is for every man, woman and child in it to do what they can do, well.'

The home, though, was the heart of *Good Housekeeping* – whether it was detailing the merits of the new food mixing machines, planning the layout of a bedroom or discussing the difficulty in obtaining a good housemaid. In fact, a committee was actually appointed to enquire into the conditions and supply of female domestic servants. With factories and shops now taking on large numbers of female workers, domestic servants had someone to compare themselves with and quickly abandoned the arduous duties and long working hours of previous decades. For the first time, middle-class women had to learn about housework and for this information they turned to *Good Housekeeping*.

Fashion has always been another staple ingredient of the magazine. Readers of the Twenties were fortunate to be able to make use of *Good Housekeeping*'s London Shopping Service whereby items of clothing displayed in the magazine were bought by the staff for those readers who were unable to get up to town. This was the forerunner of the hugely popular *Good Housekeeping* Shopping Club which still exists today.

But *Good Housekeeping* wasn't simply a serious magazine catering for middle-class women. It enjoyed provoking, teasing even, its readers as well as offering them lighter moments and great fiction, which unfortunately due to lack of space, we cannot reproduce here. Beverley Nichols probably aroused a few women to anger with his assertion, *I Would Make a Better Housekeeper Than Most Women I Know* (page 84). He firmly believed that no woman wants a good servant. 'Have you never seen a woman's eyes light up in ecstasy as she describes the nefarious practices of her cook? If a deaf man were to be present while a body of women were discussing the utter vileness, brutality, horror and criminality of their domestic staff, he would imagine by the radiant happiness of the women's expressions that he had intruded upon a gathering of literary ladies reciting passages from the lyric poems of the late Algernon Charles Swinburne.'

The change in women's perception of themselves, as well as society's perception of women, is described by Arnold Bennett in 1927. He recalls how, when he was asked to be editor of *Woman*, then a penny illustrated weekly paper, in 1896 (*Editing a Woman's Paper*, page 78), the general editorial conviction was that the chief interest of an educated woman was her personal appearance, followed by housekeeping, furnishing, health and hygiene.

Thirty-one years later, he reflects on the changes wrought by war, the advent of long skirts, short hair, the foxtrot and careers for women. He attributed the change in women's magazines to women's increasing awareness of themselves and their capabilities.

Two things are immediately apparent when leafing through the ads of the Twenties: the copywriters' art was polite, instructive and logical, without pushing the hyperbole too far. Humour was rare – the headline was all-important, and the short, sharp phrases of today were practically non-existent. The second factor was the impressively high standard of the commercial art.

Constipation and successful bowel-actions were deemed to be of the utmost importance if the number of advertisements discussing such activities are anything to go by. The motoring advertisements are mouth-watering – not only in price but also in style. Hot health drinks, salts and stomach powders were miracle workers while housewives were seen reacting in an ecstatic manner to their husband's Christmas gift of a vacuum cleaner.

Testimonials were popular with advertisers, particularly those from the lips of stage actresses and society beauties. Beauty advertising was fairly sparse and tended to concentrate on face powder, soap, unwanted hair and shampoos, with only an occasional whiff of eau de cologne. Floor polish, light bulbs, grates, dry-cleaning, charladies, housemaids and mattresses are all there in profusion. Intimate subjects were frequently discussed, often as dialogue between women or mother and daughter. And no child of the Twenties will restrain a lump in the throat at the sight of the Pathescope film projector, or the Hornby train sets.

Alas, we have had to curtail our advertising selection otherwise the book would have been enormous, and not all the subjects mentioned above are represented. Those that are, are seldom adjacent to the original editorial or even in the same issue or year. However, they do come from the same decade, and are as representative as possible, giving the flavours and charm of commercial life in the Twenties.

NOËLLE WALSH
BRIAN BRAITHWAITE

Halcyon Days

Early Housekeeping Days

There is time just to pause to take a piece of Mackintosh's, and as she enjoys it, continuing her duties, she determines that Mackintosh's Toffee-de-Luxe must feature in the weekly budget.

Sold loose by weight at 8d. per ¼-lb.; and in "Baby" Tins 1/3 each, "Tall" Tins 1/3 and 2/6 each, and in 4-lb. "Family" Tins. All the flavours are favourites with everyone, everywhere.

Egg and Cream-de-Luxe.   Chocolate Toffee-de-Luxe.
Cocoanut-de-Luxe.   Almond Toffee-de-Luxe.
Cafe-de-Luxe.   Mint-de-Luxe.
Plain Toffee-de-Luxe.   De-Luxe Assortment.

*Mackintosh's Toffee-de-Luxe has
the largest Sale in the World.*

MACKINTOSH'S
Toffee-de-Luxe

The Quality Sweetmeat

The Reason For
GOOD HOUSEKEEPING

*"Neither do men light a candle, and put it
under a bushel, but on a candlestick; and it
giveth light unto all that are in the house"*

ANY keen observer of the times cannot
have failed to notice that we are on the
threshold of a great feminine awaken-
ing. Apathy and levity are alike giving place
to a wholesome and intelligent interest in the
affairs of life, and above all in the home. We
believe that the time is ripe for a great new
magazine which shall worthily meet the needs
of the homekeeping woman of to-day.

There should be no drudgery in the house.
There must be time to think, to read, to enjoy
life, to be young with the growing generation,
to have time for their pleasures, to have leisure
for one's own—to hold one's youth as long as
possible, to have beauty around us—line and
colour in dress, form and colour in our surroundings; to have good food without monotony, and good service without jangled tempers.

It will be the aim of GOOD HOUSEKEEPING to
meet these needs and to forestall them. The
daily life of women—what concerns them and
interests them most profoundly and most intimately, what they talk about, think about, and
wish to read about in their favourite magazine
—will be the first concern of GOOD HOUSEKEEP-
ING. The burning questions of the day will
be reflected each month in articles by women in
the public eye, known for their sound grasp
of their subject—by women who can lead
women, and who are fearless, frank, and outspoken. All sides and phases of women's interest—art, music, and the drama, and the
social side of life—will find a place on our
platform, and both sides of every open question
will be given a hearing, though partisan politics
and parties will be rigorously excluded. Women
writers, whose words are waited for and whose
views are valued by other women all over the
kingdom, will be among our honoured contributors.

The house-proud woman in these days of
servant shortage does not always know the best
ways to lessen her own burdens. Household
management will be a feature of GOOD HOUSE-
KEEPING, and every new invention that is practical and economical in use will be brought to
her notice after careful examination month by
month. The time spent on housework can be
enormously reduced in every home, without any
loss to its comfort, and often with a great increase to its well-being and its air of personal
care and attention.

Fashions will be an important feature of
GOOD HOUSEKEEPING. They will be in two
sections—French and English. A very exclusive and complete service of French fashions,
such as has not been hitherto supplied to any
English magazine, will be sent over by our
representatives in Paris, where we have an
office and staff who will keep in closest touch
with all the great French houses and contribute
sketches that will anticipate every change in

line. They will supply designs that we venture
to think will be found of extraordinary value to
those whose business it is to study fashion as
well as to those whose pleasure it is to follow
it. Our French fashion service will be something quite unique in the history of Women's
papers. English fashions will be seen reflected
in sketches from the great London houses.
They will also be an important feature. English fashions have steadily improved in taste
and design, and it will be the pleasant duty of
GOOD HOUSEKEEPING to show how very good
they are—and to help those of our readers who
are out of reach of the London shops to buy
the very best that is being shown in them.
There will be a shopping service in connection
with the sketches from the London shops, and
this service will be available to all our readers.

Home cookery is nearly always good, but
the family menu is sometimes a little monotonous because the housekeeper has no time to
test new dishes and has a certain suspicion of
the *untested* recipe. Well, in the offices of
GOOD HOUSEKEEPING, a modern and properly
equipped kitchen has been installed, and there
every recipe before being printed will be tested,
and only those recipes which have passed the
test of a widely known practical cookery expert,
skilled in the knowledge of what a family wel-
comes, will be given. These dishes, old and
new, will be closely described, and there will
be nothing casual about their choice or their
explanations. They will be well worth keeping
in the note-book that is always found on the
good housekeeper's kitchen shelf.

House decoration changes with other
fashions, and the house-proud woman likes to
know what is being done in big and little houses
—how cretonnes are coloured and patterned for
country house and town house, how furniture is
being made for bedroom and living-room, what
periods are influencing cabinet-making and the
little accessories of the house from toilet mirror
to footstool. These things, too, will be described month by month in GOOD HOUSEKEEPING,
so that the house itself shall always have that
up-to-date look that other women recognise.
For though women are supposed to dress themselves to please their men-folk, they deck their
houses most often for each other.

Fiction is one of the pleasures of most
women's leisure, and good fiction only—wholesome and suited to a magazine that will find
its way into thousands of homes and that will
be read, we hope, with equal pleasure by all the
members of the household—will be given, and
will be from the pens of our greatest and best-
known novelists.

The good housekeeper is "the keystone of
the arch" and "the pillar of the house." She
is worthy of a great magazine, and it will be
our aim to make GOOD HOUSEKEEPING worthy
of her.

Woman knows that if anything deprives her of her work public opinion quietly but obstinately propels her back towards the shelter of the home, and that if she is driven in she may never get out again

WOMAN NEW

Woman Earning

By

W. L. GEORGE

WOMAN, being vastly adaptable, ha advanced as rapidly as the time and is now in 1923, thanks to the wa probably what she would have been i 1943. But things have gone too fas and she finds herself to-day in a positio full of complexity. In the new world sh has not maintained all the conques she made in the old. Some conques

factory system, which demanded larg quantities of cheap labour. Woma supplied that in England, in Americ and elsewhere, because she was willir to work cheaply if only she was give work to do. But all this is very nev it is all still on its trial. Whereas the is not to-day any great difference treatment between the shop assistant whom his employer gives board ar lodging, and the shop assistant wl unrolled bales of cloth on the count of a merchant in Rouen six hundr years ago, there exists an immen difference between the woman work of to-day and her grandmother.

What has happened is that whi men have gone on working for wag as they did throughout time, ever sir the days in Babylon where a goldsmi who could not find a clever slave decid to hire as a workman another goldsmi who had fallen upon evil days, wom have been working outside the home f little over a century. Therefore, whi men have merely been earning the living, women have been earning the economic freedom.

This is an important distinction, b cause a woman's living takes upon its a sort of political air; her wage com to her every week pinned on to h ticket of leave. She escaped from t home such a little while ago that h wage is still to her a reassurance, promissory note in which society unde takes that she shall not be herded hor again. It follows that the big even of the world affect women different from men. When there is a pestilenc a revolution, a war, the man risks t loss of his wages because industry m be destroyed, or commerce imped But he knows that eventually, if survives, society will rearrange itse that once again he will receive l wages. The woman's position different. If anything deprives her her work, she knows that public opini

THE two titles of this article are likely to arouse dissent, or at least comment, in many women who may be inclined to challenge the arrival of the new world, or to look upon the attainment of a living by women as an old story. In the United States, where the woman worker has for three generations played a definite part in the commercial activity of the great republic, women may say that for a woman to earn her living is no new thing. But one might reply that men have earned their living in the wage market for many hundreds of years, while until recently women entered it mainly as a domestic servant.

The fact is that only recently have education and opportunity enabled women to compete with men in their own spheres, and indeed to conquer spheres of their own. First it was nursing: even in the later days of the eighteenth century, apart from the nuns, sick nurses were male. Next it was teaching, then shorthand and typewriting. These things have developed one from the other. The growing education of women enabled them to seize the opportunities that came. Most of these opportunities arose out of the

i n t h e
WORLD
Her Own Living

Illustrated by
Franklin Booth

she does hold. It rests with her period, more than with herself, whether she holds them for all time. W. L. George, who has studied woman with a zeal and understanding which is rare, does much in the following article, the first of a series from this brilliant writer, to disperse the fog surrounding woman's position in the immediate future

quietly but obstinately propels her back towards the shelter of the home, and that if she is driven in she may never get out again.

Therefore great movements of mankind, like a European war, which tend to remake the face of the world can affect women more than they do men, because they leave men where they are, while they make for women a new world with which they must cope. Here many will say that this is not a new world, and the cynics may add that the new world is the same old world, more so. In a sense that is true, for mankind, starting, let us say, thirty thousand years ago, has developed very slowly through famine, massacre, the rise and fall of empires, and the progress of science. On the whole, mankind has not apparently been affected very much by great confusions. Only, and here is a peculiarity, this round earth is rather like a stone rolling down a hill. It goes faster and faster, and though it may gather little moss, it moves with visible speed towards a place which we do not know but which we hope may be a better one. Briefly, while the people of 775 were much like the people of 783, it is not true that the people of 914 are identical with the people of 923.

One does not want to exaggerate. When we think of primitive things, hunger, love, ambition, there is probably no difference between John Jones in the street and Ioannes hanging about the Acropolis. But it is not the big things matter in life; it is the little ones. We do not regulate the big things, because we cannot; the little things, money, security, social status, these make up life, and those change.

From that point of view there is, not exactly a new world, at least a renewed world, or better a world which had been speeded up. It is commonly said that war brings out what is best in

man, which is quite true, and it is not so commonly said that it brings out the worst, which is also true. It brings out, it does not create. It is an illusion to think that war breeds in people anything that was not there. It merely accelerates or delays something that was already there. The plucky become heroes, the timid become cowards, the kindly become saints, and so forth, war acting as a sort of magnifying glass. Such change as has come over the world is merely the change which would have come without any war, but it has come quicker. We are in 1923, thanks to the war, probably what we should have

been in 1943. We are a little ahead of ourselves, and therefore we come everywhere upon difficult readjustments which are causing strikes and agitations in India, California, Ireland, China, and Peru. From the same source come the agitations for saving child lives, for birth control, for the opening of the harems, for the prevention of disease, for the settlement of the Anglo-American relations, for the right of woman to live outside marriage, to smoke in public, big things and little things, all tumbled together by a torrent which rolls rocks and pebbles in a common flood.

In the readjustment of woman's work in the world the enormous field of the crafts will more and more fall to her because her natural taste for decoration is likely to expand there

Mr. G. A. SERVICE
on the Saving of Labour.

"That's good-bye to unnecessary drudgery

"... good-bye to all the work and trouble of fire-making, cleaning grates, and removing ashes. The gas fire, madam, can be lighted in a second and it starts, stays, and finishes clean.

"You'll find it's the same with all gas appliances. In fact, madam, whenever *heat* is needed—whether for warming rooms, cooking food, heating water, or burning refuse — gas is the ideal fuel for the ideal home."

* * *

The B.C.G.A., representing the British Gas Industry, is at the service of the public, without charge, for advice and help on any subject, large or small, connected with the economical and efficient use of gas in the home.

Mr. G. A. Service will welcome enquiries sent to him at the address below.

GAS

for Homes of To-day

THE BRITISH COMMERCIAL GAS ASSOCIATION, 28 GROSVENOR GARDENS, LONDON, S.W. 1.

A plan that has been found to work excellently is to give the " daily " maid a list of the silver, valuable china, and fine linen in daily use, making her responsible for their care, with instructions to report mishaps at once

Daily Maids in the *Small Town House*

By Margaret Benn

HOW much valuable space, obtained at a premium, is given up, more especially in the small town house or flat, to provide bedrooms for a resident staff! So long as this can be spared, so good. But a time may come when the needs of an expanding household will necessitate the redecorating and adapting of his accommodation to some such uses as a dressing-room, night nursery, or bedroom for an older child.

The reluctant decision once made, a vista of inconvenience opens up, and to the mind's eye the daily maid appears as ovenly, unpunctual, perhaps actually dishonest, introducing burglars, and herself vanishing from sight or, it might be, not appearing at all on some critical occasion. Chosen with care, the " daily " will fulfil none of these fearful expectations. Frequently she is a woman of a competent and superior type, the wife, perhaps, of a disabled soldier, obliged to return to service in this form, and highly recommended by the better-class registry which supplies her.

Whether cook or house-parlourmaid, it is a first essential that she should have a sense of responsibility, a quality be fostered and tacitly acknowledged by the giving of responsible work. Special pains must be taken to attach her to the household so that she will not feel herself to be a mere casual worker. A plan which has been found to work excellently in this connection is to give the house-parlourmaid a list of the silver, valuable china, and fine linen in daily use, making her responsible for their care—and with instructions to report mishaps at once. And to the cook, if she is that pearl of great price (and experience) who will do all her own marketing, give on a certain day the sum of money allowed for food, cleaning materials, and ordinary expenses. Provide her with a book to be

kept up to date, balanced, and, above all, inspected at a regular time every week. If selection has been made of a cook whom catering interests, or of a house-parlourmaid proud of her pantry, that second essential, the sense of co-operation, is thus secured, and she feels that her part in maintaining the general health and well-being of the household meets with the appreciation and respect due to the good performance of skilled work.

That there are inconveniences cannot be denied. Bells must perforce remain unanswered after " kitchen hours," and adjustment may be called for in order to ensure that during these hours—perhaps between 7.30 a.m. and 9 p.m.—someone shall be on duty. For the small house a workable scheme consists in engaging a cook for the earlier " shift " who will, if necessary, leave dinner so far advanced that it can be easily served by the house-parlourmaid who comes and goes proportionately later. Another drawback is the somewhat higher rate of wages asked by the woman who has to find her own rent and laundry. That this is met on the balance will be shown presently. In any event it should be a matter for thought to a daily employer,

whether commercial, industrial, or domestic, to pay an employee less than a living wage—particularly if that employee is a woman entirely on her own resources.

It is not an inconsiderable piece of social work to-day to make of domestic service a more pleasant profession. Of late years it has broken down, except in the case of very large establishments where the society of other servants, and some good degree of comfort, and off-time were not wanting. It has broken down mainly because it asked too much and gave too little. It gave, for one thing, an insufficiency of fresh air. It demanded the whole time, and gave back, as a concession, an afternoon now and an evening then. Thus even the concentrated strain of the factory and the office have come to seem preferable, for some part of the day at least brings back the outside world.

The mistress of daily servants will find first and foremost that the morning and evening journey infuse a new tone and vigour into the daily round. Not only is it healthy, but it gives variety and makes for cheerfulness. She will find, too, that where everything has to be done within hours, the day's work will tend to be better arranged and generally better done. Meals are ready to the instant, and dinner is served with perfection and dispatch. But best of all compensations (if any are needed), as the door closes finally the chancellor of the domestic exchequer may sigh with contentment, for she knows that below stairs everything invites inspection. The kitchen table has the whiteness of a dreadnought's deck. The larder is fresh and clean. And she knows, too, that the kettle will not boil again until to-morrow, that the kitchen teapot will remain on its shelf, and the tea undisturbed in its tin. The lights are out and the fire is low. Nothing but the rent runs on.

FASHIONS

Fashion Proclaims Herself this Spring a Devotee to Limitless Variety in Silhouette, in Colour, and in Fabric

By Anna Van Campen Stewart

"GOOD HOUSEKEEPING" OFFICE,
2 RUE DE LA PAIX, PARIS.

LAST-MINUTE NEWS FROM PARIS

The silhouette shows great variety, but in general the straight line prevails. For the street skirts remain short, reaching ankle-length or even floor-length in the evening. Many skirts are flounced. Drapery associates itself with the front and back of frocks, the waist-line remaining, usually, at the top of the hips, which are tightly swathed. Much foulard, organdie, changeable taffeta, and printed and embroidered crêpe and cotton is used for spring frocks. Long tunics in printed fabric are worn over plain underslips. Inspiration from the "period" frock has been gleaned by many designers. The vogue of the small hat prevails. Suits and cloaks are slender in line and show embroidery. A new light red, green, cyclamen, brown, and mastic are leading spring colours

GERMAINE-PAGE

EVELYN VARON

INSTEAD of one silhouette for spring, we have several. In general the straight line prevails, and skirts, while short for the street, are ankle-length or even longer for evening wear. In many cases the waistline is at the top of the hips, but in some models this line is only vaguely indicated, being lost under a fold or two of drapery. Again, a very wide girdle is employed, very flat across the hips, while associating itself with drapery in the front or back.

This season, instead of drapery or loose panels falling from the hips on the sides, many skirts show movement in the front or back—tightly swathed hips with folds falling out in the middle front, or flat-fronted skirts with folds drawn slightly upward and falling out in the middle back, suggesting the styles of fifty years ago.

Brown is a colour still cherished by the Parisienne, and is that chosen by Germaine-Page for the little hat of picot straw flying immense loops of brown satin ribbon

Mastic crêpe de Chine is used by Molyneux for a frock that expresses, like all his creations, perfection of line and colouring. A clasp of red galalith holds the girdle

The much-talked-of Second Empire frock, minus baleine, is a thing of quaint beauty—the full skirt, plain or flounced, falling softly to the ankles or touching the floor at the back, and the slender corsage not too tight. Many of these frocks are developed in the new soft crêpes, but some are prettily fashioned of changeable taffeta, muslin, or lace. Hats of changeable taffeta are smart also, trimmed with little knots of flowers or quilled ribbon.

Many simple frocks are made of the new foulards in delightful colourings. Not tightly fitted and not too loose, outlining the hips closely, the sleeves short or long or puffed, and the skirts draped, flounced, looped, or otherwise arranged, these gay little gowns are exceedingly smart. Often odd collars of white or tinted organdie are added, with charming result.

Spring itself finds expression in the wide-brimmed hat that Evelyn Varon makes of green and yellow changeable taffeta, with blue and pink asters among green leaves for trimming

MOLYNEUX

Many skirts are flounced—the picot-edged flounces circular in cut and irregular in length, sometimes passing only half-way round the skirt, sometimes lifted a trifle in front and drooping across the sides and back. Odd little wraps of crêpe de Chine or foulard are often worn with them—the wrap appearing to form a part of the frock itself.

Quaint, full-skirted frocks are made of Rodier's gay-printed cotton, with smart accompanying jackets of similar print enriched with embroidery, and broad straw hats of vivid, harmonising colour. Parasols are also made of these printed cottons—very decorative with thin summer gowns. Changeable taffeta is employed for parasols as well, with printed shantung and other gay silks.

Odd are the plain crêpes embroidered in imitation of printed cottons. Silk crêpes embroidered all over in relief are made into simple frocks trimmed with

The straight gown of silver cloth in a small brocade pattern shown below is sponsored by Georgette, and is trimmed with white cock feathers

AGNES

Agnes makes the turban above of Rodier embroidery in white and colours on a very dark blue ground

Philippe and Gaston created the graceful frock of red beaded lace with a quaint puff across the front of the girdle

bands of plain crêpe de Chine. So many of the new stuffs are embroidered or printed with colour this season that a frock of plain crêpe de Chine is a distinct pleasure. One new model of mastic crêpe is trimmed with an arrangement of flat crêpe de Chine bands—the flat, short loops falling loose.

Chanel embroiders a straight brown knee-length crêpe de Chine coat with red and mastic silk thread, and lines it throughout with a sort of fur of knitted red fringe—the fringe falling a bit below the edge of the coat and showing prettily here and there with each movement of the wearer.

Everywhere this season designers have been inspired by the "period" frock without at all reproducing it exactly. Frocks inspired by the Directoire are not tightened closely below the bust,

Pale rose crêpe georgette is used for the fascinating frock whose skirt is simply a series of picoted flounces cut in deep irregular scallops

Heavily studded with brilliants, the white mousseline frock that Doucet makes has an underskirt of silver cloth edged with silver lace

GEORGETTE   PHILIPPE & GASTON   DOUCET

Flounces are not allowed to monopolise our skirts entirely; for instance, in the black satin frock above a looped fold attracts all our attention

There is no denying the fascination of the flounce, especially when it is pleated as in the frock of shell-coloured crêpe de Chine above

being rather straight and tube-like—the high waistline merely indicated by some sort of trimming. Second Empire frocks fall softly. Frocks modelled after the fashions of the early "seventies" are so discreetly modified that the bustle is merely hinted at, no more. The frocks of 1830 are gently imitated in tulle or taffeta or muslin, the skirts widening but falling softly from the waistline, which is girdled so simply as to appear almost childish.

Tunics are worn again this season—some of them might be called overskirts—and are especially pretty in embroidered or printed stuffs, slit on the sides, decoratively girdled or not belted at all, and worn over plain underslips. For summer a tunic of white cotton embroidered in yellow, for instance, is worn over a skirt of plain yellow, the girdle being yellow also.

There is a new light red which promises to be smart in the coming season,

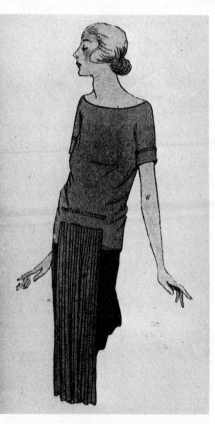

An unusual note is struck in the pleated "apron" front of this green crêpe de Chine blouse worn over a skirt of ochre crêpe

We have heard a lot about lovely new embroidered cottons, and here is one—white embroidered with blue—worn as a tunic over a blue serge skirt

Printed silk crêpe is much in the mind of French designers, and appears above as the upper part of a frock in ochre, green, and other dull colourings

not coral or geranium, but a sort of pale red which suggests both. Very smart are the frocks of black foulard or crêpe printed with a design in ochre. Other crêpes are effectively embroidered with ochre and trimmed with plain ochre crêpe bands. Very dark blue crêpe is embroidered all over with different shades of lighter blue and white, and similarly trimmed with bands of dark blue crêpe.

Premet employs much alpaca for spring frocks. In general reps has replaced serge, which has now an old-fashioned look. Besides reps, there are many new thin wool stuffs which are used instead of serge even for sports garments. The spring collections are particularly colourful, promising a frivolous season. It is difficult to be frivolous in black. However, each house shows a number of models in black or black and white. And if not frivolous, black is always *distingué*.

Managing a Husband

SOMETIMES he is grumpy, other times too languid to walk or talk, doesn't eat or sleep well, seems worried and depressed. What is a wife to do?

Men *are* curious—but the *wifely* wife knows he is the victim of headaches, indigestion, or some other ailment, which means that he is run down and needs toning up. So she places ready at hand what she knows will gently but surely restore him to better spirits and better health.

She chooses ENO'S "FRUIT SALT" because it is pure, sparklingly pleasant, free from harsh mineral salts, and has a world-wide reputation extending over half-a-century. 1/9 buys a bottle—she gets it and places it in the bathroom, where it is handy for use every morning.

It's a pleasure to drink

ENO's "FRUIT SALT"

TRADE MARK

1/9

The shape and size of the "Handy" 1/9 bottle make it ideal for the traveller—for office use—for the week-end case.

The Household size at 3/- is most suitable for regular family use. Ask your chemist for the size that suits your needs.

C. ENO LTD., "FRUIT SALT" WORKS, LONDON, S.E.

A 12

HOW YOU CAN HELP THE EMPIRE

YOU can make a point of asking, when you go shopping, for Empire goods from home or overseas. "What difference," you may wonder as you ask, "can words of mine, spoken across a shop counter, make to an Empire that covers a quarter of the known lands of the world?"

It is just such simple words as yours that find their way to the ends of the earth; and if everyone spoke as you have spoken, not a farm nor a factory in the Empire could miss the signal of encouragement. Is that a difference worth making? If it is, then ask, when you go shopping, for Empire goods from home or overseas.

BUY EMPIRE PRODUCE
from Home and Overseas

Issued by
THE EMPIRE MARKETING BOARD

Illustrated by Charles Crombie

Problems *for the* Citizen

Rose Macaulay

is sorry to say there is only one solution for the problems that afflict the minds of dutiful citizens, and that is not a comfortable solution. But, such as it is——

IT seems time, after discussing several of the problems of private life, to consider some of the problems incidental to one's life as a citizen; for we are all, as Aristotle remarks, political beings as well as private persons. The chief problem in the life of the citizen is, of course, how to exist with reasonable comfort while yet obeying just so many of the regulations of the Government under which we have the misfortune to live as to escape molestation by the minions of the law. This is not easy; perhaps it is impossible, while we have laws about paying away our hard-won earnings in taxes, not travelling in trains without buying a ticket, not obstructing the traffic, occasionally even muzzling our dogs, having to obtain a troublesome and ridiculous signed paper permit whenever we leave our native lands, and so on and so forth. One can only do one's best about it, and a poor, unsatisfactory best it is.

Consider, for instance, income tax. Ever and anon, as we have all found, horrible buff envelopes arrive at the house of the citizen, containing (as we shall see if we are rash enough to open them) impertinent inquiries as to how much money we possess, or have possessed during the last three years, and where we got it from, and how many, if any, dependents do we support, and all kinds of other intrusive inquiries. Take no notice at all; you can safely put the form (stamped envelope enclosed and all) into the waste-paper basket; be sure you will receive another before long. I am told that it is wise to attend to the third such form you receive, or unpleasantness may arise, and the good citizen should never cause this. So at

last the day comes when you will have to sit down to the thing and fill in this revolting form. You must then invent some kind of a likely and coherent tale about how much money you have earned (or obtained without earning, if you are lucky enough to get your money that way) during the last three years. Of course this is all guess-work, and all you need do is to make the lowest guess that you think will be believed. Do not make it much too low, as publicans are, as a race, lacking in simple faith, and have prying dispositions. We have been told that they will enter heaven before the Pharisees; all I can say is that the Pharisees must have been very bad indeed.

The next trouble will be that your assessment form for the current half-year arrives, asking for an exorbitant sum out of your small income, which you can ill spare, and, in fact, which you probably do not possess. Again, take no notice. You will receive presently plenty of other forms, similar in content, though they change in colour as time goes on and as the impatience of the publican increases; I am told that it is safe to ignore them all until they turn slate-blue. When this occurs, it is advisable to call on your local publican and tell him that you cannot pay him at present, as you are living on an overdraft which your bank will not increase, but that you expect in a month or two to sell a book, or some newspaper articles, or a motor bicycle, or what not, and will then endeavour to oblige him. If he still demands a cheque, give him a post-dated one and stop it before the date arrives. But there is one true and melancholy fact about taxes; you will have to pay them eventually, put off the evil day as you may.

Concerning passports, there is more

hope. With a little skill, you can forge a passport. You can obtain the binding quite easily; you can also obtain the stout pink paper required, and then all you have to do is to cover it with some kind of hieroglyphics to deceive the eye. You then fill up the paper with any story about yourself, your father's first name, and where your mother was christened, that you prefer; it does not matter in the least what you say, for you may be sure it will not be read. That is the bright spot about passports!—they are scarcely ever opened or looked at. Stamp them over with something that has, at a distance, the air of being the visa you require, and take the risk. It has been known that a map of Europe has served the purpose. You may possibly be found out by some inquiring foreign official with overmuch time on his hands, but this is improbable. Officials are, as a rule, extremely pressed for time and extremely stupid. Anyhow, take the risk; it is worth it, for the sake of evading what is perhaps the most imbecile of our European laws. At the worst, you can but, I suppose, be deported home again.

Now let us consider the citizen as a political being, a creature with a right to a say in his country's government. Even women, above thirty years of age, have this right now. It does not seem to amount to very much; the Government seems to go on along its own way without much reference to public opinion. But every now and then there is a parliamentary election, and then every voter has to decide which of the various candidates who offer themselves as representatives of his constituency he least dislikes, and considers least foolish and useless. Be sure that they will all be quite foolish, quite useless, and quite unable to show any reason why they should represent (Continued on page 22)

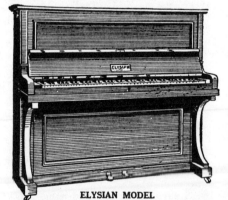
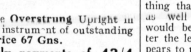

Problems for the Citizen

(*Continued from page* 21)

you. This cannot be helped. Members of Parliament are like that, and that is partly why governments and constitutions are as we see them. But the citizen must, unless he prefers to leave the affair to proceed without his assistance, make up his mind which candidate he will vote for. Parties matter very little. All political parties seem equally to be lacking in both intelligence and good intentions. Unless the voter prefers merely to vote for the candidate with the more amiable smile and pleasing address, he had better discover which of them will make the greater number of promises concerning the amelioration of the condition of the constituency. Judicious approach will be found to elicit a remarkable number of these promises from both sides. The promises will not, of course, be kept, but they are good things to have in writing, as they enable the member's constituents to make his parliamentary life a burden to him with reproachful letters.

There are several important points for voters to remember about elections. First, it is better, if you wish to accept a bribe (such as a ride in a motor-car to the polls or a present in money or kind) from one side, to vote for the other; and if you accept bribes from both (or all three), to vote for none of them. This looks better, as incorruptibility is a virtue well thought of, and the candidates' agents will never know how you voted, nor refrain on that account from bribing you next time.

Another point to remember is, that it is not thought good form to vote for a female candidate, unless she is the wife of your former member, who has disqualified himself from standing by means of death, peerage, or his conduct of elections. A little thought will show you that all lady members of Parliament obtain their seats in one or another of these ways. It is not thought very nice for a woman to get into Parliament merely on her own account; there is something a little unwomanly about it. This should be remembered always by women who may have the ambition to be M.P.s. There is only one path to this position; they must marry a member and then put him, somehow, out of action, by whatever method seems most suitable.

Having by these means, if you are a woman, by any other means if you are a man, obtained a seat in the House, your task is achieved. There is no need to attend the sittings of Parliament, still less need ever to speak. In fact, it would probably be a great pity were you to do so, since there is already quite too much speaking in our house of legislature. Very nearly everything that is said there would be at least as well unsaid; and quite everything would be much better said at a quarter the length. A great love of words appears to prevail among our legislators, who lack the art of condensation. In fact, if you are to be a normal and esteemed member of the House, you must always remember never to say in ten words what can be said in a hundred. There is no reason why the House should not be a very happy place for you to spend a certain amount of your time in, as the seats are commodious and you can go to sleep or read a novel as much as you like. You will not be perfectly comfortable unless you sit on one of the two front benches (which is not likely to happen to you), as only those who do this are able to put their feet up on the table. Hence, there has always been a good deal of competition for the positions in the Government or Opposition which entitle members to these seats. The three ladies at present

(*Continued on page* 24)

The blessed half-holiday

WHEN the autumn sun is hidden behind leaden skies, when the streets are grey and muddy, and all the fun seems to have gone out of life, then it is that the jaded town-dweller longs for quiet woods, for a walk across the blue-grey hills, for a week-end cottage in Devonshire; for a motor-car, a bicycle, a train—anything that will take him or her away to the peaceful countryside.

At last, sweet relief! Saturday comes round, Saturday, the blessed half-holiday.

Weariness vanishes as if by magic, energy returns at the thought of escape from the cramped routine, from the noise of buses, and the interminable round that is workaday life.

The country calls!

Shady, wooded walks; little valleys where sweet-smelling flowers bloom in glad liberty; silent forests where only leaves and birds stir; lonely river nooks where the brilliant kingfisher shows his beauty unmolested; still waters over which like fairies the dragon flies skim.

They are so simple in use

Everywhere peace and rest and refreshment to the soul. That is what Saturday means to the tired worker.

On the stroke of the clock, books close with a snap, drawers bang with a happy noise that seems to say, "There! that's that till Monday. Monday must come, but still to-day is Saturday. To-day is holiday!"

But there must be no waste of time in getting together the very necessary provisions for the expedition to fairyland.

Sandwiches, of course, though most sandwiches take time to make; but not if they are Sailor Savouries.

Made with Sailor Savouries they are but a moment's work, and what more delicious repast than fresh, crisp sandwiches? What more appetizing, nourishing and convenient form of food?

Lunch, tea, supper—all can be provided from this delicacy, made in many varieties (fish sandwiches, meat sandwiches, chicken and ham, salmon and shrimp, turkey and tongue, and several others), equal in nutritive value to a considerable quantity of meat.

A perfect holiday! Ideal surroundings, ideal refreshment. Life goes by smoothly and happily, "the world forgetting, by the world forgot." Angus Watson & Co. Limited, Newcastle-upon-Tyne.

£500 *guarantee of purity*

23

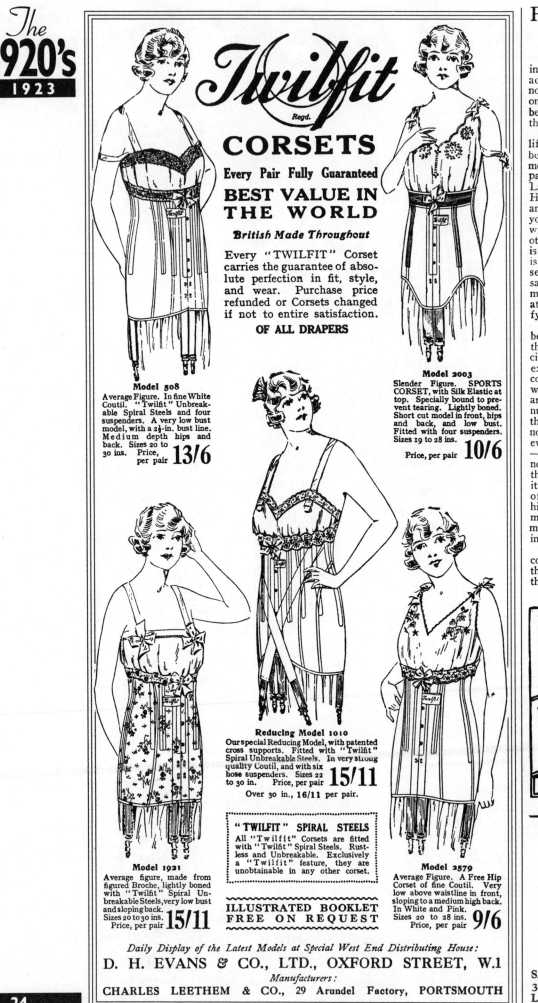

Twilfit Regd.

CORSETS

Every Pair Fully Guaranteed

BEST VALUE IN THE WORLD

British Made Throughout

Every "TWILFIT" Corset carries the guarantee of absolute perfection in fit, style, and wear. Purchase price refunded or Corsets changed if not to entire satisfaction.

OF ALL DRAPERS

Model 508

Average Figure. In fine White Coutil. "Twilfit" Unbreakable Spiral Steels and four suspenders. A very low bust model, with a 2½-in. bust line. Medium depth hips and back. Sizes 20 to 30 ins. Price, per pair **13/6**

Model 2003

Slender Figure. SPORTS CORSET, with Silk Elastic at top. Specially bound to prevent tearing. Lightly boned. Short cut model in front, hips and back, and low bust. Fitted with four suspenders. Sizes 19 to 28 ins.

Price, per pair **10/6**

Reducing Model 1010

Our special Reducing Model, with patented cross supports. Fitted with "Twilfit" Spiral Unbreakable Steels. In very strong quality Coutil, and with six hose suspenders. Sizes 22 to 30 ins. Price, per pair **15/11**

Over 30 in., 16/11 per pair.

"TWILFIT" SPIRAL STEELS

All "Twilfit" Corsets are fitted with "Twilfit" Spiral Steels. Rustless and Unbreakable. Exclusively a "Twilfit" feature, they are unobtainable in any other corset.

Model 1921

Average figure, made from figured Broche, lightly boned with "Twilfit" Spiral Unbreakable Steels, very low bust and sloping back. Sizes 20 to 30 ins. Price, per pair **15/11**

Model 2579

Average Figure. A Free Hip Corset of fine Coutil. Very low above waistline in front, sloping to a medium high back. In White and Pink. Sizes 20 to 28 ins. Price, per pair **9/6**

ILLUSTRATED BOOKLET FREE ON REQUEST

Daily Display of the Latest Models at Special West End Distributing House:

D. H. EVANS & CO., LTD., OXFORD STREET, W.1

Manufacturers:

CHARLES LEETHEM & CO., 29 Arundel Factory, PORTSMOUTH

Problems for the Citizen

(Continued from page 22)

in the House have not yet obtained this advantage. The Liberal party is also just now deprived of it, as the Ministers on one side and the front-bench Labour members on the other enjoy the monopoly. But this should always be the citizen's goal.

Further, the pay is quite good, and the life unexacting, even if your feet have to be on the floor. It is best to be a Labour member, as then your election expenses get paid for you by your party, and also the Labour members have more fun in the House, as they make much more noise and get more frequently turned out. If you are a Labour member and disagree with something said by a member on the other side, it is correct to call out, "That is a dirty lie," or something similar. This is not held to be good form for Conservative or Liberal members, who have to say, more mildly, "I venture to think that my honourable friend has spoken inaccurately," which takes longer and is less satisfying.

If you cannot become any kind of member of Parliament, which is the fate of the majority of both male and female citizens, you will have to be content with exercising such political rights as may come your way as a private person. These will not be many; the rights of a citizen are few; but his (or her) duties are very numerous and onerous. To escape them, the only way, so far as I know (for it is of no use to go abroad, citizens abroad being even more hampered than in this country) —the only way is to become a tramp, of no fixed abode. Even so you will not evade them altogether. And, in this connection, it should be remembered that it is not one of the rights of a citizen to sleep in the highways and hedges of his country; he must either have a bed, or some visible means of support, that is to say, some money in his pockets.

In fact, the citizen's is a hard and discouraging life. The animals manage, on the whole, better, though they are also, on the whole, much more uncomfortable.

Cut crusts of stale bread into small pieces and bake in a slow oven until a golden brown and crisp

The Humble Crumb Disguised

CRUMBS are one of the most useful and most adaptable commodities in the equipment of the modern housewife. To begin with, there is a well-founded sense of economy in the use of crumbs, for they are usually made from left-overs—scraps of bread, biscuits that have been broken, or cake no longer fresh enough for service at table.

If the left-overs are dry and crisp, they may be rolled or ground down in the mincing-machine, then sieved and stored in a jar for future use. The air should not be entirely excluded: the best plan is to cover the jar with muslin or cheese-cloth held in place with a rubber band. If the pieces are not dry, they should either be sieved and used at once or dried slowly in the oven and then ground down.

There are many different ways in which crumbs can be utilised. They will often extend a vegetable or a small amount of meat in such a way as to make it serve several persons. Bread-crumbs used with egg will form a coating on articles that are to be fried. Sprinkled over a *gratin* dish they add both to its flavour and to its appearance. They may also be used to thicken soups that are made with milk, besides doing good service in the many recipes which require crumbs of different kinds as the basis of the dish.

Crumb Omelet: Soak a teacupful of white bread-crumbs in a teacupful of milk for 15 minutes. Then add pepper, salt, and 3 well-beaten eggs. Melt 1 oz. butter in a frying-pan and grease the sides as well as the bottom. Pour in the egg mixture and cook slowly, shaking the pan and pricking the omelet frequently with a fork so that all is cooked. When brown underneath place in a moderate oven, 350° Fahr., to finish cooking the top. Fold over, turn out on a hot dish, and serve immediately, garnished with parsley. A little brown gravy or fried potatoes might be served separately.

Bread Rarebit: Soak 1 cupful white bread-crumbs in 1 cupful milk for 15 minutes. Melt 1 oz. butter in a double boiler, add the soaked crumbs, 1 slightly beaten egg, salt, and a little cayenne. Cook until the egg thickens, stirring constantly, and remove from the fire. Add ¾ cupful grated cheese and beat until the cheese melts. Pour on to hot toast or crisp biscuits and serve at once.

Girdle Cakes: Soak 1 cupful biscuit-crumbs in 2 cupfuls milk for fifteen minutes. Meanwhile mix and sieve 1 cupful flour, 2 teaspoonfuls baking powder, ½ teaspoonful salt, and 1 tablespoonful sugar. Add these to the soaked crumbs, along with one beaten egg and 1 tablespoonful melted fat. Stir well until smooth. Bake in spoonfuls on a hot greased girdle until brown on both sides.

Chocolate Cups: Dissolve 2 oz. chocolate in 2 cupfuls milk in the double boiler. When quite melted add a cupful of fine biscuit-crumbs, a good pinch of salt, and sugar to taste. Remove from the fire, add 1 beaten egg and ½ teaspoonful vanilla. Pour the mixture into greased cups, place them in a tin, pour in a little hot water, and bake in a moderate oven (350° Fahr.) until firm—about 45 minutes. Turn out and serve with milk, cream, or hard sauce. Serve either hot or cold.

Spice Pie: Add ½ cupful sweet biscuit crumbs to 1 cupful hot milk. Beat up 1 or 2 eggs and add them along with ½ teaspoonful cinnamon, ¼ teaspoonful nutmeg, ½ teaspoonful ginger, a good pinch of salt, 2 tablespoonfuls treacle or syrup, and 2 tablespoonfuls brown sugar. Mix well together and pour into a pastry-lined tin or dish. Bake for ten minutes in a hot oven (450° Fahr.), then reduce the heat to 325° Fahr., and continue the baking until the mixture is firm and the pastry cooked—about half an hour. Sprinkle with sugar, cut in pieces, and serve hot or cold.

Holiday Pudding: Soak 1 cupful stale cake-crumbs in 2 cupfuls milk for ten minutes. Then add 1 beaten egg, a pinch of salt, the grated rind of ½ lemon, and sugar to taste. Mix well, pour into a greased pie-dish, and sprinkle the top lightly with ground cinnamon. Place in a tin with a little warm water and bake in a moderate oven about 1 hour.

Baked Apple Pudding: To 1½ lb. apples allow 6 oz. browned bread-crumbs, 2 oz. butter or margarine, 2 tablespoonfuls golden syrup, 1 gill water, and the grated rind of ½ lemon.

Peel, core, and slice the apples very thinly and put a layer of them into a greased pie-dish. Sprinkle some of the bread-crumbs over this, and lay on a few small pieces of butter. Repeat these alternate layers until all the apples and bread-crumbs are used up. The last layer should be crumbs. Mix the syrup, water, and lemon-rind together and pour them over the top. Sprinkle with sugar and lay on some more pieces of butter. Stand in a tin with a little water and bake in a moderate oven about 1 hour, or until the apples are cooked. A little cream or custard may be served separately.

Caramel Ginger Pudding: Soak 2 cupfuls of cake-crumbs in 1 cupful hot milk for 15 minutes. Put ½ cupful sugar into an iron or aluminium saucepan with enough water to moisten it and let this melt and become a golden brown colour. Pour immediately into one large or ½ dozen small moulds that have been well greased. Then add to the moistened crumbs ½ cupful flour, ½ cupful sugar, 1 teaspoonful ginger, ½ teaspoonful cinnamon, and a good pinch of salt. Mix thoroughly for a few minutes, add 1 or 2 beaten eggs and 2 tablespoonfuls treacle and beat again. Sprinkle over 1 teaspoonful baking powder, stir it in, and pour into the mould or moulds. Cover with greased paper and steam from ¾ to 1½ hours according to size. Stand a minute or two after removing from the saucepan, then turn out on a serving-dish and the caramel will run down as a sauce.

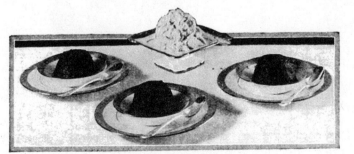

Using biscuit crumbs as the basis for Chocolate Cups results in a delicious dessert

This is a linen damask table-cloth of very fine quality with an ornamental border and wreath and stripe centre. It is available for our readers at a very special price: 2 by 2 yds., 20s. 6d., post free; 2 by 2½ yds., 25s., post free; 2 by 3½ yds., 35s., post free. Napkins to match, 22 by 22 in., 23s. 6d., 24 by 24, 27s. doz., in each case; orders of a dozen post free, orders of ½ dozen postage 6d. extra

(Centre) A useful collection of autumn gloves at low prices. First on the rail is a pair of sac nappa gloves in dark tan with strap wrist at 4s. 11d. per pair, post free; next is a pair of elastic wrist mocha suède in brown or dark grey, 4s. 11d. post free; and separately a pair of white or natural chamois gloves with fringed wrists at 6s. 6d. a pair, post free.

Below is a well-cut and recommended rainproof coat made in gabardine and lined throughout in checked proofed lining and finished with useful pockets and belt, and a collar which can be fastened high. Colours available are fawn, grey, navy; lengths, 46, 48, 50 inches. Special price, 45s. 6d., carriage paid in U.K.

At centre below is shown a very attractive French artificial silk jumper with a collar that can be worn high or low and suited for out of doors, under a coat, or house wear. It is available in white, navy, beige, sable, black, almond green, shrimp, or silver. Price 25s. 9d., postage 6d. extra.

Blanket cloth is the ideal fabric for a comfortable dressing-gown. Here is one in fine quality made with a shaped collar, edged silk cord, with a useful pocket and manly girdle, in cardinal, saxe, rose, fawn, or prune, at 21s. 6d., post free.

Returned Goods

If any reader desires to return goods purchased through the Shopping Service, the following rules must be observed. The goods, together with the reader's full name and address, and a reference to "Good Housekeeping" Shopping Service, should be returned to the shop. Postage must be paid on goods that were correctly sent in the first instance. All correspondence regarding the goods, with all instructions concerning them, must be sent to "Shopping Service, Good Housekeeping, 1 Amen Corner, London, E.C.4.

Will readers who use the Shopping Service kindly carefully read the instructions on this and opposite page before ordering goods

A set of aluminium pans are shown to right, price 15s. 6d., postage 1s. Also an aluminium preserving pan, size 14½ inches, price 6s. 6d., postage 9d.; large size, 16 inches, price 9s. 6d., postage 1s.

Everyone is using aluminium now; it is such a cleanly, quick way to cook food. Here is a ½-pint steamer with double pan which will have many household uses. Price 9s. 11d., postage 1s. 3d. Next to it is a folding travelling spirit-comfort, very easy to pack with a folding handle. It holds 1½ pints. Price, 9s. 11d., postage 6d.

Specially recommended is this complete three-piece set (knickers, chemise, and cami-petticoat) in artificial silk, available in white, black, pink, lemon, sky and lilac. Price 29s. 6d. for the whole set, postage 9d.

Below is a very attractive light-weight wool stockinette frock, suitable for early autumn, made in the new cross-over style. It is bound with braid round the collar, has stitching to tone, panels in contrasting colours and silk-covered buckle to self belt. Colours, navy-grey, café-filbert, delft-grey, grey-navy, nigger-filbert, black-white, filbert-café, black-grey, filbert-nigger, and all white. Price 43s. 6d., postage 9d. extra.

(Below) A smartly cut coat-frock, made of a superior quality gabardine suiting, trimmed with silk braid. The collar can be worn buttoned to the throat or with revers thrown open to show a vest of crêpe de Chine in contrasting colour. Sets of fine pleats are at either side of the back and in front of the skirt. It is available in black, navy, nigger, grey, in s.w., w., and o.s. sizes. Special price, 59s. 6d., post free.

OUR SHOPPING SERVICE is designed to help those who are out of reach of the London shops. Any of the articles illustrated in these pages we shall be happy to buy for you without extra charge, on receipt of money order and your name and address. Money orders from the Colonies should include cost of postage and insurance. Cheques and money orders should be made payable to the National Magazine Co., Ltd. In the case of millinery 1s. extra for the box should be enclosed. When ordering any article please give a choice of colours. When ordering a hat please state exact measurement (i.e. circumference of head) required. All letters should be addressed to "Shopping Service," Good Housekeeping, 1 Amen Corner, London, E.C.4

Will readers who use the Shopping Service kindly carefully read the instructions on this and opposite page before ordering goods

28

Towards the end of the last century, we are told, women did not want to work. They preferred the rôle of the devoted wife and warm, tender mother, always ready with stores of affection

Should *Married* Women Work?

By *Mrs. Alfred Sidgwick*

Author of "*The Severins," "Lamorna," "Below Stairs,*" etc. etc.

NO, they should not. They should sit at home while their husbands work for them. The nursery and the kitchen should be their kingdoms and the church their solace. We all take pleasure in the picture, but know in our hearts that it does not fill the bill. Some of us think the question itself tomfoolery. Who is to lay down the law for a class, the members of which are so diverse? Not public opinion in an age that is trying to liberate women, and not legislation in a country that no longer places them with children and lunatics.

At the end of the last century, a well-known novelist, interested in social questions, said that women did not want to work. They wanted to marry a man who worked for them. In the Ideal Home the man earns money in the market-place and the woman spends it in the house. His wishes are her law and his comfort her preoccupation. Where there are children, she devotes herself to them night and day, having neither wishes nor business of her own, but, becoming by marriage the contented slave of her family. This, again, is a picture we accept without question and admire exceedingly. We figure the smiling, slightly embonpoint matron, for ever busy, often tired, still the devoted wife, always the warm, tender mother, ready with stores of affection for the grandchildren about to come. A very pretty picture and, for all sorts and conditions, greatly to be desired.

The troublesome truth is that most pretty pictures bear an imperfect likeness to real life. They turn a blind

THOUSANDS of women everywhere, married women, engaged women, un-engaged women, are trying to answer this question. It entails for many of them a choice to be made now, or for the future, between economic freedom and domestic slavery. It is a difficult question, and but rarely has it been discussed so impartially, yet so wisely and helpfully, as by Mrs. Alfred Sidgwick. Her article is one no woman should fail to read

eye to all the cases that are not pretty. If married women must not work outside the home, what are those women to do who have little mouths to feed and whose husbands fail them? Some men are ne'er-do-wells, some spend, some drink, some inconsiderately die. Their wives cannot sit at home, their children on their knees, singing little songs to them and teaching them their letters. They have to go out and earn what they may at any work they can do. I know one such who was a first-rate cook, earning high wages in rich men's houses and living in great comfort. She married a sickly little man, bore him three children, lost him, and now works as she never worked before, to add a little to the parish relief she gets and so keep her poor home together. For she cannot go back to her cooking because, even in these servantless days, people will not take a cook with three children attached: and the valiant creature will not leave them.

Other women find that their work makes just the difference between pinch and plenty in the home. The husband earns the bread and the wife puts butter

on it. He pays the rent and she buys new cretonnes for the drawing-room. As a rule, marriages of this kind are harmonious and successful, for women who make money are not usually those who waste it; but all women want to spend it in ways that men may endure but cannot approve. I remember a case of a young couple taking a house in which the passages and the hall were papered with an atrocious varnished marbled paper in good repair. The woodwork was grained and in good repair too. The man and a legal friend advising him saw no reason for changing these things. The woman would have been depressed and exasperated by them constantly. In that case the husband was good-natured and let his wife have the white paint and fresh paper or distemper that she wanted. But even he, good-natured as he is, thinks his wife is extravagant when she buys new sheets or tablecloths. He would not like ragged house-linen, but he never wants to replenish the linen cupboard. So when that wife began to earn a little money, she had the pleasure of getting what was needed for the house without having to convert her man to her opinion —often a difficult process. He still twits her with her extravagance, but likes the look of a new stair-carpet when she puts one down because the old one was in holes.

Bachelor establishments are notoriously comfortable and do not have stair-carpets in holes: so bachelors must spend much what women do on wear and tear. But no one tells stories about their extravagance because they are spending their own *(Continued on page 30)*

Should Married Women Work?

(Continued from page 29)

money. A man who unwillingly pays for cretonnes reflects that the money might have backed a horse or bought a case of whisky.

Everyone who takes an interest in the welfare of women knows that their happiness and freedom hang on their economic independence. A woman should either own money or earn it. Otherwise, in honour or dishonour, she has to be maintained by men. But a woman who has trained carefully for a trade, an art, or a profession, and achieved success in it, does not always want to give it up when she marries. That she often does give it up is a common reproach. Money spent on training women is said to be wasted money, because when they are trained they usually marry and cease to practise what they have learned. Better, I say, that a thousand women should forget a wage-earning craft than that one, left destitute, should have none for her use. Every woman born without a silver spoon in her mouth should know how to get her daily bread. As for marriage, there are many vicissitudes in that estate, and it is not only the working-class woman who finds herself stranded, although a man has endowed her with his worldly goods.

In short, the question is unanswerable in terms of yes and no. Some married women should or must work, and some should not. It stands to reason that a woman who undertakes to make a home for a man, and rear as well as bear his children, should fulfil her contract: but it does not stand to reason that she will in all cases do this best by refusing to earn money. Often enough her time would hang on her hands.

Married women of energy, means, and leisure do an immense amount of voluntary work in this country and do not neglect their homes in consequence. Take a home from which the children have gone forth to school and in which servants do the work. How is the mistress to employ herself all day? We know very well how she does. She rises late, she writes a few letters and perhaps arranges a few flowers. After lunch she goes out for *to see,* either to shops or to friends. In the evening she sits at home with her husband, except when he or someone else will take her out. We all know how busy these women think themselves, how little time they have for anything they are asked to do, and how their trivial pastimes clash with their duties just as much or more than a working woman's work does: and by a working woman I do not mean what the Reds mean, but any woman, high born or low born, who pursues a craft, an art, or a business indoors or out and gets paid for her work.

The worst wives and mothers in the world are the gad-abouts and the fools—women so set on pleasure that they neglect all their duties, or so incapable that what they do is badly done. It is not the steady, intelligent women helping the family exchequer who have miserable homes. It is those who are set crazily on pleasure, or those who toil and moil to no purpose, nagging at their servants, muddling away money, stinting where they should be generous, buying bad bargains, spoiling good food. Regular work educates. No one can do it well without developing qualities of sense and application that are agreeable qualities in a house as well as in an office or a studio. That is partly why women trained to a job so often marry and give up their work. Men recognise that they will be helpmates and not hindrances in the struggle of life. Little bits of fluff marry too, no doubt, and they are not always what they seem.

They sometimes turn out good housekeepers.

But in this controversy, and in others allied to it, I should like to know what those contending mean by "work." Some say servants are scarce because work in a private house is hard and enslaving: yet, if the mistress of the house does that work, she is "fulfilling her mission," and not neglecting it for paid work. Whether it is "work" when a wife, and not a servant, does it and whether she should be legally entitled to payment are questions asked sometimes, but not yet answered. No one minds, as a rule, how much a woman drudges for her husband and children, but if she earns money in order to pay others to drudge she is a shirker and her employees are slaves. What nonsense! The best thing for a nation is for every man, woman, and child in it to do what they can do, well.

But women have never taken a step forward without a dust and a pother being raised around them. They have had to fight for education, for admission to trades and professions and, in our memories, for the Vote. Whatever they wanted was going to unsex them. When I enter a quiet balloting-room with my husband, put a cross on a slip of paper, say "Good morning" to the schoolmaster sitting there, and walk out again, I always think of old speeches and prophecies representing this business as a disintegrating one performed by Mænads amidst a crowd of hooligans. The objections to married women working are just as futile.

Nature has settled the place of women in the universe and always will settle it. "A woman wants a proper alliance with a man, a man who is better stuff than herself," says Ann Veronica. "She wants to be free—she wants to be legally and economically free so as not to be subject to the wrong man: but only God, who made the world, can alter things to prevent her being a slave to the right one." However, Nature and modern civilised conditions are constantly in conflict and compromise ensues. The woman finds her man and goes on with her work, too, because she wishes it, or because together they need what she can earn, or because she is sane and sees work to do everywhere, outside her home as well as in it. Let women settle this question for themselves, each woman doing the duty nearest to her, after which the next will have become clearer. If her home fills her time and thoughts, so be it, for that woman. If her neighbour chooses otherwise, more power to her. We must live and let live.

" . . . Young girls drinking cocktail after cocktail in public restaurants and showing themselves quite learned in the choice of champagnes"

The 1920's
1924

What Should a Woman Drink?

By Dr. Cecil Webb-Johnson

Illustration by W. S. Lakeman

T is a scientific fact that women are more easily affected by alcohol than are men, especially when they are young. The nervous system is ss stable, and the thyroid gland is more tive, and it has been well established scientific observers that alcohol is ot borne well when that gland is over-tive. During thyroid treatment a gle glass of claret has been known to ing on all the symptoms of into;ica-n. It would be well to examine the se for and against alcohol, as far as e female sex is concerned. The effects alcohol upon the human organism are well known to be recapitulated in any tail. With the ingestion of a small antity of alcoholic uor cheerfulness is in-eased, a sense of well-ing pervades the sub-ct, who revels in bodily d mental comfort. The dinary cares and rries of life assume ry small proportions, they do not fade from emory altogether, and e drinker is soon of inion that " all's for best in the best of all ssible worlds." The ture is full of pro-se and the past is ped out. This delight-state of affairs is also a temptation the weak-willed; the desire to joy these pleasing sensations on a bsequent occasion is soon yielded

Upon my theme I rightly think
There are five reasons why men drink—
Good wine—a friend—or being dry,
Or lest I should be by-and-by,
Or any other reason why

to, and then a fatal habit is formed.

This, however, is not the place in which to discuss the female inebriate; these unhappy beings are in most cases incapable of reclamation. Many men who have given way to habits of intoxi-cation have been rescued and made happy and useful members of society, but the woman who " takes to drink " is seldom cured. Even if apparently a cure has

SOME WINES AND			
THE PERCENTAGE OF ALCOHOL THEY CONTAIN			
Chablis	7.88%	*Mâcon (or Volnay)*	11.00%
Château Margaux	8.75%	*Rudesheimer*	11.60%
Leoville	9.10%	*Champagne*	11.75%
St. Julien	9.28%	*Madeira*	19.11%
Larose	9.85%	*Port*	21.91%
Johannisberg	10.00%	*Sherry*	22.90%

been effected, it is not permanent; sooner or later a relapse is bound to occur. This is the great danger in alcohol for women: the formation of a habit which

may end disastrously. In this connec-tion Dr. Arnold Lorand says:

" It is an interesting fact that in those with degenerated sexual glands there is always a greater liking for alcohol; thus women, after the menopause, have a greater predilection for spirits, and the greatest number of cases of drunkenness in women is to be observed among such. . . . If women, after the menopause, exhibit a greater inclination to drink, we think it cannot be explained solely by their seeking to drown the sorrows of lost youth and by substituting the plea-sures of sexual life by those of the bottle. This may certainly influence them to a certain degree, but, in any case, it is certain that without the possession of healthy sexual glands the desire for stimulants is greater; and it would seem also that in ad-vanced age they can take alcohol more freely than in their prosperous younger days. Such persons have a partiality for strong, sweet liqueurs. Happily, such women are in a great minority. All we wish to point out is that it is among the older people that this craving exists, as in the younger ones alcohol cannot be so well borne."

No young woman, in fact, ought to touch alcoholic (*Continued on page* 32)

If you seek the loveliest silk-like undies ask for

THESE lovely garments, all made of the beautiful 'Mylesta' Fabrics, now await your choice. The charming correctness of their design will be at once apparent, and their silk-like texture and delicate shades will claim your admiration. Yet this lingerie is not expensive and it wears and washes truly well.

'MYLESTA'
TRADE MARK
LINGERIE

What Should a Woman Drink?
(Continued from page 31)

liquor—at any rate, till she is over twenty-five years of age. It is a saddening sight to see quite young girls in the public restaurants drinking cocktail after cocktail, and showing themselves quite learned in choosing champagnes—and other wines. For a woman, there is danger in even the moderate use of potent alcoholic beverages. If that use is continued for long, degenerative changes take place in the tissues: the stomach and liver suffer first, then the kidneys, lungs, blood-vessels, and brain. The nervous system also is harmed, the alcohol acting upon it as a direct poison. Chronic gastritis, catarrh of the stomach, cirrhosis of the liver, and Bright's disease, are among the results of a steady indulgence in cocktails, liqueurs, and whisky-and-soda, even among those who have never "drunk to excess" in their lives. The mucous lining of the stomach becomes hardened and thickened, the flow of gastric juice is rendered scanty and irregular, and, consequently, unhealthy fermentation takes place, causing loss of appetite and various other unpleasant consequences.

If the practice of "nipping" is carried on to anything approaching excess there often follow degenerative changes in the brain, including loss of memory and of the power to concentrate, confused and cloudy thinking, and the like. The moral changes which occur in persons addicted to drink are well known, and examples may be seen in any prison or criminal lunatic asylum, but we need not dwell on this distressing aspect of the question here. Curiously enough, sexual immorality is not necessarily a consequence of excessive drinking—probably this is because of the degenerative changes in the tissues brought about by excess of alcohol. Small quantities of alcohol, on the other hand, may have the effect of stimulating the sexual glands, thus leading to immorality.

Time was when alcohol was prescribed for delicate young girls and women, chiefly in the form of Burgundy or Guinness stout. It was supposed to "build them up" and make blood; but this kind of thing has nearly disappeared from medical practice. In some cases the alcoholic habit has been formed through some well-meaning friend having recommended some medicated wine during convalescence. The alcohol in the wine brings about a transient sense of well being very pleasing to the convalescent and, subsequently, recourse is had to the decoction whenever the subject "feels low." The fact that the wine is obtained from the chemist's establishment and not from a public-house makes the transaction seem quite respectable; and the subject does not realise that she is just as much a dram drinker as the working-woman who slips into the private bar for her "drop o' gin." These wines are no doubt very useful in their place, but were not meant for beverage purposes.

In cases of acute illness, when a powerful stimulant is required, brandy is invaluable, and medical science has as yet discovered no satisfactory substitute. This spirit is especially valuable in heart-attacks, and in bad cases of pneumonia a tablespoonful of brandy may be given every three hours. If brandy is not available, whisky is the next best thing. Old matured whisky is the most wholesome spirit in the world, being distilled from the finest malted barley, but the so-called product of Scotland, of which the basis is wood-alcohol or potato-spirit, is liquid death. Aged people sometimes find that a little good Scotch whisky helps the enfeebled digestion to do its work and creates appetite; but it is not for the young and healthy woman.

Give her Pleasure — Give her Leisure

Give her an ELECTROLUX for Christmas

RILETTE

The wonderful Cleaner that every woman covets!

The moment a woman with a house to look after sees the Electrolux suction cleaner at work, she longs to possess it. Such easy, effortless, efficient cleaning of every nook and corner! Dust banished—germs destroyed—the very air of the room sweetened and purified in a few minutes. Hours of labour saved. Dust cleared from under the heaviest furniture without stooping, carpets thoroughly cleaned without being taken up.

There is no cleaner like Electrolux—none so powerful, nor yet so handy and compact. Electrolux is the very last word in up-to-date domestic efficiency.

Give her an Electrolux this Christmas—it means a New Year of leisure and freedom—and not only *one* New Year but a lifetime of them!

The NEW

ELECTROLUX

THE _CLEANER_ CLEANER

ELECTROLUX, LIMITED, 155, Regent St., London, W.1.   Works: Luton.
Showrooms throughout the Country.
Makers also of Electrolux Motorless Refrigerators and Water Softeners.

The well-to-do, leisured wife often consumes far more money than she could possibly earn in the labour market by the services she is rendering in her home

Violet Bonham Carter *Asks—* Should

Decorations by

STATED in this form the question sounds like one which could only have troubled the mind of a Feminist—and of a Feminist-spinster at that. It seems fantastic, after two people have pooled all the really important things of life, their time, their children, their taste, their luck, that their money should not for all practical purposes be pooled as well, whatever the law may say. But amazing as it may appear, it is a fact that in marriage, that contract of reckless mutual surrender, money has remained the one iron reservation. Happy, harmonious, devoted husbands and wives are prepared to share everything, except their banking accounts; and these, though they sound a trivial and irrelevant factor, have played an unfairly important part in the destiny of many *ménages*, and even in the lot of their children.

With the fate of the well-to-do, leisured wife I confess that I am not particularly concerned. She has legal safeguards in the form of settlements, Married Women's Property Act, etc., to protect her from material hardship or real injustice. And in most cases she is a drone, an expensive parasite who consumes far more money than she could possibly earn in the labour market by the services she is rendering in her home. Her household and clothes are looked after for her, her children are brought up by proxy. All she has to do is to order meals and pay, with her husband's money, the weekly books, on which she is, as a rule, so totally unequipped to shed a ray of scientific criticism, that the task often has to be performed for her by a secretary, who comes in once a month for the purpose. To allot to such women by law a proportion of their husbands' hard-earned gains would be to ask the State to pledge itself not merely to the support, but to the endowment of idleness.

I do not for a moment wish to suggest that these leisured "Drone-Wives" contribute nothing essential because they do not toil or spin in the technical sense of the word. "Consider the lilies of the field." If they can afford it, most men prefer the company of a wife whose glory surpasses Solomon's to that of a good book-keeper. And from the wife's point of view, to provide "relaxation" for someone else may be quite a strenuous occupation. Besides this, there is responsibility to be borne, there are decisions to be taken, "arrangements" (blessedly comprehensive word!) to be made, fun, comfort, beauty and atmosphere to be provided, "human needs" to be catered for and ministered to by sympathy, attention, suggestion silence.

But it is equally true to say of these things that they have no market-value, and that they are beyond price. At any rate their worth cannot be assessed or rewarded in terms of £ s. d. It may be necessary that decorative and sympathetic drones should be kept—it cannot be necessary that they should be paid

But if we look at the other end of the social scale, we find that the contribution of the Wife is of a very different nature. Here she is not a drone, but a drudge; not a luxury, but a vital necessity. Her function in the home, and in consequence her service to the State, is an indispensable one, and one which at present goes quite unrecognised and unrewarded. In Miss Rathbone's brilliant book, "The Disinherited Family" (the most eloquent and convincing statement of the case

Even in a coal-mine there are shifts.
But it is literally true that the work
of the working-class wife and mother
has no beginning and no end

The
1920's
1924

Wives have Wages?

Steven Spurrier

gainst the present economic position
f women and children that has yet been
nade), she gives a time-table of the
ay of a South London wife who kept
ouse on about £1 a week. She had
our children between eight years and
few months old, but as she had her
vater-supply on the same floor, and
1 old mother who came in to help
aily, her time-table, we are told, is
ne of the easiest recorded. This is
:

4.30.—Wake husband, who has to be
at work about 5 o'clock. He is a
carman for an L.C.C. contractor.
Get him off, if possible, without
waking the four children. He has
a cup of tea before going, but
breakfasts away from home. If
baby wakes, nurse him.

7.15.—Get up and light fire, wake
children, wash two eldest ones.
Get breakfast for self and children.

8.0.—Breakfast.

8.30.—Tidy two children for school
and start them off at 8.45.

9.0.—Clear away and wash up; wash
and dress boy of three; bathe and
dress baby.

10.0.—Nurse baby and put him to bed.

10.30.—Turn down beds, clear grate,
scrub floor.

11.30.—Make beds.

12.0.—Mother, who has done the
marketing, brings in the food; begin
to cook dinner.

12.15.—Children all in, lay dinner,
and with mother's help tidy children
for it.

1.0.—Dinner, which mother serves
while Mrs. G. nurses baby, who
wakes about then.

1.30.—Tidy children for school
again.

1.45.—Start them off and sit down
with mother to their own dinner;
wash up; tidy room; clean themselves.

3.0.—Go out, if it is not washing day
or day for doing the stairs, with
baby and boy of three.

3.45.—Come in and get tea for children. Put boy of three to sleep,
nurse baby.

4.15.—Children come in.

4.30.—Give children tea.

5.0.—Wash up and tidy room. Tidy
children and self.

6.0.—Go out for a " blow in the
street " with all four children.

7.0.—Come in and put children to
bed. Nurse baby.

7.30.—Husband returns; get his
supper.

8.0.—Sit down and have supper with
him.

8.30.—Clear away and wash up. . . .
Get everything ready for the
morning. Mend husband's clothes
as soon as he gets them off.

10.0.—Nurse baby and go to bed.

One can hardly imagine a harder day
than this. Even in the depths of a
coal-mine there are shifts. But it is
literally true that the work of the working-class wife and mother has no beginning and no end. It is given with
ungrudging generosity, for it is a labour
of love as well as of necessity. And
because it is a labour of love she would
probably be just as shocked as the most
detached and ignorant sentimentalist at
the bare suggestion of receiving for it
anything as sordid as Wages.

But what it does seem to me that
she has a good right to demand, and
to receive, is the material which is
essential to carrying it out. At present
a mother has a thousand duties, but
no rights.

The male parent should
family life. Thus he might
not spend the entire time

Are PARENTS

*M. Grant Cook answers this
with a decisiveness worthy*

PARENTS are always the subject of much discussion. Should or shouldn't they have children? Do they know anything about them? Are they the best people to look after them, or would children be better off in other hands? People who are not themselves parents, elderly aunts, friends of the family, school teachers and so forth, have no doubt at all about the answer to this question. Teachers, indeed, often feel that parents are not only no use, but positively dangerous. Even children, in this free age, are sometimes dissatisfied with their fathers and mothers, and parents are seldom quite contented with their sons and daughters.

The question of how to adjust parents and children to each other so that each will be better satisfied is becoming an urgent matter. In the press of modern life home and mother, and, eventually, children and father, are threatened with extinction. The home must be preserved. Without it there can be no national stability. Year by year relatives in general tend to become fewer. Grandparents have unobtrusively but definitely vanished from family life. Great-aunts and great-cousins play no part in the family calendar or the list of Christmas presents. Some children nowadays have few aunts and no uncles. Almost no modern child—unless in an occasional vicarage—has fourteen brothers and sisters, once so usual a nursery complement. Parents, too, are a diminishing class, disappearing in the countries where divorce is easy with alarming rapidity. Something must be done about it, and that soon.

It may be argued that parents have had a long trial and do not seem susceptible to improvement but I think all

the same that they have improved. The earliest case of parentage recorded in British history is that of Adam and Eve. It was certainly not conspicuously successful. A first child is often spoilt; how then could Cain escape? Abel's character is always admired and his fate deplored, but it is more than possible that he was a most tiresome child and brother, and that his parents

Parents, it may be argued, have had a long
trial and do not seem susceptible to improvement. Something must be done about it

made new and different mistakes in his upbringing, and so precipitated the disaster.

Being a parent at all is a gamble, and that of course is the other side of the difficulty. Many parents are disappointed in their children. Where they

hoped for curly hair and dimples, they get wiry locks and angles. Where they would welcome obedience, gentleness and pretty behaviour, they get uproar and squalls, and a hatred of washing By this time everyone's ancestry has got a bit mixed and no one can count on the appearance or character of their offspring. Arrogance, greed, and dullness which no parents can account for, may exhibit themselves very early in the young. Little Isabel may have Aunt Anne's small round eyes and tendency to rudeness; little George may display the least endearing traits of Uncle Albert, although these relatives have never been near the house. It is to the parents credit that they make the best of such trials. There are children whom no parents should tolerate A coal-mine would be too good for them.

Mothers hitherto have had most to do with the children, and yet how seldom can they guarantee that a child will always be perfect in health, looks, and conduct. In the eighteenth century mothers took this to heart, and believing that perfection was within reach, worked hard to correct nursery defects Preserved dandelions were administered for "the hickup"; a brew of garlic, scraped tin, treacle, and burnt oyster shells was kept at hand to be drunk freely if the child was bitten by a mad dog; for other and more probable infantile ailments a "posset" was prescribed, to be swallowed by the pint, composed of black snails and the powdered skull of a male skeleton, frog livers dried, peony roots, and lichen scraped off a churchyard wall, the whole steeped in ale and sack in equal parts So much for health.

As to looks, the child was told that

36

always take his fair share of
realise that his little ones do
trailing clouds of glory

*Illustrations by
Stuart Hay*

Any USE?

*burning question of the hour
of its great importance*

he was as God made him, and nothing more could be done about it except to preserve a modest demeanour and emulate his elders. Conduct was regulated in many horrifying ways, one of the most favoured being (as we know from the chronicles of the Fairchild family) a short walk to see the corpse of a malefactor hanging on the gallows, even infants in arms being carried to see this edifying sight, and the whole group urged to take warning by it.

These ways of making the young more bearable in the home have gone out, and mothers are more and more inclined to leave the moral and mental improvement of the family in the hands of specialists, while they improve their tennis and other games. Or perhaps they simply go shopping to get away from the strain of the home, or attend cinemas, or read novels. Too few of them have fully realised that in order to halve the worry and double the pleasure—if any—of children, the co-operation of the elusive father should be sought, and indeed, insisted upon.

Fathers seldom see anything of their children except at bedtime and in the holidays. The English father has an office in "the City," to which he is obliged to retire, and the American father is submerged "down town" for many hours a day. There are also clubs. The father's influence, then, in most homes, is confined to a few brief hours of play, during which time, as mothers have been heard to complain, he makes himself the more popular parent by overlooking lapses of all kinds, and so undoing the lessons patiently taught by the mother. She should demand that the father take a home course at least once a year, during which time he should be constantly with his offspring, seeing them through the fractious days of convalescence after measles, keeping order at table, restoring peace in the nursery, getting little Pamela off to her party, and accompanying Peter and Michael to the dentist. Thus the male parent

The English father has his office in "the City," to which he is obliged to retire. His influence in the home is restricted to a few hours per week

would take his fair share of family life, and he might realise with something of a shock that his little ones did not spend the entire time trailing clouds of glory and making naïve and delicious remarks.

Children indeed—like Old Masters, "the Classics," witty things said at Oxford and Cambridge, most great reputations, and life in general—have been greatly overrated and over-praised. The "child's world," of which we hear so much from psychologists, poets, and other people who take pains to keep well out of it, is a very limited, trivial, and tiresome place to stay long in, and the dreams and fairy beliefs of the child are mostly made up by sentimentalists or are merely the expression of pure infantile egotism. Occasionally children say a naïve, literal, or logical thing that is very charming—but how many things they say that are utter nonsense. Fathers forced into unusual and prolonged intimacy with their nurseries, and anxious to add to their repertoire of quotations from Pamela and Peter, are quick to find this out, and they are sometimes unfairly annoyed about it. Shocked at finding themselves bored, they take to shopping, and buy all the toys that they covet for themselves. Frequent presents seem to these misguided men the way to keep things quiet and happy in the nursery. The immediate effect is satisfactory, but children who are "made happy" by too much indulgence and constant presents, are noticeably antisocial and selfish when they meet other children and can't have things all their own way.

This is in a great measure the defect of the Montessori child, or one should more justly say, of the child whose mother has grasped, more or less, a few Montessori principles. Most mothers of young children have done this, and many have added a little elementary Freud, a thought or two from (Continued on page 38)

37

Are Parents Any Use?

(*Continued from page* 37)

Jung, and a trifle of Coué to their general fund of "child psychology," with the result that home life is freer and livelier than it used to be. One young mother rather nervously described herself as following "the Montorosso system or something, because everybody does it where I live." It not ill expresses the jumble of ideas (often opposed to each other) that are tried on the post-war child.

For example, Richard, aged three, is the child of "Montorosso" parents. They will go nowhere without him; they will deny him nothing, for fear—as they explain—of rousing in his three-year-old breast, feelings of injury and resentment which they would have no means of allaying. Between Richard and a common or garden "spoilt brat" there is little difference to be discerned. Richard clamours for a slab of pink coconut sugar, in the High Street, at eleven in the morning, and, lest his little subconscious be irreparably damaged, his father rushes in to a grubby little shop to buy it for him. Richard wants all the toys at his own party, and the other children are urged to give them up, for the good of their characters. Richard does not want his bath, or wants to blow a trumpet at six in the morning, or sits in a puddle, or throws the coffee-pot out of the window, and his "Montorosso" mother, a trifle harassed, says that

---

Our Shopping Service

In addition to the articles illustrated on pages 62, 63 of this number, any of which we will buy for you on receiving your order and cheque, our Shopping Service staff will gladly purchase for you any article shown in the advertisement columns of the magazine

---

it is all helping his nature to develop without an inhibition. It is characteristic of earnest "Montorosso" mothers that they are quite careless of the rights or inhibitions of other infants. They hope that Richard will never blame them for anything, but it is more than likely that the feelings of injury and resentment may be retroactive, when the grown man finds that he can't have everything he calls for, and has a digestion ruined by coconut bars.

The mother who is half-baked Freud, or Neo-Jung, is, on the whole, worse than the mixed Montessorian. She will not allow her child to kiss his aunt or open the door for his grandmother in case of a "complex" ensuing, and her whole idea is to keep the infant trotting from dawn to dark. His day is divided into periods of work and organised play, school lessons, pottery, eurythmics, woodcuts, country-dancing, drill, and painting. The Freudian child has never an instant free. I once met a little girl of twelve in a country boarding-house, who had been left behind while her family retired with a young brother suspected of having scarlet-fever. She sat completely idle all day and looked seraphically content. There was nothing she wanted to do. "I am *always* doing things — violin, carving, maps, chemistry. My children will never be taught anything," she said to me, her hands folded. She was the product of fussy semi-Freudian parents who continually were trying to sublimate imaginary tendencies to evil, unconscious that they were fostering rebellion and hatred, and

a regrettable indifference to what are calle the natural affections. Her parents, sh told me calmly, were rather like 'bus conductors—always hurrying her. She wa glad they had gone away and left he Later, when I knew her better, she showe me scraps of poetry that she wrote i secret. They were sentimental verse about family life, and her ideal was ver different from reality. Her Victorianis would have horrified her parents, coo chary of caresses, and devoted to physic activity and independence. In her rhyme she almost excelled that famous poem dozens of verses long, of an earlier age :-

"Who ran to raise me when I fell
And kissed the place to make it wel!
My Mother!"

In the opinion of the usual thre noun Freudian, there are two words express the psychological condition of th author of that poem. A poem mor fraught with complexes was probably nev penned. The over-sublimated little gi shared every one of them. She probabl thought her parents the great disadvantag of her childhood. A 'bus conductor ma be an admirable father, but surely no tr parent should, in the imaginative sens seem like a 'bus conductor to his chil

Are parents in general, then, any use They never learn from experience—or, least, they never learn much—and they hav no fixed standard at which to aim. The invariably inspire in their children a dete mination to bring up the next generatio *quite* differently. And yet, there is no ge ting over the fact, children like the parents almost always, and overlook the failures. A single parent is not of ve great value. Taking any family in sectio we find most probably that the father rather futile, and the mother—considere as a hereditary mother since Eve—a failu at her profession. We find the childre tedious, usually spoilt (though it is no called self-expression), always clamoro and egotistic. (In case I am accused disliking children, I hasten to say that most cases they are infinitely nicer tha their parents, and that I prefer their con pany, within limits, to that of other people

But if the component parts are so u satisfactory, why trouble to preserve th particular social group? The answer that, although apart these single membe are only tolerable, let them but fuse in that unit which we call the family, and have at once something irresistibly charr ing and precious. There is nothing el quite like the warmth and gaiety of a re family. (Highbrows, the young of Un versity professors, and Montessorians, u less thoroughly mixed as they usually ar do not come under this heading.) The jokes, their squabbles, their ways and cu toms, have a quality that is at least old as the race, and something in each us responds to it.

And without parents obviously the could be no children. And without Pame Peter, Michael, and even Richard th slave-driver (miscalled a free "Mont rosso" child), and all the other little cre tures who lose their teeth and won't was and bid us not "to be so proud of grow ups," everything would be a good de duller, and Christmas-trees would be use at all. Let parents take more ho days together if they need them. L the father co-operate in the nursery necessary. Let the subconscious of the i fant be occasionally forgotten. And parents and children have a natural affini for each other, let them continue to flouris

They will anyhow!

"*Splendid, Mrs. Rawlins!*"

"*You really have done those things beautifully, Mrs. Rawlins. These tablecloths.... so crisp and glossy.*"

"*Well, mum, I'm glad you like them. But I always say the credit's due as much to Robin Starch as to me. And it's that easy. The iron glides over the things like one o'clock.*"

Robin gives the expert touch to table linen. And not only table linen, but everything that needs a laundry finish. Many people run their sheets through a thin mixture of Robin Starch. It seems to keep them fresh-looking. From large things down to the small things, Robin is the easy starch. Easy to manage, easy to mix, easy to use, and the name easy to remember— "a packet of Robin please!"

ROBIN *Starch*

The problem of running a small house with the help of two or more servants is greatly simplified by careful organisation of the routine work, and by utilising every proved labour-saver. The duties of the maids should be made interchangeable as far as possible; in this way each maid has more freedom without inconveniencing the family

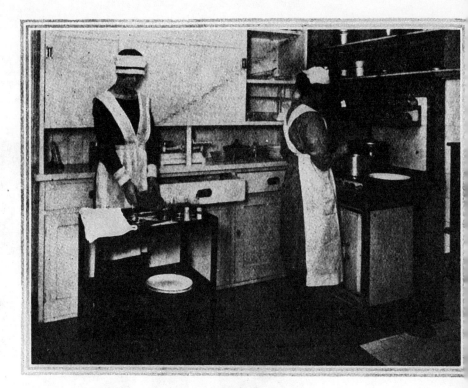

Part II of—

Running a Home

The facts given below are based on the actual working experience of a household run by a mistress and her two maids

UNTIL 1916 I experienced few housekeeping difficulties, always having had one good maid to depend upon even if the second one was indifferent. Since then I have gone in for labour-saving appliances, such as a washing machine, electric iron, vacuum cleaner, stainless knives and central heating, but find that the more I consider the maids the less work they do. I am not a beginner and am most anxious not to over-work my servants, so shall be glad to know what you consider a fair day's work for each maid."

This letter, addressed to the Institute, pointing out some of the difficulties experienced by mistresses throughout the country, is typical of many received. So much was written in the daily papers on the apparent reasons for the unpopularity of domestic service at the time the Committee appointed to enquire into the present conditions and supply of female domestic servants was sitting, that it is unnecessary to discuss the subject from this standpoint; but some suggestions and information relating to the duties of individual maids should prove helpful to many worried housewives.

With few exceptions, well trained and thoroughly efficient maids are difficult to obtain. In my opinion, this state of affairs exists not because housework in itself is dull, uninteresting, or badly paid, but chiefly on account of the lack of freedom and the long hours.

Many mistresses realise this, and consider their maid's comfort on every possible occasion, and such employers are not difficult to please. Others, on the contrary, are thoughtless and selfish, often without being conscious of the fact. Many of the difficulties and misunderstandings that frequently arise would be solved if the mistress occasionally put herself in the maid's position, and judged whether, in the event of having to earn her own living, she would be content and satisfied with her lot.

I consider that every individual, irrespective of his work or station in life, should have at least two hours of freedom daily, in addition to half-holidays. The shop assistant, factory girl, and clerk generally have the whole of Sunday, one half-day in the week, and every day after 7 p.m., in which they are entirely free to please themselves. It must be admitted that the lot of the domestic servant compares rather unfavourably.

The solution of the problem is by no means easy, for it is only natural that the mistress who pays liberal wages to two or more servants and studies their interests, demands willing service in return, and frequently this service is required after 6 p.m., when other people are enjoying their leisure.

An arrangement, which I know answers satisfactorily in more than one household, is to make the duties of the maids interchangeable, and, in this way, each maid can be spared more readily, and thus has more freedom without inconveniencing the family. Before the War, when the wages of five maids—a cook, parlourmaid, housemaid, kitchen and scullery maid—only amounted to about £100 per annum, there was little need for the work to be regularly interchanged, e.g. when the cook was off duty, the kitchen and scullery maid did her work, and when the parlourmaid had her evening out, the housemaid waited at table, so that the mistress was rarely inconvenienced.

To-day things are changed: the same money only pays the wages of two servants, a cook and housemaid, who demand more leisure, so consequently fresh methods must be adopted.

First and foremost, utilise every proved labour-saver and cut out all unnecessary work in the home.

Secondly, be absolutely frank with the maids when engaging them; if possible show them a rough plan of the work required, and state definitely what free time they will receive. Further, explain that, with a view to giving them greater freedom, they must be willing to interchange duties whenever necessary. When two maids only are kept, it is an excellent plan to engage each one for general duties, although they would carry out their respective duties until the latter part of the day.

In the country an "all-round" handy man, who combines the duties of chauffeur or gardener with the heavy household tasks, often proves more satisfactory than an additional maid, particularly if the house is old-fashioned and without modern conveniences. The cleaning of windows, carrying in of coal, laying of fires, cleaning of brasses, *(Continued on page*

(Continued from page 40)

orch, steps, and the polishing of floors
re some of the heavier tasks which he
ould undertake.

With unemployment so prevalent, it is
ot uncommon to engage a man and wife to
ndertake the entire work of a house. The
rife invariably undertakes the cooking and
pstairs work, the remainder being shared
etween both.

It is quite impossible to organise the
outine work, and plan a time-table that will
e exactly suitable for any one house, as
onditions vary so vastly, according to the
umber in family, the age of the children,
ne size and type of house, and whether it
provided with the conveniences obtainable
a town, etc., but the time-table below may
e used as a guide and altered to suit indi-
idual requirements. The plan is given for
ne arrangement of work in a house consist-
ng of dining-room, sitting-room lounge,
all, five bedrooms, or four bedrooms and
nursery, bathroom and kitchen-scullery,
be shared between a cook general and
ouse-parlourmaid.

It is presumed that the mistress will at-
nd to the flowers, linen, ordering of stores,
d will assist with light duties, such as
usting and bed-making, when there are
sitors in the house.

THE DAILY DUTIES OF A COOK GENERAL

These should be completed before the
ecial duties of the day are commenced.
6.30. Rise, open own bed, and air bed-
om. Light kitchen fire, or stoke the
iler, fill kettles, unlock front and back
ors. Sweep hall and front steps, clean
em when necessary. Polish front door
asses. Lay and light dining-room fire, if
cessary. Brush up and tidy dining-room.
8.0. Prepare kitchen and dining-room
eakfast. Wash up breakfast things.
veep and tidy kitchen and scullery. Meet
istress to receive orders for the day. Pre-
re luncheon for dining-room and kitchen,
d commence any cooking required for the
ening meal which takes a long time,
g. stocks and soups, jellies and creams.
10.30-12.30. Special work, such as turn-
g out rooms.
1.0-1.30. Lunch. Wash up luncheon
ings, tidy kitchen, get in coal.
2.0-4.0. Free time.
4.0-7.0. Prepare and cook dinner. Wash
crockery and cooking utensils. Make
ffee.

OUSE-PARLOURMAID'S DAILY DUTIES

6.30. Rise, open own bed. Sweep and
st and generally tidy up the sitting-room
unge, clean the grate and lay fire when
quired. Make and take up early tea, call
family. Lay the breakfast.
8.0. Kitchen breakfast.
8.30. Whilst the family are having
eakfast, open beds and windows.
9.30. Remove the breakfast things,
eep up crumbs. Make the beds, tidy each
om in turn, attending to the wash-basins
d taps; mop the floors and dust.
10.15. Clean and tidy the bathroom and
atory. Sweep and dust landing and
irs.
10.30-12.30. Special daily duties.
12.30. Dress, and lay cloth for lunch.
1.0. Lunch. Wait at table if required.
1.30. Kitchen dinner. Remove the lun-
eon things. Help cook to wash up.
here there is a butler's pantry, the house-
rlourmaid may undertake the washing up
silver and glass. Be prepared to answer
door.
.0. Carry in afternoon tea. Remove
wash up same.
.0-7.0. Free time.
.0. Lay the cloth for dinner, 7.30 p.m.
ht up house, draw blinds. Wait at table.
responsible for the cleaning and putting

away of silver and glass. Serve coffee.

COOK'S SPECIAL WEEKLY DUTIES

This work is planned to be carried out
between 10.30 a.m. and 12.30 p.m.
Monday. Do any washing required. The
amount of laundrywork done at home
should be clearly stated when engaging a
cook-general. It will probably be necessary to employ additional labour to do the
washing, if the family is large. If the cook
does no washing, she should clean and polish
all metals, e.g. copper or aluminium, cooking utensils, tins, cooking knives, spoons,
etc. Turn out cupboards and drawers.
Tuesday. Clean the gas cooker, giving
special attention to the oven. Prepare
everything in readiness, plan simple cooking as far as possible and give detailed instructions to the housemaid regarding the
dinner.
2.30-10. Free time.
Wednesday. Weekly clean of porch,
steps, window sills, and hall. Polishing if
necessary.
Thursday. Turn out dining-room.
Friday. Weekly clean, kitchen, stove,
and flues when necessary, scrub pantry.
Saturday. Weekly clean, scullery; do
extra cooking, baking cakes, pastry, etc.

HOUSE-PARLOURMAID'S WEEKLY DUTIES

Monday. Collect linen for the laundry
and assist the cook with washing the small
things if required; otherwise turn out the
sitting-room lounge.
Tuesday. Turn out the principal bedroom, and one small one. Ironing if required. After 2.30 p.m. attend to the cook's
duties.
Wednesday. Turn out the two other
bedrooms.
Thursday. Weekly clean maid's bedroom or nursery; special work is light as
the housemaid should be free after lunch
(2.30-10 p.m.).
Friday. Turn out the sitting-room
lounge if not done on Monday.
Saturday. Weekly clean bathroom, lava-
tory, landing and staircase. Check linen
returned from the laundry.

In larger houses where four maids are
kept, the work is divided rather differently.
The cook does not undertake any general
house cleaning other than the kitchen and
its equipment, and the scullery, pantry, larder, back steps and passages. If fancy
cooking is required, or the family is large,
she would need the assistance of a kitchen
or scullery maid.

The *parlourmaid,* in a house where one
or more housemaids are kept, attends to
the laying of the cloth and waiting at table,
the care of flowers, cruets, table linen, wine,
dessert, etc. She also takes charge of the
dressing-room and library, turning them
out weekly, serves afternoon tea, answers
the door, and valets the master of the house
when a man servant is not employed.

The *housemaid* undertakes the general
house duties, and is entirely responsible for
the bedrooms, bathroom and the downstair
rooms not attended to by the parlourmaid.
In addition, the housemaid calls the family
in the morning, taking up early tea and
hot water, and waits on the mistress of the
house. In houses with more than six bedrooms and two sitting-rooms to be cleaned,
an under housemaid or between maid would
be necessary.

Mrs. W. L. Courtney

writes about—

Step-mothers

in Fiction and in Fact

Illustration By Bert Thomas

WHEN did it begin, that fiction of the cruel step-mother? Hardly in the days of polygamy, for official step-mothers were then as unnecessary as maiden aunts— if there were any maiden aunts. Has the fiction any basis in fact, and if so, is jealousy at the bottom of it? Sarah was jealous of Hagar, because the bondwoman had given her lord a son while she was yet barren. But Sarah was the legitimate wife, and Hagar was a younger rival. On the whole the idea seems to have been of Teutonic, not Semitic, growth. Cinderella remains the classic instance. Unless, of course, Cinderella is an Aryan nature - myth translated westwards; one never knows!

Anyway, there it is. Step-mothers have got a bad name, and undeservedly. As a class they are as long-suffering and as ill-requited as legitimate mothers. They cook, and mend, and wash, or they struggle to find hired help to do these things, and at the same time they have to put up with a chorus of grown-up domestic criticism, from which real mothers are long exempt. Because, if you are a mother, your children may come into the world wailing, as Shakespeare lamented, but they do not come fully grown grumblers, whereas a step-mother may have to take over a family at any age, even the most critical.

Moreover, in more ways than one she inherits a tradition. First and foremost she has to get over the prejudice inherent in step-motherliness. Then there are the traditions of her adopted family, the "things we like," the way "things have always been done." And it is astonishing what haloes adorn de-

Step-mothers have got a bad name, and undeservedly. They have to put up with domestic criticism from which real mothers are exempt

parted mothers when a legend concerning them is a weapon with which to wound their unfortunate successors. Let daughters have chafed ever so much under maternal despotism, let them have breathed ever so freely during the interregnum of widowerhood—it needs but for their father to take unto him a second wife for the earlier régime to assume the glamour of the Golden Age. The step-mother's innocent and unwitting innovations are at once an offence; before she is well established she has earned her natural epithet of "cruel."

Even philosophers help the illusion; indeed they are more responsible than

anyone else for connecting step-motherliness with natural cruelty. Did not Kant talk about "our step-mother Nature," who enjoins upon us unwelcome moral sanctions? And then, having got step-mothers and Nature mixed up, did not Tennyson and other Victorian poets proceed to define that "step-mother" as "red in tooth and claw"—in fact the cruel tyrant the fairy-tales had already made her appear? No, the step-mother has really not had a chance. Nobody has ever looked at her just as she is— patient, unoffending, humble, striving after the impossible ideal of her predecessor's legendary achievements. If only some innocent child would one day look at her, as he did at the naked Emperor, he would see that really she was as hard-working, as domestic, as conciliatory, as any creature upon earth.

But she is often tried too high. Picture her unprotected condition when she comes first into a grown-up family. She has a nominal protector, no doubt, in her husband; but, if he is not the victim of illusions to begin with, he very soon becomes the prey of circumstances. Either he fancies his daughter "little girls," though they may be young women well on in the twenties or he is entirely ignorant of the malice and uncharitableness that can fill even a flapper's breast. To begin with, the step-mother is expected to go wrong her position is admittedly "difficult," and every false step is eagerly awaited and unrelentingly noted. She is but human; she has had a past existence she may occasionally allude to it—possibly with complacency. She meets with stony silence, or with a false show of interest

(Continued on page 43)

Step-mothers in Fiction and in Fact

(*Continued from page* 42)

intended to draw her on. She yields to the temptation, having a natural liking, poor soul, for a little friendly gossip. At once invidious comparisons are drawn; it is history against legend, and the legend wins.

Then, consider her domestic trials. The first wife, married in youth, made her early mistakes in housekeeping with only a young and indulgent husband to criticise her. And her housekeeping was on the limited scale thought suitable for young couples. But the step-mother walks straight into a large establishment with, perhaps, children of all ages, numerous servants, furniture and equipment which she did not choose and probably would never have chosen. She must either ruthlessly "scrap" a good deal of the household tradition, or painfully adapt herself to it. Probably, for peace sake and from a natural desire to save an upset, she chooses the second alternative, leaving the "scrapping" process to come later. Praiseworthy, but injudicious! She had better have had the row first; peace would have come all the quicker. The inharmony which exists between her own possessions and the incongruous framework she has struggled to fit them into, only symbolises the spiritual inharmony which keeps the machine jarring. Yet hardly any step-mother begins with a clean sweep; she has too much conscience and too strong a natural tendency to self-sacrifice. Yet, by tradition, she is "cruel."

It isn't only a question of furniture and servants. Between every husband and wife there are occasional differences, trifling in themselves, but magnified when reflected in listeners' faces. Think of the proverbial "third person" always at the board, and that a grown-up step-daughter! And then dare to say that step-mothers are not long-suffering in every sense of the word.

No one, however, is going to help them, until they first help themselves. They will be driven to form a union. For in isolation how dare they stand firm against the family traditions, however ill-founded and expensive? But united? Not just in a sneaking, tea-party sort of way, with a sigh and a murmured plaint, *sotto voce*, to another, when a sympathetic gleam appears in that sister-step-mother's eye, but a real union, a body with rules and a policy and a flag to wave before the world. "Step-mothers, unite! Strike one blow for the right to your own taste, your own opinions, your own soul, your own domestic interior!"

I am not quite sure yet what the rules would be, but a complete month in the year away from the step-family would be one of them. Another would be the abolition of all allusions to "what was always done." The policy of the "clean slate" in matters domestic would be formally and officially adopted. Members would rank according to the number and age of their step-children; babies under three would put their new "mother" only into the lowest grade, that of apprentices; children from three to ten would belong to "learners"; ten to fifteen would require "skilled" supervision; whereas daughters "out" and sons with latchkeys could be undertaken by none but master workwomen. Only at their own risk would aspirants to step-motherhood enter any grade for which they had not been certified. The union would examine them on marriage, or better still on betrothal, and award them classified certificates for tact, temper, social accomplishments, good appearance, and all the qualities likely to help to success in their undertaking. If they got a third-class certificate and yet insisted on taking first-class work—that is to say, if children under ten were thought enough for them, and they married to a family of grown-ups—the union would give them no support when the inevitable failure threw them on its sympathy, if not on its funds. But when the well qualified and duly certificated were yet worsted in the struggle, help, support, strike pay, holidays, even temporary quarters in a special "rest" or "guest" house, should all be theirs. And in that house, no one should so much as breathe the words "This is always done." It should be Liberty Hall!

Seriously, this relation between the step-mother and her adopted family is often an extreme case of the tyranny of the young over their elders—the only real "oppression" left in the modern world. Two daughters lately had a discussion, which was repeated by the more ingenuous to her own charming and successful mother, a Society favourite. "Margaret says that she has to go her own way because her mother is so out of date, but doesn't know it," confided the youthful Phyllis. "Well, and what did you say?" asked her mother. "Oh, mother, of course I said that you were out of date too, but you were so clever that you knew it." Clever enough to acknowledge our deficiencies, that is the best we can hope to attain, we who have left forty behind us. Or is it clever enough to attain our own ends under a show of simplicity? Perhaps; but we don't tell the young our secret. It is not only in the secret service, or the spy-melodrama, that feigned imbecility comes by its own. And the wise step-mother, with more of the serpent about her than the dove, may yet elect to show the dove's docility until her position is assured.

A Career for Women—

H.M. Inspectors of Taxes

By A Civil Servant

Decoration by Anne Rochester

THE Civil Service Commissioners opened the door of another profession to women when they announced their intention of permitting women candidates at the examination held in London in July 1923 for the situations as Assistant Inspectors of Taxes in the Inland Revenue Department.

This branch of the Civil Service offers remarkable chances of promotion. There is no likelihood of it ever closing down or becoming a defunct department, on the contrary its importance is rising by leaps and bounds; every year sees its volume of work increasing by a substantial percentage and the formation of new districts requiring inspectorate and staffs. The war was directly responsible for women being allowed within its precincts; even then they were only employed as clerks, so that this concession is distinctly a step in the right direction.

At the present time the number of women Assistant Inspectors can be counted on one's fingers. The ambitious girl is therefore assured of a profession not already overcrowded and not likely to be for many years hence. One who has an aptitude for accountancy and mathematics, and who is at her best when attacking difficult problems, will find the work entirely to her liking. As no woman has yet been appointed as an Inspector, it remains to be seen whether any will be given the responsibility of the charge of a district or whether they will be retained merely as an Inspector Assisting. But one can rest assured that the constant changes in the Income Tax Laws will render the position immune from monotony.

If the restrictions of a Government office are found to be too irksome, it is always possible for the expert to obtain a highly remunerative post as Income Tax Advisor to a firm of chartered accountants, land agents, or, providing one has the necessary capital, even to commence in business as an income tax expert and repayment agent.

The entrance examination is a competitive one composed of usually five compulsory subjects and optional subjects three or six according to the number of marks allotted. In the last examination the compulsory subjects

It is often difficult to persuade a taxpayer that the amount charged is a fair sum

were: Essay, English, Present Day, Everyday Science, and Viva Voce. The optional subjects included Languages, History, Mathematics, Geography, Law, and in all comprised twenty-three subjects from which the candidate had little difficulty in making up the required quota. The fee is usually £6.

Previously a University education was essential, and the candidate was required to be nominated by the authorities of a University to which she was or had been attached as a whole time student. Thanks to the enormous pressure brought to bear by the various Associations on the Commissioners, this point has been waived and is not likely to be re-enforced. The only qualifications now necessary are that a candidate must be unmarried or a widow and between the ages of twenty-one and twenty-four, also a natural-born British subject and the

child of a father also a natural-born British subject. Any person upon whose training for the occupation of a teacher public money has been spent cannot be appointed unless the consent of the appropriate Education Authority is first obtained.

The result of the examination is usually made known after an interval of about six weeks' or two months' time, and successful candidates may be appointed to any district, the United Kingdom for the purpose of convenience having been so divided.

Upon entering the office of H.M. Inspector of Taxes, the Assistant Inspector, for she will be known as such, will find her training a very thorough one, at this stage perhaps almost to a point of boredom, the first work assigned to her possibly being that of post clerk. She will find, however, that brains must be exercised to be even an efficient post and filing clerk in a Government office. Gradually she will learn how property and salaries are assessed, how the occupation of land is dealt with, and the various rules of the Income Tax Acts applicable to the different sources of income. The manner in which the duty is collected and paid over to the Revenue, how repayment is made and a hundred and one other details which make up the machinery of our intricate Income Tax system will form part of her fascinating studies. Statistical work in this department is very heavy and is a duty usually reserved for newcomers. But although monotonous, it serves a useful purpose in that the information assists the Chancellor of the Exchequer in his preparation of the Budget for the ensuing year and it also affords the assistant an excellent opportunity of acquiring good working knowledge of the various streets and parishes comprising the district and of the taxes administered therein.

One of her duties, and not the least dull by any means and which calls for considerable tact and patience, will consist in interviewing callers. It is often extremely difficult to persuade a taxpayer labouring under a sense of grievance that the amount charged is a fair sum and that all allowances to which he is entitled have been duly made. Moreover, (*Continued on page 45*) however ill-mannered and discourteous he may be, it is not in the interest of the Service that he should be allowed to go away dissatisfied, and the apt retort which rises to one's lips must be quashed before it has time to be uttered. Nevertheless, the situation sometimes reveals unexpected humour.

Another very interesting side of Income Tax, and one which will appeal to the woman who is interested in the study of the Empire, are the laws relating to relief granted to persons who have suffered double taxation by reason of their income being derived from a country forming one of the British Dominions. This is a subject very little understood by those chiefly concerned.

The Preliminary Examination taken after about eighteen months' service is entirely departmental, and includes questions only on those branches of Income Tax which have formed the daily work of the assistant. The Final Examination deals wholly with the duties of an Inspector, and includes questions on company accounts and all profits assessable under Schedule D. The assistant is given opportunity to acquire all the knowledge necessary, her Inspector often gives valuable help and advice, and to pass is merely a question of having studied both wisely and well.

Inspectors of Taxes to His Majesty are entitled to six weeks' holiday a year and all Bank Holidays. The offices are open to the public from 10 a.m. to 4 p.m., excepting Saturdays, when closed at 1 p.m., but the number of hours worked varies in each district. The commencing salary of an Assistant Inspector is £150, rising by annual increments to a maximum of £250, but on being appointed as an Inspector the maximum is £500. There are, of course, a few higher posts where the remuneration is munificent. These scales are exclusive of bonus, instituted during the war period, which varies with the cost of living.

Like the majority of Government appointments, each year's service counts towards the pension on retirement at the age of sixty. On marriage a woman is entitled to a sum equal to one month's salary, and not exceeding twelve months' salary, for every year of service, providing she has been appointed not less than six years. Special provision is made for sick leave, and in cases of prolonged illness and consequent inability for official duties a pension according to the number of years' service may be granted.

There is probably no other department whose leisure hours resemble so much that of a happy family. In the summer-time there are boating, cricket, tennis, and rambling clubs, and in the winter-time golf, hockey, football, and dancing clubs under the auspices of the Civil Service Sports Association, of which H.R.H the Duke of York is the Patron.

Both from the standpoints of remuneration and intellectual advancement it is well worth while for the woman who knows she has the necessary ability and education to consider the question of becoming a candidate at the next examination, all particulars of which, including syllabus, can be obtained from the Civil Service Commissioners, Burlington House, Burlington Gardens, London, W.1.

By St. John Ervine

A MONG the many changes which the War brought to the West-End theatre, was one which made a violent breach in a peculiarly English tradition. The increase in the cost of production made the performance of pantomime at Drury Lane financially impossible, and so an entertainment which was as native as plum pudding was brought to an end.

There were people, mostly from the country, who made two visits each year to the theatre. They came to town for the Cattle Show, and again at Christmas time. Father and mother and children, all were rosy and plump, and Philistine and simple. They had no notions about art, except those that they got from coloured supplements, and only one idea of literature, that it should be as like Dickens as possible: full of fun and sentiment and good-nature and abundant feeding, with villains who *were* villains and heroes and heroines of an incredible purity and sweetness. None of your epileptic heroes and hysterical heroines and psycho-analysed villains for them: they liked their meat good and strong and unmistakable.

They went twice a year to Drury Lane theatre. In their eyes there *was* no other theatre. They saw the melodrama and were thrilled to their several marrows by the hairbreadth escapes of the virtuous from the sensational death-traps laid for them by the villains, and were well and truly stimulated in the end by the spectacle of villainy foiled and defeated by virtue. The late Cecil Raleigh, who wrote many of the plays, told a Select Committee of the House of Commons that " virtue triumphant is my

The Passing of

Finance has struck at the Roo

income." The second visit to Drury Lane was made to the pantomime to see Dan Leno, one of the world's funniest comedians, and Herbert Campbell, who was not very funny except as a contrast to Leno. The audience at a Drury Lane pantomime was so typically English that an intelligent foreigner could have made a good summary of the characteristics of the English people by merely looking at it.

Those country play-goers would no more have thought of missing their two visits each year to Drury Lane than they would have thought of missing church on Christmas morning. I would have said that whatever else perished, the pantomime would survive, but the War was no respecter of traditions, and it had as little mercy on Drury Lane as it had on more imposing institutions. Sensational melodrama and the pantomime are seen there no more. The first was killed by the cinema, and the second by finance.

The cost of a play at Drury Lane is so great that a run of three months, even if two performances are given each day

for the best part of that time, is n sufficient to recoup the management f the expenses they incur; and a thr months' run is about as much as a pantomime can be expected to have. soon as the school holidays are over t days of the pantomime run begin to numbered. It cannot hope to achieve t success of *Rose Marie*, which h already run for twenty months and expected to run for another year. Abc two and a half millions of people ha seen it performed, and the total recei from it must now be about seven hu dred thousand pounds. It will ha secured more than a million before run is ended. Dan Leno would astounded if he could hear of the figures.

I may seem to be attaching excessi importance to the Drury Lane pan mime, and to be unwarrantably gloo when I assert that pantomime is passi out of popularity. " It may be dead Drury Lane," the reader will say, " it still flourishes in the provinces." T is true, but for how much longer will continue to be true? We die from t

PANTOMIME

of this Landmark of Childhood Days

art outwards. The branches of a tree may seem to be healthy when its core is rotten. The run of provincial pantomimes is much shorter than was the average run of a pantomime at Drury Lane, and most of them are stock pieces which have been performed, year after year, after any necessary repairs to scenery, and a furbishing-up of topical jokes, last year in Liverpool, the year before in Newcastle, this year in Manchester, and next year in Bristol. By this means the cost of producing pantomime is greatly reduced.

The strange thing about pantomime, as we know it in England, is that it is known nowhere else. Attempts have been made from time to time to introduce it into America, but all of them have failed. I do not know whether pantomimes are performed in Australia, South Africa, or Canada or New Zealand, but I cannot remember ever to have heard of any being performed there. Essentially this entertainment is an English entertainment—a formless, incoherent ragbag of a thing, as mixed and as English as a plum pudding. I

doubt if any other people in the world but the English would so incongruously mix their materials as the materials are mixed in pantomime. How ludicrous seems the conjunction of fairies and red-nosed comedians! Yet we have always done that. Shakespeare, without any qualms, did it in *A Midsummer Night's Dream.*

That play, indeed, might be regarded as the model from which all pantomimes were drawn. There are the fairies, and the comedians, and the royal lovers! And is Bottom, the rude mechanic, not transformed into an ass, and yet given some vision and nobility in the process? How very English that is! Even when we make an ass of a man, we allow him to have "a most rare vision."

The French are incapable of mixing the tragic and the comic, the fantastic and the ludicrous, the imaginary and the real in the way in which the English mix them, and to this day the plays of Shakespeare still bewilder French play-goers. They are accustomed to the austerities of Racine, who does not permit one of his tragic characters even

to smile, and they feel themselves outraged when, almost at the moment of the murder of Duncan in *Macbeth,* the porter comes and makes his jokes. That sense of astonishment and outrage was present in many a French soldier during the War, when, very sombre and serious, he found himself " going over the top " with soldiers from England, who sang comic songs as they went to their death and shouted to each other, " This way for the early doors! "

Christmas plays now are more definitely for children than the pantomimes were. *Peter Pan* has, perhaps, as much to do with the death of the pantomime as any other cause. It changed the fashion. But even these plays are not easily produced, for they suffer more severely from the end of the school holidays than the pantomimes did: they are too strictly plays for children. The pantomimes were plays for children and adults, although too often they became plays for adults alone. And not very satisfactory adults!

It is the brevity of its run which makes so much difficulty in the way of producing a children's play. Men of the theatre say that a children's play does not begin to pay its way until it has been performed for four Christmases. By the end of the fourth year, it has become known to parents and then may enjoy a long life of short revivals. The reader can test the truth of this statement for himself by observing how many old and familiar pieces are produced in London about Christmas time: *Peter Pan, Where the Rainbow Ends, The Windmill Man, Charley's Aunt.*

By A. B. Cunning, M.B.

The Wish for an Heir

In every woman's heart is an exquisiteness that is potential mother-love. To many its unfulfilment represents the greatest sorrow of all—no heir—no immortality

IT is as natural for a little girl to play with her doll as for a woman to bath and dress her child. Play is a forecast of life. A boy chooses engines and boats and guns, while a girl plays at house and looks after her dolls.

And if as the years go on the woman has no child, there is a sadness. She realises that over the things that matter most in life, we have little control—or should I say, little knowledge?

"I wish one could go into a shop and buy those," said a man as he passed a perambulator where sat a beautiful boy. One felt that he lived in a silent house where there was no patter of little feet, no happy chuckles, no mischief anywhere.

But one cannot buy a child like a dog or a horse. And when after marriage there are no children, the little mother in the woman realises that she is up against the unknown; and from all times and in all ages she has gone down on her knees to her gods.

In India there are sacred shrines, famous as those where prayers are answered for the birth of sons. In China, Eastern women pay adoration to Kwan-Yin, the Buddhist Queen of Heaven, the Hearer of Cries, the Holy Mother. In Russia they pray to their Ikons.

In myths and fairy tales and legends we get the same idea; people implore some supernatural power to grant their wish.

Lafcadio Hearn, in a translation of an old Japanese ballad, tells us of one Takakura Dainagon, who was wealthy in all worldly things but had no heir. This was a great sorrow, and at last, on the advice of his trusted servant, Ikenoshoji, he travelled to the shrine of the deity Tamon-Ten, on the holy mountain of Kurama. He fasted and prayed for days, but in vain. Then his faithful retainer made intercession for him and vowed to make wonderful offerings in bronze and silver and pure gold, "if to my lord an heir be given." On the third night the deity revealed himself and promised a son with the soul of a god. And within the year the promise was fulfilled.

We read of Hannah in the Bible going up to the Temple and taking her offering and praying for a child; and also of the promise to Abraham and Sarah, greater far than that of Canaan, that some day they should have a son.

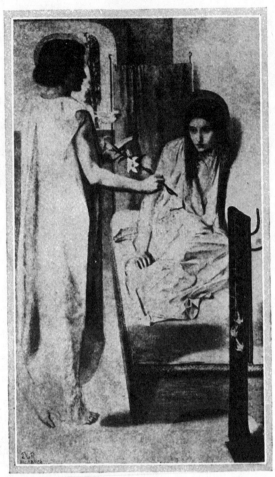

From the National Gallery collection

Rossetti's "Annunciation"

To be barren was looked on as a disgrace amongst Jewish women. To-day in our own British world, I have heard it spoken of as the greatest sorrow of all—no heir—no child to follow on—no immortality.

"I have got over having no children," one woman said, "but I shall never get over having no grandchildren."

I have seen bachelor women growing old, adopt children and love them as their own, because of the unsatisfied longing for someone to mother, someone on whom to shower a heritage of love. After all, motherhood is a woman's *raison d'être*, and a married woman who has no child is apt to look on herself as a failure.

But the age of miracles is not yet past. Every day science is discovering new facts and new ideas. Lady Barrett, M.D., considers that if a woman has

superabundant health and vitality, and given that her reproductive organs are normal, she should be able to bear a child. She must be able to manufacture in her cells all the energy for the growing of an infant, and the new little atom requires every ounce of vigour and nourishment possible.

Some women can conceive a child, but they have not the vitality for its growth and they suffer bitter disappointments. Or it may be that some illness, such as influenza, intervenes and the mother has not the strength to fight that and to nourish the child as well, and so the infant is lost.

In India, if during pregnancy a woman has cholera, it is said that the mother or the child always dies. After any long serious illness, such as typhoid fever or pneumonia or rheumatic fever, a woman cannot expect to conceive a child for some time. All her energy is needed to recuperate.

Again there are women who would like to carve a career for themselves and rear a family for their husbands at the same time, but this dual achievement cannot be done. An embryo child is a jealous creature, it can brook no rival. A woman who wishes to lead her own life, should not marry. She will need all her energy for her work.

Thus it is largely a question of energy, and anything that saps a woman's vitality may prevent her having a child. It may be that she wears herself out in her enthusiasm over games or charities or parties or some pet hobby. Late hours, hot, overcrowded rooms, indoor life, lack of sunshine, all tend to make a woman as fragile as a hothouse plant. Or there may be some physical trouble, such as chronic appendicitis or septic teeth or some other focus of poisoning that is sapping the energy and keeping the health below par.

Women of the working class often have large families, while the more gently bred the woman, the fewer children she may expect. This is peculiarly interesting to me, for during the past year as the domestic working woman is disappearing with the dole, I have been running my house with a staff of lady servants. They are charming to deal with, their manners are beautiful, but their vitality, their energy, their capacity for hard muscular work, is as chalk to (Continued on page 49

(*Continued from page* 48)

cheese compared with that of the working class. When I think of my charwoman, who is the mother of ten, and who arrives at the back door looking like Vigour personified, ready to scrub out the kitchen and larder and scullery and passages; and then ask what else there is to do, I feel that the problem of perpetual energy has been solved. And I think that through her I understand a little why the healthy, muscular working woman has many children and why the gently nurtured cultured woman has so few.

An old wife's saying tells us that a woman after one child can always have another within a year or so. It is as though the chemistry of one pregnancy prepares the body for another. The tissues have become accustomed to manufacturing the surplus energy and can go on doing so. And so women can get into the way of having one child after another as our grandmothers did long ago, when motor-cars and aeroplanes and hustling were unknown, and they led their quiet, simple lives, sewing and knitting, seeing to their households, and rearing wonderful families.

And here it might be mentioned, without serious digression, that the chemistry of pregnancy is a very wonderful thing. It has magical power to arrest, for the time being, cancer and tubercle. Just as the Spanish invaders, in the siege of Haarlem, did not molest the house where a little piece of lace on the door told of the expected visit of the stork, so the demons of cancer and tubercle seem to respect motherhood. But once the child is born, these fell diseases are often as hounds let loose. They gallop. Perhaps some day the serum of a pregnant animal, or the extract from an embryo, may be used to fight these troubles. It is also feasible that such a preparation might help to bring about conception, if the chemistry of one pregnancy prepares the woman for another. But this is mere armchair pathology.

Vitamins or living elements in the food have been proved recently to affect fertility. Miss Muriel Bond, M.Sc., of the London School of Medicine for Women, experimenting with the vitamins contained in fat, found that butter increases fertility more than bacon fat, and bacon fat more than lard. Another scientist has shown that rats fed on food containing no vitamins had no litters. When one per cent. of yeast was added to the diet they had litters containing 35 per cent. of males and 65 per cent. females. More yeast was added and the litters contained equal numbers of each sex.

These things, however, are all in the experimental stage. And so far as we know at present, a woman who wishes to have a child, should do everything that makes for perfect health. She should live and sleep in the open air as is the practice at sanatoria. Her skin should be brown as a gipsy's from the sunshine. Sea bathing is a wonderful tonic. Exercise should be sufficient but not exhausting. Her diet should include raw fruit, raw vegetables (such as lettuce, tomatoes, cucumber, spring onions, celery), butter, wholemeal bread, honey, cheese, fresh eggs and any other substances rich in vitamins. Her clothing should be light but sufficient for warmth.

This life, of course, suggests that of the primitive savage. But there is no reason why a person leading such a life, should not cultivate her mind and use her brain. There is no need to be a mere animal. And perhaps if perfect physical health and physique were attained, though it might take generations, it is conceivable that the ordeal of motherhood would vanish and child-birth be painless as it is with the savage.

That
surprising
Craig girl!

FORSTER

Pam Craig's latest is winning the half-mile punting singles. Pam could always be trusted to do *something* unexpected and startling—she beat the county's lady tennis champion in straight sets only last week. But everyone said she'd find the half-mile really too much, for she was the only girl competitor.

You should have seen that race! Round the bend, by the willows, they came, Pam half a length behind Tom McBride, with a swing and a thrust that was as strong as it was graceful. And Tom looked troubled. He was splashing a trifle. Pam was a couple of feet behind. A foot behind. Tom made a huge effort—too late. The gun went. Pam had done it.

"That surprising Craig girl again!" said everyone.

Surprising? Well, maybe. But then again, girl or no girl, there really isn't anything surprising about perfect physical condition winning. It usually does. And if you ask Pam how she came by the splendid vigour and endurance which enabled her to win her race, she'd tell you: "Sensible living, of course, plenty of fresh air, plenty of exercise, plenty of sleep—and eating proper food—*that* especially."

And she's right.

Proper food is absolutely essential, for it provides those vital elements which the body must have to be vigorous, healthy and energetic.

That's the secret of Grape-Nuts. It does provide those essential elements in **an easily** digested form.

Eaten with milk or cream, Grape-Nuts has **a** rich, nutty flavour—**different** from anything you've ever tasted **before.** It is a crisp food —a food you will **enjoy** chewing. Chewing promotes good teeth, tending to prevent cavities and toothache. Get a package from your grocer *to-day*, or post the coupon below and we will send you *two* sample packages of Grape-Nuts free—enough for two breakfasts, and "A Book of Better Breakfasts," by Mrs. D. D. Cottington-Taylor, A.R.S.I., the famous Health and Cooking expert. It contains delightful menus which will help you to form the habit of more healthful breakfasts. Send it now!

Grape=Nuts

— Do you know the Grape Nuts Secret?

Helena Normanton, B.A., asks

Why There are not More

SUPERWOMEN in BUSINESS

Routine Work is the Inevitable Bridge to—More Routine Work

TO a certain extent I could give myself an Irishman's answer to my own question by saying that there are. Every few months we read in the papers of the death of some successful commercial woman. Only the other day one regretfully heard of the loss of the late Louisa Thomson Price, who lifted a great firm of London caterers from the shallows of approaching failure to great heights of prosperity. Further back still there was old Mrs. Greig who, it is said, was the making of that firm of multiple cheesemongers.

Still with us we have such women as Lady Boot, the driving force of the chemists. Lady Rhondda we all know as an omnipresent company director. And in the old days of our fathers which were before us we had our *Veuves Clicquot* and our Elizabeth Lazenbys.

But I return undauntedly to my muttons and ask: Why are there not more big · business women? Our few examples in the business world are very nice—but they are very little (feminine) bread to the monstrous deal of (masculine) sack —as Sir John would remind us.

Being very puzzled in the matter I have taken counsel of some of the men I know. To begin with here is a great clarity and charity about business men, for all, one finds, unite on at least *a* point. That is as to the nature of the business in which women can succeed.

Any business man will tell you at once whereat women may succeed. It is in any job but his own. The theatrical manager agrees that women can manage engineering works or laundries (it then becomes tactless to murmur such names as Miss Horniman, Miss Baylis, or Sarah Bernhardt). The manufacturer of hardware thinks that women could manage millinery factories. The wholesale milliner thinks not. No, hardware perhaps, if the woman in question finds it attractive. And so on all over the place.

Often enough the individual commercial man will suggest that for all the lower grades women can do well. But just here I am not worrying about low-grade and mid-grade jobs. I am thinking, as I must own I always do, of the superlatively big jobs. Routine and formula work always strikes me as being such an excellent bridge to— more routine and formula work. Nice in its way for those who dread responsibility, but some of us would never run hard nor fast in that direction.

Clearing away such preliminaries as the foregoing, we women must ask ourselves another big question: Can women achieve success in commerce in

Personal SERVICE

to our readers is one of the principles on which the entire fabric of GOOD HOUSE-KEEPING is built. The advice of experts is available on any subject from A to Z of the complete science of home-making, and through this correspondence a very real personal contact has been established. In proof of this, we quote a letter sent by a reader in hospital to the Shopping Service. " If I wanted, would you allow one of your shoppers to come and see me and do a little shopping for me ? Also, would you allow her to dig into some boxes for me at —— Hotel, ——, as I am an invalid and unable to go out yet, but require some clothing out of my boxes, and have no one to ask to do it ? . . ." This request does not come within our usual scope; but we met it, to keep faith with such confidence

just the lines that men succeed upon? Or will their big successes come (as one is confident they are due to come) perhaps along somewhat different routes?

To answer that we must look at our big business men calmly and coolly. How have they succeeded? Every observer will allot different orders of merit to their respective virtues, and concede the possession of those virtues in different proportions. Many will differ from any list, as one is well aware. But for what it may be worth, here is my list.

First, I place far above all other commercial virtues — courage. Lovely, shining, exhilarating, ardent virtue. Add to that just enough of its opposite number—caution. Not too much

—just the slice of cucumber in the cup. For the ideal cautionist will be too aware of life's dangers even to get out of bed in the morning. Courage is needed to leave a rut, to throw down a routine blind-alley job, to pursue a different path from one's companions, to explore and discover new markets, to risk capital on new goods, to maintain high standards of commercial honesty, to trust subordinates wholesomely and yet not blindly, and to face up to the responsibilities of heavy payrolls in times of falling markets.

I was once told by the wife of a great commercial magnate how years ago a south-country farmer divided, in extreme old age, his farm between his two sons. One sold his half for £1,000, and went North. The great commercial enterprise he developed from that £1,000 is worth many millions to-day. The other half of the farm is worth now about what it was then. Courage won the difference.

I know of a woman who has in New York a chain of tea-rooms worth now an enormous sum. She began with thirty-eight dollars, according to an interview she gave the press two years ago. Courage again. A Scottish woman with under £100 founded a great set of tea-rooms of which the selling value would be, to-day, many thousands.

But you will observe that the two feminine examples have gone into a trade which buys from men and employs women. The man employs *men and women*. This is probably the secret of founding a really colossal fortune. Until women acquire sufficient courage to employ *men* as well as their own sex they will finish in the six figures. I want to see them in the sevens. There must be big railway magnates, big newspaper proprietors, big shipowners and shipbuilders, big chemical manufacturers, who are women. Not so much of the "Ye Shoppe" touch, and more of the Henry Ford! Less retailing and more wholesaling, and dealings in raw material in bulk.

For such an ideal to be obtained there must be evolved or discovered (the latter, I fancy) women of superb mentality. One knows it is the fashion to decry the business man, and when he gets off his beat and tries to be a politician or (Continued on page 52)

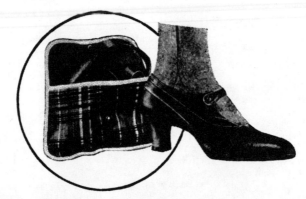
Superwomen in Business
(Continued from page 51)

magnate has begun with an initial failure. Here again comes in courage. A big man can learn from his first blunders. Can all women? Some can and some do. And some do not.

The great mentality that accumulates vast aggregations of capital, and that makes for an employed populace instead of a half-starved one, is a very overlooking, well proportioned, hovering type of mind. Detail it can know and understand, but it can soar above detail to grasp what the general proportions of a huge concern should be like. That means delegation. Delegation is the very life blood and marrow of largeness of dimension.

You may know the small and twaddling mentality for the amount of finger-in-the-pieness which it finds essential to happiness. There is never any poise or dignity about such people. They inspire no confidence because they proffer none. Their conceit leads them always to think that no one can do a thing like themselves and that whether technically qualified or not their opinion is always of great moment and value.

"Large, fat, slow-moving men who would sit in chairs and plan," was what one captain of industry told me he liked for his big chiefs. "Little, fussy jumpers," for subordinate positions and for smaller doings.

Over-conscientiousness is the bane of too many women. What a splendid systole and diastole of extreme energy and beautiful indolence distinguished the supermen! Think of Napoleon lying in a hot bath for hours. Think of Darwin leaving alone his experimental field of earth worms for forty years undug. Think of the late Sir James Ramsay, the Duchess of Atholl's father, accumulating his history material for years and not publishing his monumental work until he was sixty. There is a certain feeling of *mass* about truly great men. The only woman who has ever given one that feeling is Queen Elizabeth, whose mentality exhibited a tremendous roundness and volume as well as alert sagacity.

Judgment is the next quality I would beg for. Some people can read signs of times and discern all the elements with which they are dealing. One investor I know began to manufacture women's hat-bandeaux just as soon as hats began to be fitted on to the female head instead of being perched. When last I heard of him, he had opened a hairpin factory just as the era of the bob was developing yet more gloriously into that of the shingle and the Eton crop. I suppose when the Day of Judgment has ended he will try to place upon the ethereal market a new line in trumpets.

Judgment is closely allied to imagination without which courage and massive mentality would be mere brute forces. To be imaginative is to be inventive, and to arouse in the human mind an image of a new want is the preliminary to making money by feeding that want.

All the copybook virtues are as necessary for a big commercial success in life as they are represented to be. But they do not fill the bill. A Rockefeller or a Carnegie in the sunset of life practising philanthropy may dilate upon this that or the other trifling point. One notices that such people rarely give the world an accurate account of the qualities and driving power which made them succeed. Probably they cannot state them. It also may sound more modest to say that a severe abstention from some pet antipathy or a sin was the foundation of the success.

If a great man tells the truth about himself, the world gets restive. A man must

not say, according to our conventions: "I built up my great business on a foundation of specialised education, acumen, driving-power, will to succeed, energy, judgment and large confidence (sometimes badly shaken) in subordinates." What the world *likes* him to say is that he never ate pork for supper or always read a chapter of the Bible last thing at night, or wrote home regularly to his old mother and consulted her on all his big deals.

The power to live rhythmically is indeed an asset. Work hard, play hard, love hard, read hard, travel from time to time, practise being able to organise so that your machine will function with your own hand off the buttons and levers—to do all this is to do what the supermen do. Can women allege that they will scale the summits of success by that other all too frequent route—the ceaseless potter?

Lack of capital is frequently alleged as a cause of women's failure. It takes ferocious determination for a poorly salaried worker, especially a woman, to save her first hundred pounds. But if she has not saved it by the time she is thirty she is nearly always one of two things—a spend-thrift fool, or an altruist sacrificing herself

to her family. "You can't do much with £100," someone will object. No, Carnegie couldn't have, Rockefeller couldn't have, you can't; so nobody could. And that's that.

So long as big business is mainly in the hands of men, women will have to observe certain tacit conventions. They must respect men's sex-solidarity. If they have to command men it must be done with tact and with no bossiness. There must be no attempt to turn the individual firm into a feminist institution—you cannot mix business and politics. Your subordinate women can be given a fair chance, but not a ha'porth more than they have earned. A business is not a baby to be fussed over nor prettified. Neither is it something for which a woman need sell her soul, her individual essence. Plain attire of good quality need not become an aping of masculine modes. Least pleasing of all is the woman who tries a masculine manner, or who imagines she has to become portentous, impressive, dominant and imposing.

To be able to take a good look at one-self and a good laugh whenever that important feeling begins to arise is one of the best prescriptions for success as it is for happiness. The power to do it makes its possessor easy to deal with—a summation of most of the other desiderata.

Helena Normanton, *B.A.*

ponders the question—

Do Men Want *Women* in *Politics?*

IN common with all the rest of the world, I have been reading *The Intimate Papers of Colonel House.* Scores of writers have already dealt with those aspects of the book that deal with the intertwining of America's politics with those of Europe during the War period, and to what they have said I have nothing to add. To me Chapters XI and XII, which deal with the campaign for the re-election of President Wilson (and in addition, certain other odd passages), furnish a very special interest of their own. I don't think they say as many as twenty words upon the subject of women in politics. But, read with an analytical mind, this section of the Colonel's *Intimate Papers* throws as much light as is necessary for a right understanding of why men don't want women in politics.

Let me deal with, and set aside, the possible objection of a direct contradiction. Men *do* want women in politics. Yes, so far as rough work is concerned, canvassing, for instance, and in short as the charwomen of the political world. Scrubbers — yes. Cabinet Ministers, Premiers, and Presidents—no. Five times at least has this old country taken a chance with a woman on the throne and trusted to the mere luck of heredity. But if Britain ever became a Republic how long would it be before a woman were made president? The United States has been a Republic since 1783 —if you do not count it as beginning at 1776—nearly one hundred and fifty years. And not a single woman has been elected President, and only one (so far as I know) has ever got as far as contesting the presidency. Britain might be even slower.

To return to Colonel House. No lengthy description fits him so well as the term "political artist" on page 342 of the *Intimate Papers,* and it is just because he is that rare thing in politics, an artist who can draw a picture and —far rarer still—one who has actually done so, that for the first time probably in history, all can read exactly how political power in the vastest democracy in the world is grasped and retained.

And what in the world has all that to do with women? A very proper question. It has this to do with them. I would ask any women who have political ambitions of a serious nature and the thousands of their sisters who wish that other outstanding women *would* have serious political ambitions to read carefully and analytically the chapters I have

Her considered answer is: They do want women—so far as rough work is concerned, in short as the charwomen of the political world. Scrubbers—yes. Cabinet Ministers, Premiers and Presidents—no

mentioned, and to ask themselves whether they think that women possess now or ever will possess, certain qualities therein revealed, vital to the running of a powerful political machine. For it is the machine which matters.

What are those qualities? They are a curious blend of what the world usually regards as good and what it

The Blasé Husk of Youth—

which hides the shyly tentative, wistful groping after the spiritual realities, giving the lie to the charge of a moribund religious sense, is the inspiration of an article specially written for our November issue by

REV. DR. NORWOOD

usually says it regards as bad.

In the first place, an eloquent figurehead had to be replaced in the most powerful position in the world. Real devotion from the Colonel to the President is constantly in evidence, and a tremendous self-abnegation. Yet the whole book demonstrates, time and time again, that Mr. Wilson had to be pushed from the rear and constantly managed from the flanks by people who knew the practical world as it is, during all his tenure of the presidency. Why, then, did Colonel House and those like him concentrate upon and select a dully brilliant pedant like Wilson for the presidency? The words of an old comic song recur to one:

" They wanted something to play with, Something to love and adore."

Wilson had an impressive aspect and

was of suitable presidential. *timbre.* N[ot] perhaps a great man, but one who coul[d] be made to appear one. Colonel Hous[e] the positive thinker, selected the instr[u]ment for the carrying out of his ide[a] in preference to being both creator a[nd] instrument.

Here comes in item number one [as] to how women differ from men. N[ot] only the power but the appearance of t[he] power, viz. the office itself, appeals [to] the feminine nature, which is creati[ve] plus executive, and so is rare[ly] content to delegate. One of the mo[st] frequent sentences on a woman['s] lips is: "If I want anythi[ng] done properly I have to see [to] it myself." That is to my mind t[he] weakest feature in the character [of] many women who would otherwi[se] be first-class. They have not streng[th] enough to delegate and to follow o[ut] the logical corollaries of delegatio[n] the first of which is to break t[he] failures and replace them by bett[er] people. Jealousy here may come t[o] readily into play. Does the leadi[ng] lady (or gentleman) too much enj[oy] the startling success of an unde[r]study? Does the headmistress alwa[ys] genuinely felicitate the first assista[nt] who has won commendation duri[ng] her own absence?

The first rule to be powerful is [to] be so strong that one can delega[te] without jealousy, without undue fe[ar] of consequences and, if need be, wi[th] a certain ruthlessness. The great[e]r kings and queens have thrown asi[de] incompetent subordinates with cool[e] impersonality.

The next quality which comes in[to] prominence in this thrilling story [of] the re-making of a President, is the gus[to] felt by Colonel House in the actual wo[rk] of the re-making. Since Warwick t[he] Kingmaker there has been nothing qu[ite] like it so openly revealed, although ma[ny] concealed parallels have gone to t[he] making of inner history of natio[ns.] "House could not resist the lure whi[ch] the technical problems of organising [an] electorial campaign presented," says [the] editor.

The lure of the campaign. The lu[re] of the technical problems of organisi[ng] one. Does any woman feel like it about elections? There may be a f[ew] consummate staff officers at the hea[d]quarters of the various political part[ies] here and in America who care for t[he] rigour of the campaign as a campai[gn] and love technique as technique. B[ut] that is not the lure of politics as wom[en] see it. No military metaphor such [as] campaign *(Continued on page 5[6])*

By St. John Ervine

Have WOMEN A Sense of HUMOUR?

Ruminations on a Question to which Men have usually One Reply

Miss Anita Loos has sounded a note that women have rarely sounded before. Is she the first of the feminine satirists?

Illustration by Ralph Barton

T is an old reproach made by men against women that they have no sense of humour, and the stock test of their failing is their attitude towards Falstaff. Someone has said that no woman can see the fun of Falstaff. This may or may not be true (it is obviously impossible to settle the point with any accuracy), but assuming that it is true, it proves no more than this, that women do not appreciate that particular sort of humour: it does not prove that they have no sense of humour at all. There probably is a deep difference between a woman's sense of humour and a man's. That would seem to be in the nature of things. Even when they laugh together, they may be laughing for very dissimilar reasons. But there must also be a sense of humour which men and women share in common, when they laugh at the same thing for the same reason.

There can be no decision about this matter, but we may amuse ourselves by considering why it is that women, generally speaking, do not laugh at certain things which make men laugh. Lately in the theatre I have entertained myself by listening to the laughter of the audience and attempting to divide it, so to speak, into sex sections. I would not for a moment pretend that my observations have any scientific accuracy, but I think I have sufficiently well observed my laughters to be able to offer some opinions on this odd subject. There are many things which make men laugh most uproariously, and yet leave women mirthless; there are some things at which they both laugh, either for the same reason or for different reasons; and there are other things which make a woman laugh loudly, but leave men looking either glum or unmoved.

One night, during the performance of a farce, I heard Mr. Huntley Wright, when told that even a worm will turn, reply, "What's the good of a worm turning? It's the same on both sides."

This jest caused as much laughter among women as it did among men. It is the sort of jest which depends for its effect on knowledge and observation. A person who had never seen a worm would probably see no fun whatever in that joke, but nearly everybody has seen a worm, and is familiar with its shape, and the jest therefore—such as it is—is as likely to excite laughter among women as it is among men, and among children as it is among adults.

This sort of laughter, which comes from shared experiences and common knowledge, is perhaps the most important of all laughter. But there are other sorts of laughter which are dependent upon the nature of those who hear or see the things which provoke it. Cruelty, for example, is a considerable element in laughter. A great deal of what is called wit (a very different thing from humour) is founded on cruelty. A witticism is nearly always a jest made at the expense of some person, and leaves him or her wounded or humiliated.

An example of this kind of wit was told to me some time ago. A certain politician was so ugly and hairy-faced that he seemed to resemble an ape. He was invited by the leader of his party to dine with him in the country, and when he arrived, a little late, for the meal, he excused himself by stating that he had had to make a troublesome cross-country journey, and the trains were not convenient. His leader looked at him and replied, "Why didn't you swing from tree to tree?"

Now, when one is told this story and remembers the appearance of the unhappy gentleman who was the butt of it, one laughs, but can any person believe that the man himself shared in the amusement of his fellow-guests? The greatest laughter in the world, per-

haps, is that which makes everybody laugh without wounding a single soul, but it is undeniable that much of the world's wit has sprung from a cruel desire to hurt someone's feelings; and although it is less common now than it was, the world has laughed very loudly at the pain and suffering and disfigurement and mutilation of many men and women.

In a London theatre recently I received proof of this fact. A play by a French dramatist, Lenormand, was being performed. The scene was laid in a sanatorium in Switzerland, and many of the characters were consumptives. As is the habit of people in hospitals, some of them incessantly talked of their illness, and an old woman in the cast spoke the following sentence: "I have had a hundred and eighty-three hæmorrhages—a hundred and eighty-three!—and two attacks of pleurisy." This statement sent young women in the audience into fits of laughter. I think I am correct in saying that the laughter was almost exclusively feminine laughter, and as far as I can judge, it was the laughter of young, healthy women. I confess I was shocked by it. It did not seem to me funny at all, but terribly painful, and I was driven to the belief that this was one of the forms of humour appealing to women in which men could not share.

I do not base a belief on this incident, because my observation was not sufficiently wide or accurate to enable me to do so. Moreover, there were women about me who were not laughing. All I assert is that I did not hear any men laugh, whereas I heard a great many women do so. I suspect, however, that the element of cruelty that is sometimes to be found in laughter does attract women more than it attracts men. Women, I think, like to laugh *at* people more than they like to laugh *with* them. That sort of laughter is commoner among Latin (Continued on page 56)

2 TOWER BRIDGES
one above the other —

*Yet the length of a Bronco
Roll is even greater.*

THE towers of Tower Bridge are
200 feet high. Two bridges, one
on top of the other, measure
400 feet. That is a great height; but
even so, if you were to stand on the
top of those two bridges and release
one end of a roll of Bronco—the de
luxe Toilet Paper—it would reach to
the river *and then have some to spare!*
From this one fact alone, you can
judge for yourself the enormous
quantity of paper in a Bronco roll.
A so called "cheap" roll contains
only about one-third the quantity of
paper a Bronco roll contains—and
what a difference in the paper.
That is why it is a waste of money
to buy any other roll but Bronco.

Bronco Toilet Paper is the best
Toilet Paper money can buy.
It has a soothing silky softness no other paper possesses,
and is, of course, antiseptic.

*Obtainable from Stationers, Chemists, Stores,
Grocers, Hardware Dealers, etc.*

**THE BRITISH PATENT PERFORATED PAPER CO.,
HACKNEY WICK, E.9.**

Do Men Want Women in Politics ?
(*Continued from page* 54)

expresses their reaction towards politics.
Rather do women wish to go out bearing
some sort of a gospel of good tidings—they
concentrate upon the programme.

"See," says the woman politician,
"what I (I, My Party) can get for you.
A better life, better food, more leisure,
more peace, more opportunities, greater this,
plenteous that, abundance of something
else." Rarely, if ever, are groups of
women organised to defend or to attack
some positive entity. Politics for women
is not so much planning a campaign or
bringing her troops into conflict—it is
much more of the nature of taking an
ambulance over the stricken field of life,
and of gathering up the casualties—or a
nursery garden for growth of choice plants.
Visualise, please, the intense distaste of
any general who wishes to get his troops
into battle with those of the other side,
and who is asked to delay action so that
people who are largely non-combatant may
stroll over the battleground, and plant a
nice lot of seeds on it !

Men do not want women in politics.
Neither do they at the Bar, nor the
Stock Exchange, nor on the Episcopal
Bench, nor in the priesthood, nor in fact
in any seats of authority. It means, for
men, too much adjustment for themselves.
The old ways have suited them very nicely
all down the centuries. Any system which
puts its devotees at the top naturally does.
Women cannot change men's natures and it
would be sad if they did. Perhaps men's
objects can be changed and the methods
of attaining those objects will naturally
and consequently change *pari passu*. When
there are more women voters than men,
and that by a really handsome superfluity,
more voters will want constructive plans
and fewer voters will want a dog fight.
Men will then (and not before then)
clamour for women in politics as being
able to help them to attain the objects and
sketch out the programmes which will lead
politicians into the golden realms of place
and power. Women will then talk less
about ideals; and men less about "the lure
of campaigns." A harmonised intermedium
will be developed in which both can utilise
their natural gifts, and that unregarded
tertium quid, the poor old British Public
may somehow, some day, receive a little
more attention.

Have Women a Sense of Humour ?
(*Continued from page* 55)

and Celtic people than it is among the
Nordic races. Latin and Celtic males get
more entertainment out of exhibitions of
cruelty than Nordic males do. An Irishman, a Welshman, a Highlander, will laugh
at suffering and physical disability more
readily than an Englishman will, and it
is said that these races, the Celtic and
the Latin races, are more feminine in their
nature than the Nordic races.

When I am told that the Falstaff test
proves that women lack a sense of humour,
I am unimpressed, for a good deal of the
Falstaff humour is concerned with drunkenness, and I imagine that women seldom see
the funny side of drunkenness. A drunken
man may be an amusing companion to
other men, especially if they are also
drunk, but he probably is a source of
horror, in greater or less degree, to women.
The number of men to-day who find
drunkenness singularly unfunny is increasing, and at the risk of being told that I
lack a sense of humour myself, I will
acknowledge that I find a drunken man
a disgusting sight, and that I have no
desire whatever to be in his company.

The humour of this form of human outrage seems to me more imaginary than
real, and I have noticed that pretended
drunkenness excites more laughter than
real drunkenness. People will laugh in the
theatre at an actor giving an imitation of
a drunken man, but they laugh less readily
when they see a drunken man in the street,
or are unfortunate enough to come into
the company of one.

A good deal of laughter, of course,
is not laughter in any genuine sense
of merriment, but an inverted sense of
horror. We commonly call it hysteria.
I have myself in France, during the War,
seen a man blown into the air by a shell.
The sight caused a brother officer to shriek
with laughter—"shriek" is the word. But
it would be foolish to assume that this
officer got any pleasure out of seeing his
friend dismembered. His grief and horror
at the sight so suddenly presented to him
took that hysterical turn.

I remember reading an article by one
of the greatest writers in England on his
experiences during a visit to the Front.
He stated that he looked out of his car
and saw lying on the ground "a gentleman
who had lost his head." It seems incredible that any sensitive human being should
write such a thing at a time when thousands of people were in deep distress, and
likely to be grievously hurt by such a piece
of flippancy. One simply does not make
jokes about a dead soldier who has had
his head blown off. How, then, does one
account for this outrageous jest made by
a man who is noted for his kindness and
his sensitive nature? I account for it by
the fact that the memory of that shocking
sight was so horrifying to him that even
when he wrote about it a sort of hysteria
possessed him, and made him laugh just as
my brother officer laughed when he saw
his comrade blown up by a shell. It may
be that much of what seems to be cruel
laughter in women is no more than that.

It is interesting to consider how the great
influx of women into the theatre in recent
years has changed its character. The old
fashioned music-hall, which was chiefly
a man's entertainment, has nearly disappeared. I doubt, indeed, if the great comedians who flourished at the beginning of
the century—men like Dan Leno—would be
popular with the contemporary and chiefly
feminine audience. They depended entirely
upon their personalities for their success;
their jokes were limited in range and were
mainly concerned with drink, interloping
lodgers and cantankerous mothers-in-law,
subjects which are not, and have never
been, funny to women.

The old-fashioned music-hall was, indeed,
a prolonged masculine jeer at women; and
when women took possession of the theatre

(*Continued on page* 5

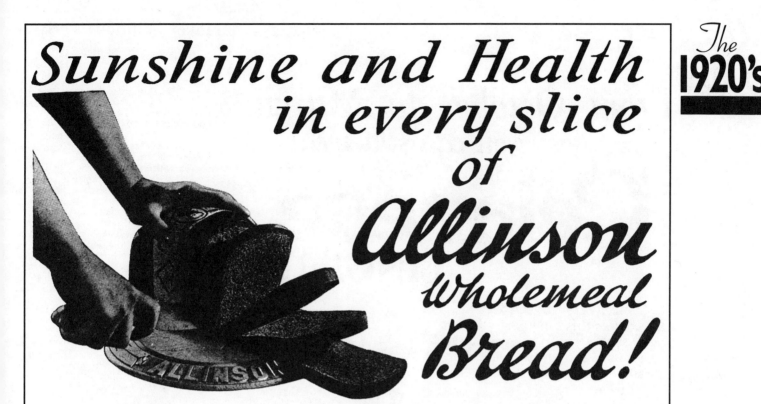

Sunshine and Health in every slice of *Allinson* Wholemeal Bread!

The Prince of Wales stresses an Important Fact

In his Presidential Address to the British Association the Prince of Wales alluded to the recent development of knowledge concerning the intimate relationship between sunlight and health. But the real importance of any acquisition of knowledge, he emphasised, exists not so much in the obtaining of it as in its application.

Now it is precisely for the reason that it represents the application of knowledge in accord with modern science that Allinson Wholemeal Bread should appeal to every intelligent man and woman. As Allinson Wholemeal Flour contains the whole of the wheat, that has literally absorbed the light and heat from the sun under which it has ripened, **Allinson Bread** may truly be said to contain the largest possible amount of energy derived from the source of sun's rays.

In the making of Allinson Wholemeal Flour—from which Allinson Bread is made—only the best Home-grown and Empire Wheats are used—rich, plump, golden grain, saturated with health-giving sunshine—these being reduced, by stone milling, to a degree of fineness that is sufficient to allow of complete digestion, yet not too fine to impart the necessary stimulus required by the bowels for their normal healthy functioning.

Also, it is unadulterated, and entirely free from any preservative.

Order Allinson 100% Wholemeal Bread from your Baker. Allinson Wholemeal Flour is obtainable from your Grocer in 3½-lb., 7-lb. and 14-lb. sealed cotton bags, *each containing a recipe book and particulars of a unique prize scheme.*

In case of difficulty in obtaining please write to Allinson Ltd., Cambridge Road, London, E.2.

Allinson Flour and Bread

GUARANTEED
100% WHOLEMEAL

The 1920's
1926

From October to March
you can still wear
'Celanese'
LINGERIE

You have loved your 'Celanese' Undies this Summer. And it *is* such a joy to know you can go on wearing the same slim, silky things all through the Winter.

It is a fact that you cannot buy more healthy Winterwear than 'Celanese.' The special insulating properties of 'Celanese' that have kept you so deliciously cool on the hottest days will keep you cosily warm in the chilliest weather, and protect you against all the vagaries of our English climate.

TRICOT : SATIN : MILANESE

Your draper can show you the exquisite styles in a fascinating colour range. They all launder most satisfactorily, retaining their lustre and softness to the last day of wear.

YOUR GUARANTEE

This woven 'Celanese' Brand Tab stitched inside every garment is your guarantee. None genuine without it.

Garment No. 3532

Sole Manufacturers:

BRITISH CELANESE LTD., 8, WATERLOO PLACE, LONDON, S.W.1

Have Women a Sense of Humour?
(*Continued from page* 56)

it was inevitable that the comedian who lived on that jeer should lose his occupation. I used to sit in music-halls and marvel at the fact that a *lion comique* could reduce the men in his audience to a condition of helpless laughter and yet leave the women rarely smiling, and perhaps even yawning in his face. The substitution of spectacular pieces and revues in which there is no personality, but instead a lavish display of dress and pretty colours and dancing and spectacle, seems to support the belief that women are not interested in humour. The commonest complaint made by men against these entertainments is that there is no fun in them.

But I suspect that women find much of masculine humour merely boring and silly. They have less patience with nonsensical behaviour than men have, and perhaps they are not so easy-going and tolerant in their attitude towards oddity. It is rare for a woman to write a humorous book. She generally takes a sterner view of the world

---

Practical Demonstrations

Fully qualified members of the Institute staff are available to give lectures and practical demonstrations on any domestic subject at private houses, Women's Institutes, schools, and institutions of all kinds. Application, giving full particulars, should be made to The Director, Good Housekeeping Institute, 49 Wellington Street, Strand, W.C.2

---

than a man does. A man would say that a woman has no sense of proportion, which is what a sense of humour really is, and that she flies from one extreme to another, from an appalling austerity to imbecile silliness; but we may take that with a pinch of salt. Nevertheless, it remains true that the laughter of the ages has been made by men. No woman has ever succeeded in ascending to the company of the great comedians. From the time of Aristophanes to the time of Bernard Shaw that region has been exclusively inhabited by men. But will it long continue to be occupied only by them? One hears the sound of laughing women approaching. Miss Anita Loos, with her *Gentlemen Prefer Blondes,* has sounded a note that women have rarely sounded before. Is she the first of the feminine satirists? Will women presently shake their sides with laughter as Falstaff shook his, even if drink be not the subject of their discourse? Anyhow, they are laughing more reasonably to-day than their great-great-grannies seemed to do, and reason is at the bottom of all good laughter.

*Photos :
Hana,
London*

*Exercise II.
Positions I and 2*

VI. Overcoming Obesity and Emaciation

By Evelyn D. Fanghanel

WHY do rhythmic health movements attack and improve both obesity and emaciation?

Exercise produces in the system two absolutely different effects. It increases the process of assimilation by which the body gains new tissues, and it accelerates the process of disassimilation which leads to the destruction of certain materials.

A muscle which works is a muscle which becomes heated, and this cannot occur without a greater quantity of blood flowing there—in fact at least nine times as much as in an inactive muscle—the blood carries oxygen, and this increased heat turns up a certain quantity of tissue. This excessive production of heat, which accompanies work, the rapid combustion of certain materials of the body and their elimination from the system as waste, cause loss of weight.

The toxine materials which the organic cells are constantly constructing are more actively eliminated, and the general effect is that the fats are burnt up and cellular functions regulated.

Muscular work is a means of regulating the nutrition of the body, because a moving muscle calls for blood to enable it to move, and in order that the brain and the nerves may carry out their orders, more blood must flush these areas. In this way an increased area is enriched and nourished because the nutritive fluid which feeds the tissues is carried in the blood stream. Also the elimination of waste matter is more active and over-storage of reserve forces is prevented by the ever-increasing oxygen present in the blood stream.

After being motionless for a long time, everyone experiences a need for action, and that fact is alone sufficient to prove the absolute necessity for regular muscular training if we are to keep perfect equilibrium in the human body.

The need for rest is called fatigue, and although the need for exercise has not received a special name, it deserves one just as much as hunger and thirst.

Some people whose life is too inactive put on too much fat, and others waste through insufficient movement. Thus the need for movement is felt by the thin and the fat, there is a need to burn the too abundant reserves, and there is a need to draw in more oxygen into the system; these are the two causes which join in producing the manifestation of the instinct to perform muscular work.

If this useful warning is misunderstood and the need for exercise is neglected, two evils occur.

If the quantity of oxygen introduced into the system is too little, the blood becomes less rich, its contact does not give to the organs that precious stimulation which makes their working more active and brings all their energies into play. The appetite fails through deficient stimulation of the digestive organs, or assimilation of food is imperfect. Even when appetite is still keen, we may eat with the mouth but still have a hungry body owing to imperfect assimilation; then the muscles lose their irritability and respond more slowly to the stimulus of the nerves, in a word the system languishes and the organs become weak.

She is not portrayed as healthy-minded—

The STAGE

By St. John

Illustrations by

IT is becoming increasingly common to find a very irritating young person of the female sex in modern English comedies who is misnamed a flapper, especially in these times when the hairdresser leaves ladies with very little to flap, but I take it that the word is properly applied to girls who wear their hair hanging down their backs, and not to girls whose hair would be up if it were not bobbed or shingled. That, at all events, was the meaning of the word before the War. To-day, however, flappers seem to be of all ages. I have actually met some that were grandmothers! One must not complain of this. A passion for youth was a natural result of the War. It was inevitable that the young men who died in the trenches should fill the imagination of their elders with a fierce and unquenchable love.

Nature, which mystically satisfies the imaginative needs of mankind, gave us a prince who, in his own person and appearance, symbolised the spirit of youth, all that "blown feature of youth," as Ophelia called it, which was lost in the War. The personal charm of the Prince of Wales is undeniably great, and it endears him to the British people, but I sometimes think that the affection in which he is held is due to a deeper cause than his own very attractive character: it is due, I think, to the fact that his boyish looks and his young manner are an unblemishable monument to the gallant lads who died in France. Youth had been spent for the redemption of the world, and Age humbly offered homage to it. The extraordinary vogue of youth since 1914 is surely explained by that.

But the dramatists seem unable to portray this modern youth with any sort of verisimilitude. I write about this subject with some diffidence, for I have myself been accused of having put into a play a tiresome modern girl. Perhaps, therefore, I am in the state of Satan rebuking sin, but that fact does not prevent me from recognising that serious injustice is being done to the flapper by the dramatist. What, exactly, do I mean by that? Well, the modern girl or flapper is nearly always portrayed as an ill-bred, pert young person, incessantly uncivil to her elders, whose manners would cause her to be thrown out of a back-street pub., and would certainly, if she had then displayed them, have caused her to be well and thoroughly spanked by her father before the War.

She chatters at great length and with immense assurance on subjects that are scarcely decent. She repeats the jargon of the psycho-analysts and explains everything in Freudian terms. She talks about complexes and inhibitions and is daring in her discussion of sex. She knows all about it! She knows, she knows, she knows! Her tactlessness is almost unbelievable. She blurts out everything, especially the more wounding and unpardonable things. In spite of her affectation of knowledge, she is amazingly dense and stupid. Altogether, she is a singularly disagreeable minx who rouses murderous thoughts in the minds of the average decent playgoer. In two plays that I saw this year in London, neither of which is now being performed, there were flappers of such an exasperating sort that I found myself, in common with all my neighbours, almost unable to refrain from storming the stage and smacking them with great force and persistence. The flapper in one of the plays was so irritating that she almost ruined the play. People in the audience had the greatest difficulty in sitting with patience through the scenes in which this character appeared. I could hear all round me murmurs of "Isn't she awful?"—"Why doesn't somebody hit her?"

Now, I do not doubt that the author of this particular play, a woman dramatist, thought that she was faithfully portraying a contemporary person. I am sure that the disagreeable qualities of the character were accentuated by the producer of the play, who instructed the young actress who took the part to act it as acidly as possible. But the author must accept some of the blame

but as ill-bred, tactless, cocktail-sipping

FLAPPER

Ervine

Aubrey Hammond

for the character since it appears just as disagreeable in print as it did in performance. And I ask myself where these ill-bred flappers are to be found. Where do these outspoken wenches who are addicted to cocktails abound? Here is a sample of the conversation in which a stage flapper indulges. It is taken from *The Widow's Cruise*, by Joan Temple, and is spoken by a girl of eighteen named Jill. Jill is discussing the world in general with her guardian, Sir Theodore Frome, and she casually informs him that she hates his wife because she had rather hoped that he would marry her:

THEODORE: But—but—but I knew you as a baby! Seen you tubbed and all that. Good heavens, whatever put such an idea into your head! Some sentimental nonsense you'd been reading, I suppose.

JILL (*loftily*): Don't insult me, Theodore! It was just—adolescence and propinquity.

THEODORE: I don't know whether it's a sign of rapidly advancing age, but the conversation of the present-day *jeune fille* sometimes makes me *stagger*.

JILL (*indulgently*): You mustn't let

yourself get dated, Theodore. Nothing labels one's period so clearly as one's mental attitude.

That is a fair sample of the sort of talk which Jill, aged eighteen, directs at her guardian, aged forty-five. Here is another sample:

JILL: Why, you've only to read these exquisite poems of his about vine leaves and naked white bodies!——

THEODORE: Jill! For Heaven's sake!

JILL: Does the word "bodies" offend you? The Victorian era must have been *very* restricting to poetic fancy!

THEODORE: You young pagan!

JILL: Who could be anything *but* pagan in a place like this? It's in one's blood. One of these moonlight nights I shall take off all my clothes—put vine leaves in my hair—and dance the moon down.

And here is a final sample:

CESCA: You mustn't be sentimental, Jill.

JILL: I'm not. Girls aren't sentimental these days. Anything but! Oh, you don't understand. I want to talk about Life, and—and Love is one of the

fundamental facts of Life, isn't it?

CESCA: We—we oughtn't to discuss such things. Nice people don't, you know.

JILL: Oh, what rot! We're none of us "nice·people," come down to brass tacks. Psycho-analysis teaches us that, and justifies the Bible.

CESCA: What do you mean?

JILL: Well, the Bible indicates the existence of what it calls "Original Sin" —and psycho-analysis shows pretty clearly its *exact location* in the human complex.

CESCA: *I* think psycho-analysis is immoral.

JILL: I suppose you'd tell a doctor he was "rude" if he told you you'd got a floating kidney. Same thing.

CESCA: Don't be coarse, Jill.

JILL: What an ornament you'd have been to the Victorian era!

Are there girls of eighteen who talk like that to men of forty-five and women of thirty? I lead a fairly varied life. I meet all sorts and conditions of men and women, rich and poor, in London and in the provinces, but I have never in my life met anybody remotely resembling Jill or, indeed, any of the flappers that I see on the stage these nights. Perhaps the girls I know either respect my white hairs or disdain to waste their eloquence on me, but I have not yet met one who has talked to me about psycho-analysis, nor has any girl mentioned "white bodies" in my presence or expressed a desire to take off all her clothes and dance the moon down! I do not know a single girl of eighteen who drinks cocktails. It may be that I am lucky or that I am living in a (*Continued on page* 62)

The Stage Flapper

(*Continued from page 61*)

backwater, but none of the flappers of acquaintance swear or smoke or drink talk about complexes or inhibitions, no they discuss sexual relationships or sp late on the relative merits of living a man or being married to one. W does this strange creature, so arde described by the dramatists, live?

What I do see wherever I go healthy-minded girl whose self-assuranc not a synonym for ill-breeding. I see tackling jobs with skill, and doing s of the work that men used to do with ra more ability than men did it. I like freshness and jollity and health and g spirits of these girls, and when I remem how gamely they behaved during General Strike in May of this year, I like taking off my hat to them. Girls incessantly sip cocktails could not have about their business with the spirit and with which the flappers of Great Bri behaved during the suppression of tr One has only to look at these girls to that they are healthy-minded women healthy bodies. It is true that they pow their noses and lipstick their mouths r than they need—though there are multit of them who do neither the one nor other—but that is a habit that women had from the beginning of the world it is a habit which they probably will re until the end of it.

Some of them, no doubt, are rude, rude girls were as common before War as they are now. But what their faults may be, they do not include faults which are discoverable in the versations I have quoted from Temple's play or those that I might quoted from other plays in London i last two or three years. I suspect tha stage flapper is a stage fiction. Mr. began the business by portraying a likeable modern girl, fresh and frank free, but not ill-mannered, not coar her conversation, not cocktail-swillir her habits. Then other dramatists, ob ing with what favour Mr. Milne's fla were received, began to embellish Milne-ry, until at last we got a cre as remote from his flappers as they remote from the flappers of fact.

What appals me is the thought perfectly decent girls, habituated to frightful female on the stage, may to imitate her. We do undoubtedly in our lives some of the things w in plays, and although it is not true the mannerless girl of the contemp drama abounds to any extent in life, i very well be that in a few years she What a calamity that will be! O other hand, it is possible that this f will vanish from our theatre be audiences dislike it so intensely. I told recently by an elderly lady, who been deceived by the plays she had that she gave a party to some girls received the shock of her life! Sh vited them to smoke, but they declin do so. She urged them not to spar grey hairs and went so far as to s a cigarette herself, but still they dec She offered them cocktails, but they not touch them. "Oh, but come," she "I'm not so old-fashioned as you to think!" Then one of the flappe genuine flapper—said, "We leave all to the war girls!" It seems that an generation has grown up, one which r against stained fingers and cocktails bad manners and loose talk. One of days dramatists will get to hear abo

If only we had some strawberries we'd have strawberries and cream if only we had some

IDEAL
UNSWEETENED
MILK

PREPARED BY NESTLE'S IN ENGLAND

Small Size 4d.   Large Size 8d.

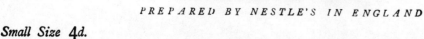

By St. John Ervine

NOEL COWARD

One of the Most Interesting Figures of the Modern Theatre

I SUPPOSE the most interesting figure that has appeared in the English theatre since the war is that of Mr. Noel Coward, who was born in 1899, and is now twenty-seven years of age. Mr. Coward is interesting, not only because of his youth, his vivacity, his great industry, and his variety of gifts, but because he has created, or perhaps one ought to say, portrayed a modern type on the stage. When one thinks of what are called "smart people," who breakfast on cocktails and dine on cocaine and inhabit night clubs and are everlastingly dancing, one instinctively thinks of Mr. Coward as the author who has put them into plays. Other authors—Mr. Frederick Lonsdale, Mr. Michael Arlen, and the late Israel Zangwill—have written about such people, but none of them has succeeded as Mr. Coward has done in making himself their protagonist.

Indeed, Mr. Coward has done this so successfully that many persons foolishly imagine that he is himself the sort of character he describes, and their humourless belief is confirmed for them by the impish writings of Mr. Coward himself, who, when accused of being a "dope fiend," merrily replies, "Yes, that's true! When I wake in the morning the first thing I do is to wail for a beaker of cocaine!" That of course is youthful impudence, and Mr. Coward is getting over it, though I confess to a fondness for his cheek. I like a young man to have an air and some audacity, and to be insolent in a well-bred way. I detect nothing fundamentally offensive in Mr. Coward's cheeky conversation, nor anything ill-natured or spiteful in his wit. He has, indeed, made some sharp replies to people who attempted to "put him in his place," but the replies have been provoked and deserved. Did not the famous Society lady who had just gone on the movies, and had appeared in a thoroughly dull and silly film, fully deserve all that she got when at a luncheon party she very offensively said to Mr. Coward, who had just had a comedy produced in London, "I saw your play, but I didn't laugh once!" "Oh!" Mr. Coward replied. "I saw your film, and I laughed all the time!"

That retort gives me pleasure. There is no cruelty in it: all the cruelty—intended cruelty—was in the lady's gratuitous insult. Not that Mr. Coward has not got his cruel side. He is young and witty, therefore he is doubly cruel.

His early plays repelled me because his mockery was almost brutal. That element in him, however, is now under control, and his cruelty is slight and almost imperceptible.

We need not concern ourselves with Mr. Coward's youthful impudence now, but consider him seriously as a dramatist not only of notable accomplishment, but as one who may become a distinguished dramatist. It is a remarkable feat for a young man of twenty-seven years of age to have written nearly a dozen plays, in addition to the writing, or part writing, and composing, or part composing, of a number of revues.

In six or seven years, he has made a wide reputation for himself in England and America not only as a dramatist, but as an actor and as a composer of light music. Established actors discuss his technique as an actor with extraordinary interest. They say that he does all the wrong things, and yet contrives to get the right effects. His performance in his own play, The Vortex, a most moving and sincere piece, was very impressive, although skilled actors stoutly assert that he did everything that an accomplished actor ought not to do. The increase in his craft as an actor was obvious in his performance of the part of Lewis Dodd in The Constant Nymph, but here, of course, he had the help of Mr. Basil Dean.

What, one asks oneself, is to be the future of this brilliant young man? His personal qualities are unusually attractive and likeable. He is loyal to his friends, he is generous and unaffected in his behaviour, he remembers those who were kind to him when he was in need of kindness, and he is full of courage and decision. He knows his mind and is not afraid to express it. He is sincere and simple and modest. His wits are quick, and he has an uncanny knowledge of stagecraft. He writes good "theatre"; his plays click; his big scenes come off. It is not surprising that he thoroughly understands theatre craft, for he has been on the stage at least half his lifetime, if we exclude the period when he was in the Army. (He reached military age towards the end of the war.) His first appearance in a play was when, an Italia Conti child, he acted the part of Prince Mussel in a fairy play, The Goldfish, at the Playhouse, London, in 1910. He was then eleven years of age. They say that he was a shy and sensitive child,

and that when he went, at the age of thirteen, to act at the Liverpool Repertory Theatre, he felt so homesick that he used to sit in Miss Conti's lap and cry for his mother.

An actor is not necessarily a capable dramatist because he is an actor; but it is a fact that when an author has had considerable experience as an actor, his plays nearly always have a tidiness of technique which is not observable in the plays of dramatists who have not been actors. Many dramatic authors have begun their career in the theatre as actors. One instantly thinks of Shakespeare and Molière, and there are others. Ibsen was not an actor, but he was the manager of a theatre, and undoubtedly acquired his remarkable technique there. Sir Arthur Pinero was an actor before he was an author, and so was Mr. Harley Granville-Barker, although one is bound to acknowledge that Mr. Granville-Barker has, one might almost imagine deliberately, excluded his sense of the theatre from his plays. Mr. Coward, therefore, is in a great line. He does understand the stage, and is able to get effects in his work that dramatists who have not been on the stage are either unable to get, or take a long time in acquiring.

The danger which besets the actor-author is that he will sacrifice verisimilitude and thought to theatrical effect. He thinks of scenes and situations rather than of people and of life. This is a danger which peculiarly besets Mr. Coward, because of his youth, and the fact that the greater part of his life has been spent in the theatre. I once defined a bad dramatist as a man who went into the theatre and never came out again. An author who has achieved success so quickly as it has come to Mr. Coward has to be on his guard against tricks. No one denies that Mr. Coward is brilliantly clever, but even the most brilliant author cannot know a great deal about life, or about people, between the ages of twenty-one and twenty-seven. These, indeed, are the years when he is beginning to learn something about life. The bulk of Mr. Bernard Shaw's plays were written after he had passed his fortieth year. The most obvious fact about Mr. Coward's work is that in spite of the great skill with which he conducts his scenes, and the verve with which he writes his dialogue, he really does not know much about people (Continued on page 66)

Portrait: Maurice Beck and Helen Macgregor

Mr. Noel Coward

66

Noel Coward
(Continued from page 64)

or life, and the little he does know he seems to know all wrong, or in the wrong proportion. When one compares an early play of his, *The Rat Trap,* which was written before he was twenty-one, with *Easy Virtue* and *The Queen was in the Parlour,* which were produced in 1926 (although in fairness to Mr. Coward one must state that they were written several years earlier), one is struck, first, by the technical excellence of all three plays, and second, by the fact that there are no signs of growth in the latter plays. *The Rat Trap* is as good a play as either of the other two, and it is as bad a play. It is this fact which alarms critics like myself, who, while we admire Mr. Coward, are not undiscriminating in our appreciation of his work. A dramatist cannot live on technique. He certainly cannot live on tricks, and the danger in which Mr. Coward now is, or so it seems to me, is that of a man who has learned one trick very well, and is content to repeat it.

When I say that there are no signs of growth in his work I am referring chiefly to his people and his themes. There is not a great deal of thought in Mr. Coward's work, and what there is of it is largely false. People do not behave in the way in which he makes his characters behave. But even in the matter of technique, there is evidence that Mr. Coward is content to repeat a formula. The characteristic of his work is a bad first act, an uncommonly good second act, and a weak last act.

In the first act of *The Rat Trap* practically nothing happens. We are informed that Sheila Brandreth and Keld Maxwell are on the eve of getting married. He aspires to be a dramatist: she has already had some short stories published and aspires to be a novelist. A friend warns her that marriage between two persons of strongly-marked character and temperament is likely to be disastrous for one of them, if not for both. The idea seems to be that either the dramatist-husband will be submerged in the novelist-wife, or the novelist-wife will be submerged in the dramatist-husband. One must yield to the other. This is a very arbitrary and disputable statement, but Mr. Coward seems to have no doubts on the subject, and he proceeds to prove that it is impossible for two able people to live together in harmony. If they are not continually bickering and finally separated, then one of them has to give up ambition!

I do not propose to be as dogmatic as Mr. Coward on the subject, but I would remind him that very able men and women in other walks of life have lived in great happiness and carried on their work with success, despite the fact that each of them was extremely able at the same job. I cite the cases of M. and Mme. Curie of Mr. and Mrs. Sidney Webb, of Canon and Mrs. Barnett, of Mr. and Mrs. J. R. Green, or Mr. and Mrs. J. L. Hammond, and surely the Brownings are as fine a refutation as one could discover of Mr. Coward's argument. Does not the theatre itself offer many instances of great ability in husband and wife that was not incompatible with domestic felicity? Mr. Coward's theme is very casually, almost unnoticeably introduced into the first act. In the second act, Keld and Sheila are married, and are already experiencing the jars of temperament. In this act Mr. Coward displays his craftsmanship at its best. We get a quarrel between the husband and wife which is conducted with remarkable ability. The third act goes to pieces, and the play ends in the most abrupt and inconclusive manner of any play I have ever seen on the stage.

The first act of *Easy Virtue* is as empty

content as the first act of *The Rat
ap*. So is the first act of *The Queen
s in the Parlour*. In *Easy Virtue* Mr.
ward does no more than assemble his
racters in the first act. Why they are
re we do not know: what they are
ng to do we cannot imagine; but re-
mbering Mr. Coward's other plays we
l fairly certain that in the second act
re will be a terrific row. And sure
ugh the row happens! It is a first-
ss row. Undeniably, Mr. Coward can
this sort of thing with immense effect.
t it is clear that he is not extending
acquaintanceship, that he is not observ-
people very closely, that indeed, he is
y observing one little group of people,
l observing them through the same
sses with which he observed them when
began to write.

le has in him the potentialities of a
y considerable dramatist. When his
y *The Vortex* was performed, even
se who disliked his work realised that
had great sincerity and feeling, and
t there were depths in him of which
n he himself was hardly aware. But
is a fair criticism of Mr. Coward that
repeats the themes of other drama-
s in terms of his own generation, and
s not improve upon them. The famous
ne in *The Vortex* where the boy brow-
ts his mother, is merely the Closet
ne from *Hamlet* again. *Easy Virtue* is
kened Pinero. *The Queen was in the
lour* is weakened Anthony Hope. And
may well inquire when we are going
see a developed Mr. Coward. His
ogue is too easy; there are passages in
plays which might almost be described
automatic writing.

Ir. Coward is now at a turning point
his career. There is evidence in his
k of sincerity, but one feels that it
n him rather than in his plays. Behind
flippancy and—the word is a harsh
but it is not used harshly—the ignor-
e of Mr. Coward there is a fine, flexible
sensitive mind questing for truth. He
tes too quickly and too much. He does
brood over his work sufficiently, nor
he adventure far enough among
ble. His youthfulness is apparent in
ing so much as his amazing belief
the virtuous woman is a dull woman,
arrow woman, an ignorant woman, and
ably a cruel woman.

ll that is youngness, and pardonable in
ne under the age of twenty-five. But
Coward is more than twenty-five, and
ust now, if he is to maintain the high
tion he has so brilliantly won, begin to
k like an adult. It would do him a
ld of good to be compelled to live in
suburbs of Huddersfield for twelve
ths, with no other society than that
is immediate neighbours. He happens
e an extremely temperate and abstemi-
man, or I would say that he should
forbidden to drink cocktails, but I
k it would be a good thing for Mr.
ard if he abstained from visits to the
assy Club and similar institutions for
ast twelve months,

I were a Mussolini I would compel
Coward to become a patrol leader in
Boy Scouts in the neighbourhood of
urn. I would forbid him to put on a
s suit or to visit a theatre for a year.
ould break his heart by making him
Gibbon's *Decline and Fall of the Holy
an Empire* with no other relief from
han dips into Hooker's *Laws of
esiastical Polity*. I would make him
ciate with mill-girls and district visi-
and industrial life insurance agents
bookie's clerks and archdeacons and
ole horde of un-clever people. And I
d make a fine dramatist of him. But
aps that sincerity that I see in him,
simplicity and lack of affectation, will
ently enable him to make a fine drama-
of himself. The stuff is in him; he
only to bring it out.

Our LONDON SHOPPING Service
Will Buy Your Spring Wardrobe for You

Left: Neat looking frock in wool marocain with panel of buff silk georgette let in in bodice. Box pleats front of skirt. Available in Air Force blue, rust, almond green or cedar. S.S.W. 42, S.W. 44, and W. 46 inches. Price 30s. Post free U.K.

Right: very attractive afternoon frock in two shades of silk and wool crêpe marocain outlined with scalloped embroidery. The bloused bodice has the front inset with beige marocain and a deep underwrap allows ample fullness to the skirt. Available in navy, almond, cedar, chamois, beech, bois de rose, sunset, moonlight blue, grey, and black. W. size, price 3 guineas. Post free U.K. In outsize, £3 17s. 6d.

Centre, below: a charming frock in small sizes only in good quality marocain. The bodice has an inset front panel and V neck with georgette collar and cuffs; the skirt has inverted tucks at back and side front. Available in navy, grey, brown, green, and all new colours. S.W. only, varying lengths 42 inches to 45 inches from centre neck at back to hem. Price 39s. 6d. Post free U.K.

Right: a very good matron's frock in marocain made on long and becoming lines suited to most figures. Vest of georgette and lace. Available in black, navy, grey, bottle green, cedar or saxe. S.W., 45 inches; W., 48 inches; O.S., 51 inches. Special price, 39s. 6d.; O.S., 49s. 6d. Post free U.K.

Below: charming frock in crêpe de Chine made with a pleated jabot of buff silk. Available in cedar, almond green, saxe, navy or black. S.W. 44 inches, W. 46 inches. Price 49s. 6d. Post free U.K.

Extreme right of group above: coat frock in all wool charmelaine with inverted pleat down corsage and skirt; trimmed with smart galon; skirt pleated at sides. In navy only. S.W. and W. sizes. Price 39s. 6d. Post free U.K.

Above: locknit jumper suit in artificial silk guaranteed not to ladder; set of fine pleats at either side of skirt. Available in pimpernel red, burgundy, cedar, navy or black. S.W. 42 inches and W. 44 inches. Price 49s. 6d. Post free U.K.

Our Shopping Service

is designed to help those who are out of reach of the London shops. Any of the articles illustrated in these pages or in the advertisement columns of this number of Good Housekeeping, we shall be happy to buy for you, without extra charge, on receipt of money order and your name and address. Money orders from the Colonies should include cost of postage and insurance. Readers in Irish Free State must be prepared to meet Customs charges on dutiable goods. Cheques and money orders should be made payable to the National Magazine Co., Ltd. When ordering any article please give a choice of colours

Will readers who use the Shopping Service kindly carefully read the instructions on this and opposite page before ordering goods

Right: attractive young-looking frock in good quality wool marocain. Buckle finishes the belt in front, and the skirt shows the new space pleating. Available in navy, saxe, grey, mauve, fawn, brown or green. S.W., 44 inches; W., 47 inches. Price 29s. 6d. Post free U.K.

Below: smart coat frock in the new wool basket-weave material. Skirt with deep pleats and suède belt. Collar piped to match skirt and finished with artist's bow in crêpe de Chine. Available in chamois, cedar, beige, almond, and bois de rose. S.W. and W. Price 45s. Post free U.K.

Left: for full figures this frock in black artificial silk marocain is becoming and cut on long lines. W. 48 inches and O.S. 50 inches from shoulder to hem. Price 49s. 6d. Post free U.K.

Below: two-piece jumper frock in fine all wool suiting; the jumper of plain suiting has band down the centre, border, collar, cuffs, and pocket of check. Deep wrap-over skirt cut with yoke. Available in beige/tango; beige/blue; beige/green; beige/cherry; beige/hyacinth and beige/brown. S.W. and W. Price 39s. 6d. Post free U.K.

Centre, above: useful coat frock in navy all wool charmelaine of good quality with collar, vest and cuffs in pastel blue. Skirt with deep inverted pleats in front. Also available in navy/beige, cedar/beige. S.W. and W. Price 39s. 6d. Post free U.K.

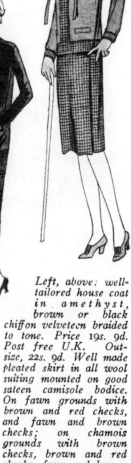

Our Country Readers

All letters, money orders, and cheques should be addressed to "Shopping Service," GOOD HOUSEKEEPING, 153 Queen Victoria Street, London, E.C.4.

Returned Goods: If any reader desires to return goods purchased through the Shopping Service, the following rules must be observed. The goods, together with the reader's full name and address, and a reference to GOOD HOUSEKEEPING Shopping Service, should be returned to the shop. If goods are not returned in perfect condition the money cannot be refunded. Postage must be paid on goods that were correctly sent in the first instance. All correspondence regarding the goods, with all instructions concerning them, must be sent to "Shopping Service," GOOD HOUSEKEEPING, 153 Queen Victoria Street, London, E.C.4

Left, above: well-tailored house coat in amethyst, brown or black chiffon velveteen braided to tone. Price 19s. 9d. Post free U.K. Outsize, 22s. 9d. Well made pleated skirt in all wool suiting mounted on good sateen camisole bodice. On fawn grounds with brown and red checks, and fawn and brown checks; on chamois grounds with brown checks, brown and red checks, fawn and brown checks. In 42-inch, 44-inch, and 46-inch lengths. Price 12s. 6d. Post free U.K.

Right: this is a good pull-on elastic belt laced at the sides with a slightly boned front. Four suspenders. Sizes 22 inches to 30 inches. Price 8s. 11d. On top is an evening brassière of pink milanese and écru lace cut very low at back and held in position by elastic covered in satin ribbon. Sizes 32 inches to 40 inches. Price 6s. 11d. Post free U.K.

In centre of group on right is shown an ideal belt for dancing of good quality pink broché; well boned in front giving support with perfect freedom of movement. Four suspenders. Sizes 22 inches to 30 inches. Price 10s. 11d. On top is a brassière of strong pink batiste in figured design lightly boned in front, hooked at side with dainty ribbon straps. Sizes 32 inches to 40 inches. Price 3s. 6d. Post free U.K.

Left: corselette of white figured batiste slightly boned at front; elastic gores at hips, fitted four suspenders and shoulder straps; sizes 30 inches to 40 inches. Price 8s. 11d. Post free U.K.

SIMPLE STORIES OF SUNLIGHT STREET

The name LEVER on Soap is a Guarantee of Purity and Excellence.

I WASH SUNLIGHT STREET SAYS THE MAN WITH THE CART THO' AT WASHING MY MISSUS CAN GIVE ME A START.

When it comes to highly-skilled washing, a man can't keep pace with his wife. With her washing is not a job—it's an art. Breakfast things are washed up—Bedrooms are tidied —Dinner is prepared—Children's needs are seen to— *and all the time it's Wash-day.* Truly a good wife brings Sunlight into the home.

In Sunlight Soap there is everything to help the good wife and nothing to hinder her. Sunlight represents a scientific combination of nature's finest cleansing oils and fats. The best materials are selected—the most efficient methods of manufacture are rigidly adhered to —every boiling has to pass an analytical test for purity.

Sunlight Street is the great Highway of Health— It is a Thoroughfare of Thorough Cleanliness.

£1,000 GUARANTEE OF PURITY ON EVERY BAR.

SUNLIGHT SOAP

LEVER BROTHERS LIMITED, PORT SUNLIGHT.

S 425—34

The Housekeeper's Dictionary *of* Facts

Hints When Using an Electric Cooker

Much economy can be effected by using hot water from the tap for filling saucepans needed when cooking vegetables, boiling puddings, etc., as much current is often unnecessarily wasted by heating up cold water on the hot plate.

For tea making use an electric kettle, which is rather more efficient for such a purpose than the hot plate elements.

As the hot plate elements of most stoves remain hot for some time after the current has been turned off, it is possible, when simmering and stewing, to switch the current off ¼ hour or so before cooking is completed.

When frying in deep fat it is important not to attempt cooking too much at a time, as if this is done the fat cools quickly and current is wasted in heating it up again.

When using the oven, it is usually advisable to switch the current on "full" for about 20 minutes, then turn it to "medium" and afterwards to "low." In most cases the oven is so well insulated that it retains the heat sufficiently to allow for the current being switched off about ¼ hour before cooking is over.

Pantry Efficiency

To avoid inconvenience and delay, household stores bought in packets should be placed in jars. If labels are pasted on to the jars and then given a coat of shellac, they will withstand immersion in water. This arrangement produces neat shelves and enables one to tell at a glance when the stock requires replenishing.

The Care of Aluminium

Aluminium saucepans are now very generally used, and they doubtless possess many advantages, being easily cleaned and kept in good condition. Fine steel wool can be recommended for ordinary cleaning, although it will not remove the dark discoloration frequently apparent. The latter is perfectly harmless but rather detracts from the appearance of the pans, and most people prefer to remove it. This can be done by boiling up with a weak acid such as vinegar and water. Soda is most undesirable for cleaning aluminium, as the soda solution has a definite action on this metal, very slowly dissolving it.

More Cookery Demonstrations

Syllabus of the Cookery Demonstrations to be given at Good Housekeeping Institute, 49 Wellington Street, Strand, on Wednesdays, April 27th, May 4th, 11th, 18th, 25th, and June 1st, at 3 o'clock sharp. Tickets 1s. 6d. each

April 27th, at 3 p.m.

SOME USES FOR YEAST.—*The making of bread, buns, waffles, crumpets and Babas*

May 4th, at 3 p.m.

HORS D'ŒUVRE, SAVOURIES AND SUPPER DISHES.—*Preparation of hors d'œuvre variés, cheese straws, sardines Piedmontaise, cheese aigrettes, anchovy toast*

May 11th, at 3 p.m.

THE PREPARATION OF FISH DISHES.—*Lobster cutlets, casserole of fish, Irish haddock, sole à la maître d'hôtel, sole à la Colbert*

May 18th, at 3 p.m.

CAKES AND SCONES FOR AFTERNOON TEA.—*Oven, girdle and treacle scones, biscuits, macaroons, Josephine cakes, almond fingers*

May 25th, at 3 p.m.

SWEET MAKING.—*Peppermint humbugs, almond rock, coco-nut ice, Turkish delight, marshmallows, fondant, marzipan*

June 1st, at 3 p.m.

PLANNING THE FAMILY MENUS.—*Typical menus and the preparation of dishes for adults, children and invalids*

Demonstrations on the Theory and Practice of Making Jam, Ices, Iced Puddings, and other Frozen Delights will be announced later

Pastry Board Hints

It is a good idea when using a pastry board to spread a sheet of greaseproof paper tightly over it, securing the corners firmly with drawing pins. This device saves frequent washing of the board, and afterwards the paper can be folded and kept for placing over the top of pies, cakes, etc., in order to protect them from burning.

When Making Shortcrust Pastry

In kitchens where it is the custom to make shortcrust pastry almost daily, time may be saved by preparing sufficient flour and shortening to last for several occasions. Sieve the flour, salt, and baking powder together and run in the shortening. It is then ready to use as required, and only requires mixing with cold water and rolling out.

To Whiten Discoloured Linen

When old linen or lace has become yellow, it can be bleached without damaging the material by stewing for several days in a solution of borax and water, to which a little soap has been added. The water should be changed every day and the solution should on no account be allowed to boil. The addition of small quantities of cold water will probably be necessary from time to time to keep the temperature low and to make up losses due to evaporation. Afterwards, the lace should be rinsed and blued in the usual way.

Lemon Curd

Beat 4 eggs, put into a saucepan with 8 oz. loaf sugar, ¼ lb. butter and the grated rind of 3 lemons and cook slowly until the mixture thickens.

To Prevent Eye-Glasses from Becoming Misty

If eye-glasses are rubbed over with a soft rag dipped in a little glycerine, moisture does not condense on them.

Keeping Parsley Fresh

Parsley should be washed in cold water, and, if withered, allowed to stand for an hour or two in the cold water. It should then be well shaken in order to remove the water, and placed in a glass jar, such as a fruit bottling jar provided with a cover. If the jar is placed in a refrigerator, or, if this is not available, in the coolest part of the larder, it will be found that the parsley keeps perfectly fresh for several days.

The Indispensable Scissors

A pair of scissors should find a place in every kitchen. They are very useful for a variety of purposes, including cutting the fins off fish, cutting up jelly squares and gelatine, toffee, and greaseproof paper for lining cake tins, etc.

To Avoid Fatigue

It is false economy to wear down-at-heel and out-of-shape shoes when performing household duties, for nothing produces greater fatigue than tired aching feet. The housewife should reserve a pair of plain, well-fitting shoes with broad low heels and roomy toes for housework, especially when she has much standing to do.

Good Housekeeping Institute

Director, D. D.

Certificate Household and Social
London; First Class Diplomas
Laundrywork, House

We Wish to Apologise to those Readers

who were unable to obtain admittance to the lectures given at the Institute during October and November, and also to those who had not made previous application for a ticket and were obliged to stand. Owing to the great interest shown in these lectures we have decided to give a series of four Cookery Demonstrations on January 19th and 26th, and February 2nd and 9th, at 3 p.m., particulars of which will be found on page 78. For the comfort of the audience it has been decided to limit the number of tickets issued. Will those wishing to attend, therefore, please apply to The Director, Good Housekeeping Institute, 49 Wellington Street, London, W.C.2 ?

The Institute is able to send fully qualified members of the Staff to give lectures and demonstrations at girls' schools, Women's Institutes, etc. Private tuition can also be given in all branches of Cookery, Housecraft, and Laundry-work at the Institute. As only a few students can be accommodated, those wishing to attend are asked to make application as far in advance as possible

---

SO many readers have asked us to give particulars of catering for a dance that we propose to devote the third and last article in our short catering series to dance suppers and refreshments.

Under normal conditions the work entailed in catering for, say 50 guests, is as much as can be undertaken in a private house. When larger numbers are invited, it is advisable to entrust the work to a reliable firm of caterers, first getting estimates from two or more firms so that the menus submitted at a given price per head may be compared.

The first thing to be considered is the particular type of meal—whether light refreshments are to be served at a buffet and handed round, or whether a sit-down supper is to be provided.

When arranging menus of any description, something quite plain in each course—e.g. tongue sandwiches, plain biscuits, etc.—should be available for any guest who may prefer it.

The following menus are suggested for light refreshments and the quantities required for 50 guests are given.

We have included methods for preparing certain of the dishes mentioned. Many people will prefer to order the ices from a reliable confectioner's as this saves time and trouble.

The cost per head of the first menu, which is especially suitable for young people, works out at between 3s. and 3s. 6d. per head according to the quality of the food, while the slightly more elaborate menu on page 73 costs approximately 5s. per head, excluding drinks.

Catering for

The Institute gives MENUS

DANCE MENU and QUANTITIES REQUIRED

Tea	½ lb. tea; 1½ lb. coffee; 4 qts. of milk (3
Coffee	hot 1 cold); 10 qts. mixed drinks—lemon-
Fruit Punch	ade, orangeade, and punch; 6 qts. cider cup.
Cider Cup	
Orangeade	50 chicken patties; 40 anchovy eggs; 35
Lemonade	plates salmon mayonnaise (4 lb. salmon).

	Sandwiches	
		150 mixed sandwiches;
Chicken Patties	Sardine, Crab and Cress	75 bridge rolls (for
Anchovy Eggs	Ham and Cress	sardines); brown bread
Salmon Mayonnaise	Cucumber and Tongue	for cress and crab;
	Cream Cheese and Celery	white bread and butter.

Macedoine of Fruit	
Coffee and Chocolate Cream	4 quarts of jelly for
Buns and Eclairs	macedoine of fruit; ¾ pint
Fruit Salad	cream; 6 quarts fruit salad.

	40 cream buns and éclairs (20
Cake—Fruit, Madeira, Cherry	coffee and 20 chocolate); 2 lb.
Mixed Biscuits	fruit cake; 1 lb. Madeira cake; 1 lb.
	cherry cake; 3 lb. biscuits (choco-
Mixed Chocolates and Sweets	late, shortbread, and mixed fancy);
	2 lb. chocolates; 1 lb. cream fondants.

Vanilla and Strawberry Ices	
Coupes Jacques	40 vanilla ices; 40 strawberry
Ice Wafers	ices; 20 coupes jacques; 1 lb. ice wafers.

Clear soup or broth should be served to the guests on their departure.

8 quarts clear soup or broth.

Cottington Taylor

Science, King's College for Women,
in Cookery, High Class Cookery,
wifery, A.R.S.I.

a DANCE

and Suggests Quantities

ALTERNATIVE MENU with QUANTITIES

Tea	½ lb. tea; 1½ lb. coffee; 4 qts.
Coffee	milk (3 hot, 1 cold); 10 qts.
Ginger Beer	mixed drinks—lemonade, ginger-
Claret Cup	beer, claret cup, cider cup.
Cider Cup	
Lemonade	

Eggs in Aspic	25 eggs in aspic
Sausage Rolls	30 sausage rolls
Lobster Cutlets	25 lobster cutlets
Bouchées à la Reine	50 bouchées à la reine
Galantine of Chicken Sandwiches	50 galantine of chicken sandwiches
Vol-au-vent of Veal	50 vols-au-vent of veal
Bridge Rolls spread with Gentlemen's Relish	50 bridge rolls with gentlemen's relish

Royal Trifles	25 royal trifles
Charlotte Russes	25 charlotte russes
Cold Caramel Creams	25 cold caramel creams
Ginger Creams	25 ginger creams
Jellies à la Suisse	25 jellies à la Suisse
Babas au Rhum	25 babas au rhum

Cheese Creams	50 cheese creams

Neapolitan Ices	
Praline Ices	150 mixed ices
Pineapple water Ices	

Lemonade.—2 lemons; 1 oz. sugar; 1 pint of boiling water.

Peel the lemons thinly and remove all pith. Cut in half and squeeze out all the juice with a glass squeezer, then put the juice, rind and sugar into a porcelain jug or basin. Pour on boiling water. Cover and allow to cool. Ice, when cold, if preferred. One or two thin slices of lemon should be reserved and placed on the top of each glass jug in which the lemonade is served.

Orangeade.—2 oranges; 1 lemon; 1 pint boiling water; 4 oz. sugar.

Prepare in the same way as for lemonade, except that the mixture is improved by simmering for 8–10 mins.

Sandwiches.—The labour involved in the preparation of sandwiches is halved by ordering sandwich loaves cut into slices from the baker. By mixing 1 lb. butter with ½ pint of boiling milk, and whisking vigorously till they blend, a considerable economy is effected. It may be necessary to whisk for as long as ¼ hour.

For the crab and cress sandwiches it is advisable to order dressed crab. All the meat can then be pounded up together and seasoned with salt, cayenne, a very little vinegar and some made mustard. Spread on the cut bread and butter and cover with a little cress which should be well washed and then dried.

For the sardines, split the bridge rolls and butter them. Remove the skin and bones of the sardines, and place one in the middle of each roll, sprinkling with paprika.

If you are a duchess and your mate is a dustman, track him down and marry him . . .

To Marry *or NOT to* Marry

By Leonora Eyles

Decoration by Bertram Prance

THERE are only two occasions on which a woman is unhappy in this life . . . when she is married, and when she isn't! I have never met a married woman yet who did not sigh for the freedom of unmarried life. I have never met a really honest unmarried woman who did not admit that she had moments—many moments—when she wondered whether, after all, there was not a great deal in "what some have found so sweet."

There is a terrible loneliness about the unmarried woman's life. There is loneliness for the married woman, too, very often, a loneliness of soul that is more terrible than mere physical loneliness. But she has, at any rate, "someone behind her." She does not get that panicky feeling of being a unit amongst thousands of thousands, that so affects the unmarried woman, no matter how many good friends she may have. There is one very sound thing about that *égoïsme à deux* that is marriage . . . it *pays* your partner, for his own interests, to look after yours. You have someone in the world, when you are married, who would actually lose by your loss. That is sound business.

As a woman without a man behind me for the last few years, I have found myself constantly at war with people who have tried to cheat me. I have been badly paid for work; I have found business people of all sorts ready to take advantage of the fact that I was a woman. There seems to be a *camaraderie* amongst men that prevents them

from underpaying and cheating each other, and makes them rather tend to cheat a woman; at the same time women in business positions of power are usually nicer and fairer to the men they deal with than to the women. It seemed ludicrous at first, to me, to know that several well-known figures amongst the most feminist women were married and said openly, " My husband does not let me do so and so." It wasn't until I got out into the world that I saw how wise they were in adopting this pose, if it is a pose at all! Cowardly, perhaps, to hide behind a man. But very sensible. " My husband won't let me " removes entirely from one the stigma of meanness when one refuses to lecture for a charitable cause *gratis,* or give a dozen copies of one's books to a Cause! And when you don't want to go out to dinner, you need only say, with a deprecating smile, " I'd love to, but you know what a man is! He *will* dine at home and he *will* have me there while he's doing it ! "

Yes, a husband is very useful as an excuse for one's little delinquencies. The unmarried woman has to stand and fall by her own mistakes. That's a frightening sort of idea, even to the boldly independent woman. There is something rather awful in being responsible for yourself, particularly if you were brought up in the Victorian way and dared not call your soul your own, but said " I'll ask Mother " or " I'll ask Father " about every mortal thing.

Sometimes this loneliness and respon-

sibility weigh you down until you fee you dare not move. Yet, come t analyse it out, what do you find? I your married friend any better off? Sh has someone there, about the house, a the time, certainly. She can tell hir that she has a cold coming on and sen him to bully the coal merchant when h sent half a ton of slate and coal dus But is he really responsible? True, h earns the living. But is a man wage earner any safer than a woman to-day No one is *very* safe. Financially, eve the wealthy are in pretty poor case t day, with credits tumbling about ou heads. The man of independent mear of to-day may be turned out on th mercy of a cold world to-morrow; U man with a good job to-day may fin that his firm has gone into bankruptc at any time.

I believe that we have, through genei ations, got into the way of thinking c a man as a rock when he is simpl nothing of the sort. Financially he i no more a rock than a capable woma and the woman who sits back and le her husband manage the financial si of the combine, perfectly sure that l will always turn up trumps, is deludin herself. Many women marry to l saved the responsibility of fending f themselves. That is not sound busines and it is very hard on the man; sin I have been the man of the family have been filled with astonished admir tion at the way in which men should these burdens of responsibility and kee the seamy (Continued on page 7.

(Continued from page 74)

side from their women-folk. If they grumble a little sometimes, no wonder! A woman in the same position often wants to grumble, but she has no one to grumble to!

You can't generalise about marriage. You can't say that such a person would make a success of marriage while another wouldn't. Individuals marry, not types, and they marry other individuals, with all the complexities of emotions, tastes, associations, and prejudices that are implied by "individuality." Individuality is always clashing, particularly in its young days—say until the thirtieth year, when they have either acquired some amount of philosophy or never will acquire it. Until philosophy comes, there is every reason for quarrelling and strife and only one reason for keeping the peace. And that reason is love.

Yet what is love—the sort of love that will make marriage possible? Why is it that some well-intentioned, clever, kindly folks make such a muddle of marriage? Lovers have married, before to-day, starting out with every augury of success, yet in the end they have drifted apart, although, to all outside observers, they are quite good friends and an ideal couple. This is such a common state of affairs to-day that on all sides people are asking what is wrong, why we are most of us so discontented or else so hectically occupied that we have no time to be discontented, although we know that we should be if we gave ourselves time to think.

The Church gives us answers to the problem that we already know and have sucked the virtue from. The sociologist talks about excessive individualisation, the speeding-up of civilisation, the stress and rush of modern life, the strife between instinct and the social sense. The psychologist has much to say, too, about old associations and differences of upbringing that cause fundamental strifes and maladjustments.

In a way, science and religion both have some sort of solution to the problem, but I believe that the right answer lies somewhere between the two of them. Minds and bodies count greatly in marriage, and can be understood by the scientist. Spirits count in marriage, too, and the spirit is not understood by many to-day. That is where the trouble lies. If a marriage does not imply union of body, mind, and spirit, it will end in disaster, either mild or fierce according to the temperaments of the parties.

It is only necessary, in order to prove the truth of this, to look round on one's married friends. A man marries a lovely girl and in two years is looking round for someone else, tired of her, hungering for change. A girl marries a man, handsome, clever, and soon finds that something in her is being starved; a man marries a girl whom all her friends have thought a fairy thing, compact of mist and rainbow, and in a few years he is turning to some plain, practical woman for her sturdy common sense.

The trouble is, we don't know all this until we have found it out by bitter experience and pain. I do not believe any marriage was ever made that did not depend, to some extent, on physical attraction. The physical side of marriage is a most important thing. It is being recognised, at last, as one of the things that make or mar marriage, and very few people can realise the ghastliness of marriage to one for whom physical aversion is felt, until they have been through the terrible experience for themselves. The mental aspect of marriage is being understood better now that women are coming into their place as men's comrades and equals, and very many more people marry for comradeship and mutuality of interest than formerly. It is that intangible thing, the

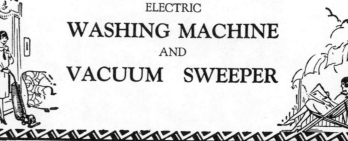

spiritual side of marriage, that is still misunderstood. Very often a marriage into which very little of the physical enters, is a success when two people marry because they share a great interest. They marry so that they can carry on the work better. But as there are surprisingly few people in this world with a " big job," this sort of marriage can almost be counted out of one's calculations; it sometimes happens between two doctors, two artists, or two writers, and, living for their work, they find it easy to let little things—the little things that wreck the average marriage—slide.

Most marriages are made under the glamour of physical attraction of some kind or the other, most, that is, if we except marriages for money that can never turn out happily or be anything but an unholy, disastrous mockery. A man meets a girl socially, at a dance, perhaps, or during some sort of playtime. He sees her at her best as she sees him. There is the glamour of pretty clothes, music, leisure; there is the irresistible draw of the body that comes of youth when the body is first realised as a mighty force to use and subdue and control. Something entrancing in the movement of a girl, something exhilarating in the way a young man looks at one—these are sufficient reasons for marriage when one is twenty or thereabouts. And they think that this white heat of exhilaration and enchantment will last when the playtime is over and the workaday world comes into proper perspective again.

Physical attraction is important. Without it marriage will fail on one side, if not on both. But it is not the main thing. It is a fierce fire that will soon burn itself out, as all fierce fires do. If it is not accompanied by the tenderness of love, of mutual trust and sacrifice and understanding, it will bring about dislike in the long run.

When physical attraction is present, it is almost impossible for two people to get on each other's nerves—and that is a big thing in marriage. We see each other's bodies more than minds or souls! One can get irritated to distraction by the way a woman pours the tea or a man blows his nose, but not when there is that mysterious thing, physical attraction.

"You are terribly honest," said a friend to me recently, when I was talking to her about marriage and totting up advantages and disadvantages. I had been saying how I loved my freedom, loved not having to wonder whether " he " would mind me doing this, that, or the other, loved being able to indulge my own pursuits. " But I miss—something," I said to her. " I miss the feeling that I matter immensely to someone, even though I may matter so much to him that he bullies me into doing as he wants me to! " I'm terrified sometimes of feeling that there is " no one behind me," even though I know quite well that very often the one behind a woman is only a stuffed dummy. And sometimes I feel that I would like to be told to do things. . . . But that is a terrible admission that very few so-called " strong minded " women will make.

I would say to women, don't marry until you find your mate. If you find him and you are a duchess and he is a dustman, track him down and marry him against all opposition. If he is your mate, your mind and your spirit will thrill at the touch of his just as a young girl's cheek flushes at the first kiss of her first lover. Because even if a woman has been thrice married, ten times in love, she retains deep virginity for the man who is her pre-destined mate, and until he finds her she is untouched.

Bread

By

GRACE NOLL CROWELL

Illustrated by Forrest C. Crooks

Some labour gathers to itself a light :
This I have found where women, making bread,
Perform anew an ancient, simple rite
That men and little children may be fed.
Something about the handling of white flour
Is beautiful : the thought of sun on wheat—
The shining silver of a quick, late shower—
A great mill glimmering through the harvest
    heat—

And old as time—a fadeless picture still :
The gold of grain crushed fine beneath a stone—
Two women grinding at an ancient mill,
And one is taken—one is left alone—
Oh, always, somewhere—women have made
    bread
That men and little children might be fed.

Illustrations by Arthu

Editing A

. . . and they always did look brainless and silly

WOMAN was a penny illustrated weekly paper for women, and I became the editor of it in November 1896, at the tender age of twenty-nine. Although then, as now, I kept a Journal, it was chiefly impressionistic, and not a diary of facts, and I can find only one entry in it which bears on the sublime fact of my ascent to the throne. The entry runs:

"To-day a business crisis which has been active for a fortnight ended with a definite arrangement that I should accept the editorship. A fortnight of secret conclaves suddenly hushed at the sound of a door opening, of poring over figures and lists of names and correspondence; of devising schemes, each one superseded by a better, a more perfect one; of planning and counter-planning; of saying the same thing over and over again to a colleague, merely because it was impossible to leave the subject and impossible to say anything fresh; of publicly expressed hopes and private pessimisms; of forced jocularities; of feverish incessant *thinking* by day and by night, awake and asleep, walking or sitting, silent or speaking. Almost my first real taste of a strictly business personal anxiety! A few years of such anxiety (the lot of many men), even a year of it, even a month, would drive me, I fancy, to clerkhood again."

(No, it wouldn't.)

I was young, but I had not the slightest idea that I was young. I thought I was quite old. The great event, according to the almanac, happened thirty years ago. But the truth is that it happened about five hundred years ago.

Women did not smoke. At least ladies did not smoke. The only women who smoked were ancient hags in the slums of industrial towns, and they smoked short clay pipes. Ancient hags no longer smoke. To earn her own living was a daring adventure for a girl, and many parents forbade it. Skirts trailed in the dust and mud of pavements. Three guineas was a monstrous price for a hat, and twenty guineas for a frock. Really imitative imitation furs had scarcely been invented. Stockings were cheap. Scent was cheap. Women never used unprintable oaths. Hansoms were a barely respectable mode of conveyance for a lone lady. Bicycles for ladies

had only recently become respectab. The fashionable craze for riding rou and round Battersea Park on a bicyc was but just beginning to fade.

Women had no general desire f the vote, and the handful of creatur who temerariously talked about getti the vote were regarded as being better, but worse, than they should Doubtful characters! Any woman, i deed, who meddled with any matter c nected with the improvement of t status of women, or who sought widen the activities of women, had struggle with the opposition of 99 cent. of the male sex and 98 per ce

. . . rouging and powdering herself in the middle of a banquet

of the female sex. The notion of a woman M.P. would have been considered exactly as preposterous and unthinkable as the notion of flying.

Women's clubs were extremely f and even worse managed than they to-day. Girls, even in pairs, did dash off unprotected to restaurants a change. They ate at home, and they ate abroad it was at a tea-sh There were less than a hundred th

Woman's Paper

By Arnold Bennett

not so much a discussion on
Years' survey of the
of Women

Women are not more beautiful than they were, but they are incomparably better dressed, nearly all of them assist, with tact and discretion, the original work of heaven

watts 27

...sand tea-shops in London. People when they did eat in restaurants found it possible to swallow the food without the help of a band of music or a variety show. Nobody danced except at balls, or "hops," as they were called. (And rightly called, because then dancing was hopping, and a dancer who kept his feet continuously on the floor would have been held to be neurasthenic, or totally demented.)

Such was the Stone Age in which I was appointed to edit a woman's paper while still under thirty. I ought to mention that I owed my august position neither to a natural taste for feminine affairs, nor to earnest and sustained industry, nor to precocity. My original situation, as assistant editor of the paper, had not been unconnected with a purchase of debentures; and I succeeded, after a very few years, to the editorship simply because the editor wished to retire and there was no one else handy to take his place. Merit or talent had little or nothing to do with my sensational rise in the world.

When I think of my editorial staff and my regular contributors (writers and artists) tears come into my eyes, as they would sometimes come into the eyes of those women for whom my smile was sunshine and my frown (so rare) rain and sleet and snow. They were all young, those ladies, but it never occurred to me that they were young. I deemed every one of them middle-aged, like myself. Without exception they were devoted to duty; and their loyalty to the welfare of the paper could not be disputed. I believe, too, that they had knowledge of their subjects—frocks, cloaks, lingerie, boots, gloves, shops, bargains, food, cookery, housekeeping, children, hygiene, smart society.

But I regret to say that they had defects. The artists could not draw. Nothing surprising in that. Fashion artists were not supposed to be able to draw. They were supposed to know by heart the curves of a certain stock figure and to reproduce the said figure in the only two attitudes permitted by the existing cast-iron traditions of journalism for ladies—standing and seated. The figures were invariably portrayed either solitary or in a uni-verse peopled solely by women. No male figure ever appeared in a fashion sketch. The figures were all taller than life and slimmer than life, with hands and fingers longer than life; and they all wore their lips sweetly parted in an

The evolution of complexion amounts to a revolution

everlasting simper. It was held proper for them to look brainless and silly, and they always did look brainless and silly. I cared not; I was not troubled by the extraordinary unlikeness of the figures to any human being created by heaven.

What did trouble me was that the writers did not know how to write, and I was passionately interested in the art of writing. I had very clear notions about literary style. My contributors knew naught about literary style; they had never heard of literary style. True, they had heard of grammar, but not one of them understood the principles of grammar. When I pointed out to them that the first business of a journalist is to write, and that in journalism knowledge and tastes are useless until they are set down on paper clearly and neatly and in a manner agreeable to read and easy to understand, the young ladies were thunderstruck. In the worst crises of work I would try to teach them grammar, but without any marked success. Occasionally they would weep—not because of my brutality, but because of their own unworthiness. I could tolerate anything but tears. When they cried, I would beg of them to leave the presence.

Once an unknown girl sent in an unsolicited contribution which was faultlessly grammatical and which I could read, if not with delight, without positive (Continued on page 80)

Editing a Woman's Paper

(*Continued from page* 79)

pain. I invited this bird of paradise to visit me, and I engaged her at a salary on the spot. Things improved.

Woman was supposed to be, and was, an "advanced" paper. Its motto, printed on the first page of every number, was "Forward but not too fast." Owing to the looseness and vagueness of the English language, this phrase could unhappily be interpreted in two very different meanings, and the ribald missed few opportunities of jeering at it. Nevertheless it did plainly indicate an editorial belief that the status and activities of women ought to be raised and enlarged.

So far so good. But we were so determined to offend the feelings of nobody that our columns almost never indicated in what direction feminine progress ought to be made. No downright opinion upon any really controversial topic affecting the relations of the sexes was ever expressed. "Safety First" is supposed to be quite a new slogan. It is not new. It was ever the private watchword of editors; it was ours; it is the watchword of all editors to-day, and it will be the watchword of all editors to-morrow and eternally.

Nevertheless *Woman* did mysteriously acquire a reputation for being in the van of progressive movements, though nobody who now examined its files could possibly conceive why. It had also the reputation of being the most intellectual woman's paper in existence. It may have been. But, if so, what must the others have been like!

Its aim was certainly to satisfy the tastes of educated women, or women who thought they were educated, or women who wanted to be educated—and not to go beyond those interests. Hence naturally politics were excluded from its pages. A woman's politics were those of her husband, if she had one; and those of her male relatives if she was unmarried. If she had neither husband nor male relative then she had no politics, as to which her mind, assuming she was right-minded and not an abandoned female, was a white blank.

The make-up of the paper was calculated to give the impression that the chief interest of educated women was the doings of exalted social circles, for these were always allotted the first place. The impression was not in accordance with facts; by which I mean that it was false. The genuine editorial conviction was that the chief interest of educated woman was her personal appearance, and articles and news and drawings intended to help her to make the very best of her personal appearance constituted the main part of the paper.

Only there was supposed to be something not quite avowable in this chief interest. There was a suspicion that an educated woman ought to have a soul above solicitude for her personal appearance, and accordingly the dress-and-looks department were not flaunted on the forehead of the paper. The day had not arrived when a perfect lady of education and taste could, by taking out her mirror and rouging and powdering herself in the middle of a banquet, with a man on either side of her, publish shameless to the world that personal appearance was her continual preoccupation and that she didn't care who saw how much of it was faked and how much was heaven-made.

Indeed, though paint and powder were by no means unknown or unemployed, a All is changed since those days, which are separated from these by two long

wars, the advent of short skirts, the advent of short hair, and the advent of various fox-trot types of activity, not to mention careers for women.

Women, however, have not changed in their essentials, though they certainly make far more interesting and intelligent companions than they did. Women are not more beautiful than they were; and I maintain this despite ten thousand assertions to the contrary. They only seem to be more beautiful. But they are incomparably better dressed and better turned out than in the recent past.

In this particular the development has been tremendous, and it has rendered life vastly more agreeable and exciting. When I see signs over shops such as "Eyebrow Specialist," and when I read of the enormous fortunes amassed by perfumers and skin-improvers, a doubt may or may not occur to me whether the development has not gone just about far enough; and I may murmur softly to myself that women are currently reported to have minds as well as bodies, and that the care of women's minds is not often referred to on shop-signs.

In any case the evolution of attire and complexion amounts to a revolution. The big shops have grown bigger on account of it, and the big daily papers likewise. In the central, fashionable streets of London and the big provincial cities, the infinite apparatus for the beautifying, setting-off, and framing of feminine beauty forms the largest, most splendid and most expensive spectacle: a magnet which fills pavements with women and the hearts of men with financial fear. Take away the apparatus from the big shops and what would remain?

Similarly with the daily papers, which nowadays flourish in the main by and for women. In most morning papers more than fifty per cent. of the advertisement space is consecrated to women; and women have also a page to themselves of editorial matter. Advertisements for men are not to be compared with advertisements for women. Nor do men receive a page of editorial matter to themselves. Indeed men have a very poor show in journalism. Soon somebody may have the bright idea of starting a bright, masculine paper for men. There are half a hundred papers for women, and there is hardly a single one for men. True, women outnumber men, but even so the disproportion must appear to the impartial observer to be somewhat excessive.

Women's papers are out of sight better than they were in the days when I sat on a throne. And the reasons for this are clearly displayed in the above paragraphs. The first reason is that women are more conscious of themselves and their possibilities, and more exigent and critical in

their demands for help in the exploitation of those possibilities.

The second reason is that advertisements have grown enormously in quantity and quality and scope. Look back at the advertisements in women's papers thirty years ago, and you will wonder that in their dullness and their ugliness and their lack of appeal they could ever have attracted anybody to buy anything. (Yet they did.) To-day advertisements have to be read because they insist on being read. They are often beautiful, they are always persuasive. Some of them would draw money out of a safe-deposit. And it is axiomatic that they add prodigiously to the charm of women's and other papers, not merely by their intrinsic attractiveness, but also by the stimulation which they give to the editorial side.

The third reason is the competition of the big dailies. The editor of a woman's paper in 1927 well knows that in order to triumph he must surpass the daily papers in the breadth of his range, the exactitude and copiousness of his information, the up-to-dateness of his information, the exclusiveness of his information, the originality of his notions, the fineness of his printing, and the beauty of his illustrations. Powerful competition has been a very important factor in the improvement in women's papers. When a woman has been examining the woman's page of her daily paper every day for a week, the woman's paper that comes at the end of the week has got to be something very much removed from the ordinary if it is to arouse afresh her partly appeased appetite.

I would not care to be put in charge of a modern woman's paper. I should faint under the severity of the strain. Modern editors for women, however, have in one respect an easier time than their forerunners. They do not have to instil into their contributors the rules of grammar and the elements of correct writing. In addition to the great feat of doubling the profits of tobacco combines, women have actually learnt grammar. I cannot conceive where they picked it up—probably not at their boarding-schools—but picked it up they have. Women's papers are now "written." And in every way women journalists are far more expert than they were. Further, women have furnished to the world some of the most brilliant journalists in existence. I say nothing of women-novelists. Any mediocrity with impudence and a freely-wandering mind can concoct a novel that people will read; but a woman who can produce a column of mingled expertise, sense, and stylistic brilliance, with a beginning and an end, really counts on this earth—where men still have the semblance of power.

THE LAW EXACTS HEAVY PENALTIES
of those who take excursions into carelessness.

The strictest laws are those imposed by Nature. King Winter is approaching with his trappings of Chill and Damp and weapons of penetrating Wind and Icy Cold. In the eyes of the Law there is no excuse for carelessness or ignorance. It is our duty to obey the Laws which safeguard the health of the Children, particularly during these most treacherous months, by clothing them in CHILPRUFE.

The prices of Chilprufe are again reduced this year, making it more economical than ever

CHILPRUFE
for CHILDREN
The Underwear Essential to Health

Ask your Draper, or write direct for a copy of the new

ILLUSTRATED PRICE LIST

If unable to obtain Chilprufe, write, addressed to the firm, for name of nearest Agent.

The CHILPRUFE MANUFACTURING Co., LEICESTER.

John A. Bolton, M.I.H., Proprietor.

Things You'll

*Decorations by
Elizabeth Montgomery*

On Handwriting

Things to Notice

YOU need not be a witch or a wizard to be able to read certain facts from your friends' handwriting. It is safe to say that you can tell by a glance at a letter whether the writer was in a hurry or not.

If he writes a careful hand he is tidy, if a very hurried writing it is almost certain that he is busy with a thousand things. Long tails to Ps, Gs, and Ys, and high strokes to Bs, Ds, and Ts, are supposed to mean a vivid imagination. A person who feels important will take a good deal of pains over his signature; perhaps wrapping it up with many flourishes.

A Tie Case

Daddy's birthday's coming again soon, and his little girl, Megan, down in her Welsh home, has been wondering what to work for him. He always likes something she has made herself. Well, now it's finished and really is a brilliant inspiration.

Just a tie case made out of a strip of pretty gay green and blue cretonne backed with rose pink silk.

Just the Thing for Journeys

On each side strips of rose-coloured elastic are sewn firmly across as you see in the picture. Through these loops the folded ties are passed to keep them folded neatly in place. The case is closed with three firm snap fasteners and it is just long enough to hold a tie.

This tie case will come in most usefully on journeys, and is really very easy to make.

On the Downs

Strange But True

SHOULD you have the luck to be wandering over one of the smooth South Downs in fine weather, you can make an interesting experiment. When on the chalky down, which you feel has been there for ever and ever, solid and sure, poke a little hole with a stick through the soil.

The Wonderful Out-of-Doors

Take a handful of the chalk and bring it home. Then shake it up in a glass of water, throw away the thick liquid, and keep what remains at the bottom of the glass. Hasten to your own microscope, or to the house of a friend who owns one, to look at the chalk, and the slide will show most probably a fair number of little shells, very prettily shaped. Once the seas covered these downs you know and love!

Bicycles are being fetched out perhaps, after a long winter rest. Be careful to look over your machine before you start for your first spring ride under the pale green trees. By the way, why not invest in sideguards? You are pretty sure to meet with April showers and muddy tracks. And sideguards save a lot of dirt.

It is a sound plan to take off your bicycle chain and to soak it in paraffin for some hours, rub it quite dry, and then oil every link. Take out any little stones in the tyres.

An Easter Party

Lights in the Doll's House

IT was a most extraordinary thing and I *must* tell you about it!

I'm Dorothy, and I'm eight, quite old, you see. Well, Cousin Lillie wa staying with us for Easter, and so slept every night then in the da nursery. One night I was just goin to sleep. I was staring drowsily acros at my lovely dolls' house when sud denly, what *do* you think . . . *light suddenly appeared in all the windows*

I sat up. I was just going to jum out of bed and paddle over to th opposite wall, where the dolls' hous stands, when I saw the dearest littl *carriage* with two white ponies drawin it, come out from behind the curtai that hides the toy shelves.

It *was* exciting! I guessed at onc "An Easter Party," I said to mysel "I wonder if they'll ask *me*."

They didn't!

Then suddenly I remembered it wa Clemmie's birthday. Clemmie was th day three years old, and she is th prettiest doll of all.

The Visitors

Perhaps I had better hurry on an tell you at once that in my dolls' hous live two very old little dolls calle Aunty Lid and Aunty Lion, a gentl man doll dressed in a green suit, calle Mr. Grass; and Clemmie, the pret little girl. There is also a very nic servant-maid called Liza; but no foo men, really no footmen. And as I la rolled over on my side, my eyes near dropped on the floor with excitemen because a real footman doll in crimso knee breeches and cutaway coat, came open the door! And out of the ca riage, which was driven by a tiny coac man doll, there stepped two lady doll oh, so beautiful! Not with trailir skirts, you know, but with fashionab bunchy silk dresses off the ground.

The door closed on them, and I w again just going to get out to loo when the sounds of tinkling mus began. There is a balcony all alor the first floor, and a tiny voice said:

"It's spring now. Ridiculous have the windows shut! Let the ba play *here*."

And a whole string of small dol dressed like bandsmen, each with instrument, came and squeezed on the balcony and played the fainte gayest little jig you ever heard.

I adored that gentle music.

A Dolls' Ball

The Queen Arrives

SEVERAL of the guests must have arrived before I had begun to watch, for I could see that, in the drawing-room, couples were dancing about, and the dear little glass chandeliers were blazing with light.

But more carriages arrived, more dolls came out, and then appeared a very special motor indeed, driven by a coachman in scarlet. A doll lady with a crown on floated up the steps, wearing the sweetest little ermine cloak. With round eyes, I guessed; a *Fairy Queen!*

Something kept me from going further; I swung one leg out, but yet something warned me not to interfere.

Out of the house, down the steps, a footman came running along the floor towards my bed. I held my breath. Then I looked down at him and strained my ears to catch his wee, wee voice.

The Cowslip Wine Problem

"A dreadful thing has happened," he cried, looking up at me. "We cannot undo any of the bottles of cowslip wine for supper, as we haven't a single *one* of those little buttonhooky things.

"The Queen has arrived and has asked for supper at once," he continued. "We've got a carpet of real violets down in the supper room, too. It *will* be a pity if everything's spoiled."

I suddenly remembered a picnic we'd been to when everything nearly went wrong because *we* hadn't one of these openers.

"Try a sock suspender," I urged. "Just the round hook at one end, I believe it would do. I'm afraid I haven't anything else to suggest."

"But I don't think that I would like to do such a thing," he answered very politely, and shook his powdered head.

Then another footman came tripping across.

"It's all right, James," he cried. "The Prime Minister has knocked the glass out of his eyeglasses and one of them does splendidly for twisting off the tops. Come back."

And so they went back, after two deep bows to me. That was all.

But I ask you; *was it a dream?*

A Spring Rhyme

Yellow Chicks in April

OH, a poultry farm is the place for me; plenty to do and plenty to see! The cocks are all crowing, and the young chicks growing, and the sweet winds are blowing in the West Countree. Oh, a poultry farm is the only place, eyes shine bright in a rosy face, as I go a-speeding to attend to the feeding, when chicks their grain are needing, in the West Countree!

This is Walking Time

Now you are able to take country walks, spy about for the lustrous white Stitchwort. Do you know the Cuckoo Flower, the Herb Robert, Spring Gentian, and Wall Speedwell?

Try this marching song, *fitting your words to your steps.*

"Right, right, right. I had a bad egg that I left, left, left. Oh, do you think I was right, right, to leave the bad egg that I left, left, left?"

Then vary it.

"Left, left, left. I have lots of letters to write, write, write. But somehow they always get left, left, left. But some day the letters I'll write, write, write, will down at the post-box be left, left, left."

Easter Sweets & Games

Pineapple Tablet

FOR this you want half a pound, or two cupfuls, of chopped preserved pineapple, half a lemon, a pound of sugar, a tablespoonful of golden syrup and what cream you can afford.

Put the sugar, cream and syrup into a saucepan, stir till it boils, then add the pineapple and the strained lemon juice, and boil briskly for ten minutes. After it has cooled for a couple of minutes, beat with a wooden spoon until it is sugary and shows signs of stiffening, then pour into a buttered tin.

A Good Game

When you are out at tea ask everyone to say aloud the first word that comes into their head when they think of the month of April. You must say, "One, two, three, *Go*," and all must speak at once.

We did this yesterday and got *Sunshine, Daffodils, Holidays, Gardening, Easter,* and *Blackbirds.* You can then take lots of other words in the same way.

Easter Eggs

If you get any Easter eggs made of pretty coloured cardboard this year, do not throw them away; they will do to bring out next Easter with a new present inside.

Little coloured flowers made of wool, in a bunch tied with ribbons, look nice for an Easter present.

I would make a Better House than Most Women

By Beverley

LORD KILBRACKEN of Killegar was a wiser man than Sir Walter Scott. Listen to this little gem of wisdom from his pen:

" *Oh woman! In our hours of ease*
Incompetent to make our teas,
Too apt with inattentive eye
And wandering wits the task to ply,
Too apt to fill the teapot up,
Just when we want our second cup!
What can we do or say when thus
You condescend to wait on us?
With gratitude of course we
take
What ministering angels make,
And yet we know it's better
when
It's made by ministering
men! "

I agree quite fiercely with Lord Kilbracken. I recalled these words last week when I was lying ill in bed, suffering the visit of a charming young thing who, I am told, would make an ideal wife. She swayed round my bedroom, a pale, lovely creature, making what I believe are called "little feminine touches"—a delicate way of describing the art of fussing. From my pillows I watched her, irritated almost beyond endurance. I ought not to have been irritated by her, for she had played to perfection the *rôle* of a modern ministering angel. She had talked in a low voice, she had put an exquisitely refreshing scent on my handkerchief, she had been cool and calm and detached. It was only when she began to criticise my bedroom that my gorge rose.

She assumed, as a matter of course, that a woman can arrange a room better than a man—a ludicrous fallacy.

"Those curtains should sweep right down to the ground," she said. "That would add several feet to the height of the room." ("And spoil the whole effect of everything else in it," I muttered between my teeth.)

"And," she added, "what a funny place to put that old Chinese vase!" (I had built a niche specially for 'it, where it gleamed green and gold in the sunlight.) "Of course," with a radiant smile, "we must put it on the mantelpiece." Which she proceeded to do, as though she were conferring a favour on me. "And these roses will look quite lovely in it." (Roses in a Ming vase! A *Ming* vase! I ask you!)

"There!" She paused, a figure of slim beauty. "Isn't that an improve-

ment? Ssh!" (A finger to her lips.) "You mustn't talk."

It was lucky for her that I mustn't.

The "feminine touches" continued. My dressing-gown which made so

In making this masculinely arrogant claim on behalf of his entire sex as well as himself, Mr. Nichols sets out to provoke the House-proud woman, but perhaps she won't take him Too Seriously!

decorative a splash of colour on the wall, reminding me of Lido days, was bundled into a cupboard. A lovely old mirror, cracked and tarnished, was put away in a drawer—"the shabby old thing." The curtains were pushed from their severe folds into terrible little flounces. Oh—I forget the rest. But I remember, as she went away, she said in liquid tones, "It takes a woman to make a home." Of all the vast concourse of lies about woman, that particular lie seems to me to be the most outrageous.

Stroll with me over my tiny house in old Chelsea. It is my first house, for I am still in the twenties, and I left Oxford without a penny. But is it not a pleasant little house? There is a window box filled with gay flowers. There is a knocker, brightly polished, which I found on a barn outside Rome. Inside, you will find no feminine touches but you will find comfort. A long room hung with old *grisailles* from a French *château*. A piano, unadorned by repulsive photographs. The

right number of chairs and couches. Two old Adam alabaster urns, which glow golden and soothing at night. A huge desk, with no tiresome knick-knacks on it.

Come upstairs and look at my linen-cupboard. I remember, at home, among feminine influences, that I regarded a linen-cupboard as a sort of limbo, designed to distract and mortify all who attempted to have dealings with it. Since the time that I have managed these things myself, I have made the startling discovery that a linen-cupboard is nothing more nor less than a cupboard to hold linen. I cannot begin to understand how any woman can spend a whole morning draping sheets round her head and biting her nails in despair before the laundry list is ready. My servant manages the whole thing in five minutes, and then, being of literary tastes, he sits down and reads a novel.

Visit the kitchen. Now, as a boy, I remember seeing my mother (who, for a woman, was an exceptionally good housekeeper) disappear behind the door leading to the servants' quarters and spend at least an hour over the vital question of what one was going to eat for lunch. It takes me, on an average, thirty seconds. You see, not being a woman, I happen to realise that there is such a thing as System. I do not go down to the kitchen with a blank mind, close my eyes, and expect a menu to present itself to me, like the shade of a departed spirit. Oh no! I write it down in a book. Whenever I have a new dish, down it goes. The list is increasing every week. Soon there will be little that I cannot offer you.

Enter the dining-room. What is the first thing that you see in it which you never see in the average woman's dining-room? (I am not speaking of millionairesses.) Ash-trays! Delicate little things too—old English pewter. If you want to smoke before the fish, you therefore do so without burning your fingers. What is the next thing you see? A cocktail outfit with a glass of lemon-juice *always* ready, so that when you desire a cocktail—which

keeper

I Know

Nichols

is essentially a desire of the moment, a passion which should be satisfied instantly or not at all —you have it. And the next thing? Open a cupboard and you will see. The proper wine at the proper angle. Women have about as much knowledge of wine as a cat has of the home life of the oyster, and they invariably, if they are allowed, stand it up on end, like a row of ninepins.

"All those things," you may say, "are very nice, but they merely prove that you possess an excellent valet."

I do. And whose fault is that? It takes two to make a good servant, remember. And if there is one truth of which I am profoundly and irrevocably convinced it is that *women do not want to have good servants.* The form of joy which they receive from the persecution of thoroughly bad servants is one of the fiercest joys in their life. For no woman is ever happy unless she has a grievance.

Consider this question a moment. Have you never seen a woman's eyes light up in ecstasy as she describes the nefarious practices of her cook? Have you never noticed how eagerly her companion's lips are trembling to tell her of the murderous instincts of her butler? If a deaf man were to be present while a body of women were discussing the utter vileness, brutality, horror, and criminality of their domestic staff he would imagine, by the radiant happiness of the women's expressions, that he had intruded upon a gathering of literary ladies reciting passages from the lyric poems of the late Algernon Charles Swinburne.

You can prove it. Listen to one of these pæans of dispraise and then put the very simple question, "Why don't you get rid of him, or her, or it?" ("it" being applied to the universally abominable stratum of page-boys.) The reply is invariably: "Oh—but my *dear,* we can't get anybody else." You begin to reply, "I know a marvellous butler. He was twenty years with the Duchess of Wrex. He hates women, is teetotal, non-smoking. . . ." But you are interrupted with a flutter of hands, and a quick excuse. Deprive her of her persecutor? Present her with a man who will not drink her best Cordon Rouge? Don't you try it. Your name will be mud in that household, if you were to succeed.

Yet I, the bachelor, who never worry about servants at all, being possessed of the ideal factotum, am informed that "I need a woman to run my house for me." Do you wonder that I clench my teeth with fury when I hear that statement? For it is only too evident to me, from my conversations with women friends on domestic troubles, that if they ever got hold of a really (Continued on page 86)

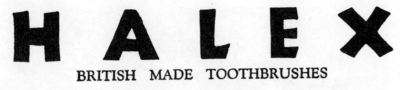

HALEX

BRITISH MADE TOOTHBRUSHES

KEEP LAW AND ORDER AMONG YOUR TEETH

6 PATTERNS 6 COLOURS 6 PRICES 9ᴰ TO 2/-. SEE THEM IN THE RED AND BLACK HALEX SHOWCASE ON YOUR CHEMIST'S COUNTER

THE BRITISH XYLONITE CO. LTD., HALE END, LONDON, E.4

I Would Make a Better Housekeeper

(*Continued from page* 85)

perfect servant they would at once be to irritate him out of his senses.

Take this question of staying out nights. It seems to me simple in the treme. But women, by their perpet curiosity, their insistence on poking i the lives of others, have made of it a f class complication. Suppose that I dining out. I say to my man, at ab five o'clock,

"I am dining with the Duke of So-a So to-night." (All the best of us, member, are snobs.) "When you h put out my things, and provided me w the ingredients for a cocktail, there see to be no object in your remaining in house."

"What time do you wish me to be sir?"

"In time, Gaskin, to provide me w a perfectly good egg and bacon in morning. Between now and then you free. Your life is a mystery to me. prefer it to remain so. You may steeped in vice. You may be qualify for a swift descent to hell. I neit know nor care."

I do not of course say these things, they are, as it were, in the air.

Now, I am apparently original in ade ing this very human attitude. A few d ago I was talking to a woman who, v the usual expression of radiant bliss, describing to me the unmitigated evil her three maids.

"They want to go to bed at all hou she said.

"Well?" said I.

"But at *all* hours. . . . How ca sleep?"

"But you don't sleep with them, you?" I asked, coarsely.

She waxed furious. "I couldn't s with the thought of them still out," said.

I ended the discussion by asking he she was jealous of them.

Let's face this. Isn't it, to say the l of it, absurd? Servants are watched v a lynx eye. If they are not in at ele woe betide them. Why? If a girl wis to indulge in girlish pranks (as Lor might have said) she can do so with ev prospect of success just as well bef eleven as after. So why worry?

That is, indeed, the theme of my pla Women adore worry. If you place woman on a desert island, with cons supplies, and no sort of interference, would find something to worry about, e if it were only the morals of the monk And a house, which to a man is merel dwelling place, which, if he is inclined, may make beautiful, is a paradise of wo for a woman.

She worries because the tradesmen not send things at the right time. M is the home I stayed in where life se to be a constant succession of "things coming." The fish hasn't "come," or ice hasn't "come," or the flowers hav "come," and so on. What on earth it matter? Does she not realise that best parties are always those which prefaced by a catastrophe of this natu I remember giving a lunch to Mr. H Walpole. He was in the house before butcher condescended to remember existence. We were abominably late, what did that matter? We drank co tails, we sang songs and we cu butchers. Which seems to me an excel method of beginning the day.

She worries, again, because of "noises" —whether in or out of the house. Why? At this very moment, a man is selling lavender in the street outside my window. He calls out, in a queer old tune, "Who will buy my lavender, pretty lavender, sweet la-a-a-vender, three bunches for sixpence, three bunches for six-pe-e-nce." And I think, though his voice is harsh, that song has echoed through the streets of London for centuries, so that I throw him a sixpence for his pains. If a woman were here I have not the smallest doubt that she would be frowning at him, cursing him for his impertinence.

She worries about "time." One must breakfast at a certain hour. If lunch is at a quarter to two, the day is destroyed. If, suddenly, one is hungry in the middle of the morning, one must wait till the appointed hour. Why, oh why? I realise that I am an animal and that when I want to eat, I eat, and that when I don't want to eat, I don't.

One could prolong the list of unnecessary worries indefinitely, but I will not do so, for by now you will have realised that I am a confirmed bachelor.

Oh—yes. I have my dreams, my longings, taunting me in the hours of loneliness. Sometimes, strolling home along Piccadilly at night, my hands deep in my pockets, my coat collar turned up, my hat over my eyes, I glance at other men hurrying past me, running to catch buses, disappearing into subways, hailing taxis, and I speculate upon their mode of existence. They, probably, have somebody waiting for them at home, somebody to whom they can tell their worries, somebody who gently and quietly can smooth the wrinkles out of their foreheads. A catchword, heard long ago, echoes through my head. . . .

"It's the midnight voice that counts . . . that is what really determines one's destiny . . . the midnight voice, whispering wisdom in the half-veiled moments before sleep."

But for me—there is no midnight voice. There is a silent little hall, some mail, a fire dying down in the grate, and silence. I throw off my hat and coat, and sink down into a chair. Opposite me is a mirror and I study the reflection in the glass. It is an older reflection than it used to be, and to-night, being tired, I can guess, even in the shadows, how I shall look in twenty years' time. A bachelor, in the forties. Not quite so popular as he was. Regarded by the young things as a bore. A solitary figure, whose principal purpose in life is to fill up gaps at dinner parties. "Let's ask Beverley Nichols," I can hear them. "He's a harmless old thing and he's always got something to say." Twenty years of dining out. Twenty years of loneliness. Twenty years! And I look at myself once again in the glass, and the reflection, for a moment, is dimmed.

Then it clears again. The reflection gradually changes, and I begin to laugh, at first almost indignantly at myself, and then almost uproariously, at the world. Of all the damned self-pity! For what are these things that I am nursing? What is this companionship, this midnight voice? Dreams—all dreams! They are the things that all men long for, the things that so few ever get. For even were I married, how should I be certain of finding somebody waiting for me? She would be waiting, of course, if she were a quiet domestic thing who liked waiting, but I am bored to tears by quiet domestic women. She would be waiting, again, if she were a dancing enthusiast whose partner had failed her (I say "partner" because even the utmost transports of love would not persuade me to take any female to a dance club), or she might be waiting merely be-

(Continued on page 88)

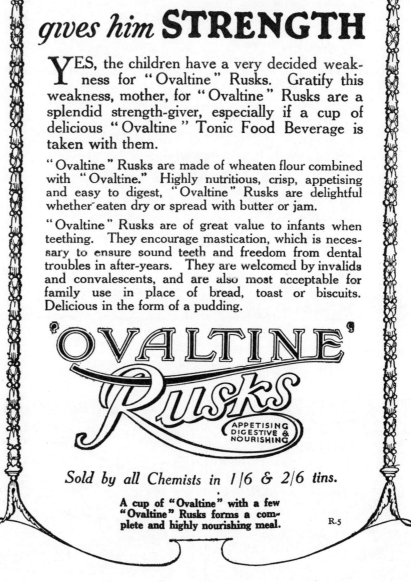

The sapling and the oak.

The sapling symbolizes everybody's child. All parents desire their children to grow strong and sturdy as the oak, to weather the storms and enjoy the sunshine of life.

Children who grow weak from the start require special feeding, no matter how good the daily food; and every child who is weakly or backward, shooting up too rapidly or failing to make normal growth, should be given Benger's extra to the ordinary meals.

A cup of Benger's Food between meals and just before bed-time has transformed many weakly infants. To-day, thousands of robust fathers and mothers are evidence of the benefits derived from Benger's in their growing period.

Adult men and women, in indisposition, sickness or in health, always benefit by Benger's Food.

Benger's is not expensive. Made with all milk it costs only 6d. per pint—two dishes—including the 7d. or 8d. per quart you pay for the fresh milk. Some children like the food flavoured with a piece of chocolate for a change.

"Mr. Benger's admirable preparation."—"THE LANCET."

Parents interested in this advertisement are invited to read the more detailed information given in Benger's Booklet. A copy will be sent post free on application.

BENGER'S Food for INFANTS, INVALIDS and the AGED.

TRADE MARK.

Sold in tins by Chemists, etc., everywhere — 1/4, 2/3, 4/- and 8/6

BENGER'S FOOD, LTD.,   Otter Works,   **MANCHESTER.**

NEW YORK (U.S.A.): 90, Beekman Street.   SYDNEY (N.S.W.): 350, George Street.   CAPE TOWN (S.A.): P.O. Box 573-

I Would Make a Better Housekeeper

(*Continued from page* 87)

cause she was tired and irritable. In any case, where is the fun of it?

All of which may sound very "modern," but then I imagine that I am very "modern" and that my female contemporaries are also very modern. I imagine—rather, I *know*—that we are breeding a race of men and women to whom marriage, in the old Victorian sense, is impossible. It was all very well when marriage was an entirely one-sided affair, when the man had merely to dictate and the woman to obey. But those days are over. And how any intelligent man or woman can expect *two* highly-strung, entirely individual natures to settle down, balancing their lives on a precarious precipice (called, by our sentimentalists "give and take"), I do not know. I for one am not going to try.

For, to sum it all up, life is half poetry and half prose. Do you find the poetry in marriage? Yes—for a little while. A year, two years, perhaps even five. But after that, the lyric falters, the rhyme becomes clumsy, the gay sweep of song dwindles into dreary prose. Don't tell me that it doesn't. It does. Don't try to put me off with pretty prints of Darby and Joan. Don't try to deafen me by the patter of children's feet. I am not to be deceived over that. All I know is that the glory dies, the radiance fades, and a bewildered mad night of enchantment turns into the most sordid dawn.

Forgive my purple passage and turn to the prose half. Where am I to obtain comfort, even peace, in marriage, unless I am to subordinate my individuality entirely to another? I have said enough to show that I consider women, as housekeepers, a back number. They have no system, they worry intensely over details, and they are usually possessed of an æsthetic taste very inferior to that of the male. Whatever else I possess to-day in my home, I possess comfort, and within my means, beauty. And it is suggested to me that I sacrifice my comfort for discomfort, and the quiet, grave "rightness" of my house for fuss. Why, in the name of reason? Why? Why?

You will find that question, unless I am very much mistaken, engraved upon my tombstone.

London Shopping for All

Our Shopping Service staff will gladly purchase for you any of the articles illustrated on pages 62, 63, as well as any article shown in the advertisement columns of the magazine. Send order and cheque, stating clearly what you require, to Shopping Service, 153 Queen Victoria Street, London, E.C.4

Women's Clubs

A Medical Man's opinion on their contribution to Health and Well-Being

By Dr. Cecil Webb-Johnson

I HAVE been asked to write an opinion on women's clubs from the point of view of health and well-being. At the outset, there is no more reason that a woman should not belong to a club than that a man should not do so. The ordinary club for women, such as one finds in the neighbourhood of Dover Street or Piccadilly, provides a handy meeting-place for women of similar tastes and takes a woman out of the rut of home affairs. This is all to the good; for constant re-occupation with one narrow round of home duties and interests not only dulls and atrophies the mental faculties, but also affects the nerves, and, through them, the general health.

The use of a good club is useful to the lonely spinster as well as to the married woman who has a household to look after. Single women who are compelled by circumstances to live in flats or rooms by themselves are apt to develop nervous irritability. The atmosphere of a club, with its constant coming-and-going, and the different interests which arise, "takes a woman out of herself," as the homely phrase goes.

Particularly is this the case with middle-aged women who no longer care for the more strenuous delights of youth: the varied activities of club-life give them something to think about. Among middle-aged people with nothing very serious to occupy them, we often observe a strong inclination to doze the days away in physical and mental idleness. The fruits of this are *ennui*, depression, and eventually decay of the mental faculties, and premature senility. Women who are addicted to what are ironically called "the pleasures of the table" are, in these circumstances, apt to think of the day in terms of intervals between one meal and another. No sooner is one meal cleared away than they begin to think what they will have for the next. This leads to over-eating, with its long train of evils, including obesity, rheumatism, gout, and complaints of the liver and kidneys.

As a rule club-life for the middle-aged woman provides just those interests and harmless excitements which keep the brain active and the faculties alert. "Among the classes of people who die earlier than they ought to from imperfect brain-work," says an acute observer, "are some who lived a healthy life up to fifty and sixty, but then began to fail from want of occupation and activity." He continues, "Another advantage of regular, even absorbing, occupation is that it prevents us from turning our attention to our own feelings and failings, to our mental and physical troubles. Many persons are apt to pay too much attention to slight ailments, imagining them to be the beginning of serious disease and suffering, and become through this mentally depressed and unhappy. These imaginings often give rise to *real* disease of mind or body, such as hypochondria and melancholia." And the beginning of all these evils is the want of something to occupy the mind—outside the home and its petty cares.

Professional women can also derive great benefit from belonging to a good women's club, and there are several, including (*Continued on page* 90)

Women's Clubs
(Continued from page 89)

the Writers' and the Lyceum, which cater especially for the busy working woman. Let us see how she can take advantage of her membership.

To begin with, the average professional woman—if she is unmarried—lives by herself in a small flat or in rooms. The exigencies of her working life forbid her, as a rule, to take advantage of a boarding-house or private hotel. Wherefore, when she reaches her "home" after a long day's work, she is generally too tired and dispirited to prepare a proper meal, and finds it less trouble to boil a couple of eggs or open a tin of sardines. Eggs follow sardines and sardines succeed eggs with sickening regularity. The consequence is that she soon begins to feel the effects of malnutrition, and her working powers become affected. Belonging to a club, she can command a nutritious and well-balanced meal, comforting and hot, at the end of the day's toil. I know it is the fashion for men to deride the catering at women's clubs, but so long as it suits the members, that is all that is required.

Furthermore, in a club, the professional woman has the advantage of mixing with congenial spirits, and indulging in the comforting, satisfying gossip without which no woman's life can really be considered complete. This is obviously better than sitting alone in lodgings or a flat, or inflicting herself on friends who may or may not be glad to see her. Thus we see that membership of some decent club is, to the woman who has to earn her own living, of inestimable advantage to both mind and body—to say nothing of its practical use in "shop" matters.

Outside the general and professional clubs there are countless special clubs which a woman might be all the better for joining. And of these, clubs formed for the practice of games are the most productive of bodily health and mental efficiency. It is pleasant to see on summer evenings the roads white (literally) with girls and women hurrying off to the tennis club. The various rowing clubs for girls —for instance, the Furnivale—also do much good; but it is needless to multiply instances. Clubs for "rambling" and Nature study have their undoubted uses in taking women out into the fresh air and in giving them something to occupy their minds. That the "something" may be quite useless is beside the point; the great thing is to keep the mind occupied and prevent that mental inertia which afflicts so many idle women.

We may now consider a very different kind of club, for which none of the above arguments can be advanced. These are the supper-and-dance clubs which stud the West End of London. The disreputable haunts which every now and then are raided by the police we need not touch upon; they do not come within the purview of this article, so can be left to work out their own perdition. The clubs one has in mind are perfectly respectable, conducted in strict accordance with the law by people of repute, and frequented by the highest in the land. Yet they do an infinite deal of harm to the growing womanhood of England. It cannot be good for a young girl to dance night after night in the vitiated and nicotine-tainted atmosphere of a club, and crawl home at three or four in the morning, a haggard, weary-eyed creature, unable to raise her head from the pillow till lunch-time the next day.

The cocktail and the cigarette are inevitable in the life of the night-club, neither of them good for girls. No young

man requires alcohol at all; and in any
se nobody ought to touch stimulants
fore the age of twenty-five. As regards
garettes, their evil effects, when smoked
excess (and the night-club girl never
es anything in moderation) are well
own. They are bad for the digestive
ict, for the eyes, and for the nerves.
any cases which come before the nerve-
ecialist are due to the excessive con-
mption of cigarettes. These seductive
t deadly articles affect the heart, first
king it beat more powerfully but more
wly, and then accelerating its pulsations
30 to 50 per cent. They also have
toxic effect on the nerve cells and by
ninishing the gastric secretions and
wing up the action of the intestines
erfere with nutrition.

Undoubtedly, too, night-club life leads
the undue consumption of alcohol. Cock-
ls begin the night-club supper and
ung girls fall easier victims to cock-
ls than do men. In fact, it has been
lared by a well-known caterer in the
est End that while a man is satisfied
give his appetite a fillip with one cock-
l, a girl invariably has two or more.
ampagne and liqueurs accompany and
ish the meal; and by the time the girl
es home her brain, nerves and stomach
all affected by the quantity of mixed
uor she has drunk; it cannot be other-
se. In due time, cocktails, champagne
l liqueur-brandy cease to have their
ial "bite." Then comes cocaine or
oin; and after that—the abyss! This
not an exaggerated or alarmist picture,
anybody familiar with the night-life of
ndon can tell one. Dancing, in modera-
n, is a healthful and pleasant exercise;
ampagne, in moderation, an excellent
mulant; and an occasional late night
er hurt anybody. But *the night-club
l can never do anything in moderation*;
over-stimulated nerves will not let her.
attered nerves, ruined digestion and
ks, disposition and temper all awry, are
portion of any girl who lets the night-
b habit gain too great a hold of her.
olesome recreation is one thing; reck-
s, feverish pursuit of so-called pleasure,
ht after night, is another.

Practical Demonstrations

ully qualified members of
he Institute staff are avail-
ble to give lectures and
ractical demonstrations
n any domestic subject
t private houses, Women's
nstitutes, schools, and
nstitutions of all kinds.
Application, giving full
articulars, should be made
o The Director, Good
Housekeeping Institute, 49
Wellington Street, Strand,
W.C.2

DŒUILLET   LELONG   CALLOT

FASHIONS *for*

By
M a r j o r i e
HOWARD

Left above: fine wool jersey in new blue-green shade with geometrical pintucks. Centre: grey-green crêpe de Chine encrusted with crêpe satin. Right: white China silk with grey-blue bias

"GOOD HOUSEKEEPING" OFFICE,
2 RUE DE LA PAIX, PARIS.

ONCE more it is the season of the winter holiday, when ever-increasing numbers break the monotony of the bleak months by journeying to the snow sports of Switzerland or the sunshine and mimosa of the Riviera, as their fancy dictates.

I have gathered from the *couturiers* the newest ideas in clothes both for winter sports and Southern, and also the latest developments in afternoon and evening wear.

Trousers are definitely established as *de rigueur* for ski-ing, and a choice of three kinds is offered—breeches, which have often the annoying disadvantage of constricting the knees; plus-fours, which can only be worn by a slim

DRECOLL   SCHIAPARELLI   MARY NOWITZKY

Winter *Sports* & Southern

person; and, finally, Norwegian trousers.

This last variety meets with general approval; in fact, the Norwegian costume is almost exclusively worn by the real sportswomen. It consists of a close-fitting, usually double-breasted, short jacket or coat, worn over a sweater blouse, or a man's cotton, linen or silk shirt, and tucked into the long trousers, which again are tucked into

Drécoll contrives a classic ski-ing costume from black gaberdine with yellow collar, cuffs, and buttons. Schiaparelli quaintly employs grey and yellow knitted jersey

The third model shows a clever skating two-piece, in which the trouser-skirt is worn over a maillot showing a sweater but forming trousers under the skirt

the ski-ing boots. The material of the costume is usually a hard-surfaced wool, or a mixture of silk and cotton, in dark blue, dark green, dark brown or black. With it are worn a scarf, gloves, and socks turned down over the tops of the boots. These accessories are in gay colours, and may be striped or checked or patterned. Big ski-ing mittens are worn sometimes on a string round the neck.

PATOU

Printed Crêpes

and Chiffons

Will Acclaim the

Sunshine at

Southern Resorts

Very straight at the back, this powder blue coat, lavishly trimmed with grey fox, has a little flare in front. The hat is of matching felt and velvet

Right: a skating ensemble, with skirt of finely pleated grey cloth and jacket of silver patterned green duvetyn. The fur is grey astrakhan

REDFERN

Beach Suits

and Wraps

Follow a Chic

Simplicity

LELONG

PAQUIN

Lelong's rather formal frock is of heavy yellow crêpe de Chine, and a matching grosgrain ribbon trims the broad-brimmed white manilla hat

The original arrangement of the blue fox trimming is the outstanding feature of this afternoon coat in dead-leaf brown cotton velvet

The King's Chef, Mr. Cédard, with
Their Majesties' gracious consent, has supplied
to the Empire Marketing Board
the following recipe for

An Empire Christmas Pudding

5 lbs. of currants	★	AUSTRALIA
5 „ „ sultanas	★	AUSTRALIA
5 „ „ stoned raisins	★	SOUTH AFRICA
1½ „ „ minced apple	★	CANADA
5 „ „ bread crumbs	★	UNITED KINGDOM
5 „ „ beef suet	★	NEW ZEALAND
2 „ „ cut candied peel	★	SOUTH AFRICA
2½ „ „ flour	★	UNITED KINGDOM
2½ „ „ demerara sugar	★	WEST INDIES
20 eggs	★	IRISH FREE STATE
2 ozs. ground cinnamon	★	CEYLON
1½ ozs. ground cloves	★	ZANZIBAR
1½ ozs. ground nutmegs	★	STRAITS SETTLEMENTS
1 teaspoonful pudding spice	★	INDIA
1 gill brandy	★	CYPRUS
2 gills rum	★	JAMAICA
2 quarts old beer	★	ENGLAND

*Recipes for a sauce and for brandy butter, also made
exclusively from Empire ingredients, to accompany the pudding
have also been supplied by His Majesty's Chef. Copies can be obtained free on
application to the* Empire Marketing Board, 2 Queen Anne's Gate Bldgs., London, S.W.1

Black woollen coats
are a good feature
of the mode. Below
is a smart example
in ermine-trimmed
velours de laine

Reboux employs red
felt for this brimless
hat, in which the
trimming of little
birds is held very
flat under the band

REBOUX

Brimless Hats Are
the Feature of
the Winter Mode

Imposing silver lace out-
lining the panels adds importance to Callot's evening
frock of very supple blue-
green panne. The shoulder
straps are of strass

The crown of the little hat
below is all covered with
shaded grey feathers, the
brim, which is caught up
with a bow over one eye,
being of pink felt

JENNY

REBOUX

CALLOT

A HOME FOR £50 CASH

BALANCE AS RENT. TOTAL COST £400

PEACEHAVEN

LIVE BY THE SEA
IN YOUR OWN HOME
ON YOUR OWN FREEHOLD LAND
IN "THE SUSSEX SEASIDE GARDEN CITY OF AMAZING GROWTH"

FREEHOLD LAND AS AN INVESTMENT ON THE VALLEY ESTATES.

WHAT undoubtedly is the finest proposition ever placed within your reach is that now being offered on the Valley Estates which form part of the great Peacehaven section of the South Downs.

The Valley Estate commands magnificent views of the Ouse Valley, adjoins the Brighton Road passing through the Estate, and is within a few minutes of the Golf Links. Freehold Land on the original Peacehaven Estate close by has increased 300 per cent. in value during the past eighteen months, and those fortunate enough to acquire plots in the Valley Estate, will undoubtedly reap a substantial benefit from their property owing to our scheme of quick development.

SIZE OF PLOTS.

The Freehold Land in our Valley Estate is sold in quarter, half, and one Acre Plots. Every plot offered for sale is properly surveyed. You are under no obligation to build until you desire to do so, but Ideal Homes can be built when you are ready from materials on the spot at minimum prices. Free deeds, no legal charges, and no other expenses.

PRICES OF PLOTS vary according to size and position.

THE FERTILITY OF THE SOIL is wonderful—a rich, natural possession. The flavour and size of the vegetables and other produce grown on the Estate are remarkable, and some magnificent results have been obtained. Success depends entirely upon your own individual effort and inclinations, and whether you go in for Small Fruit Growing, Poultry and Bee-keeping, or Small Holdings, you can easily make a secure income a certainty, besides which your investment will bring you a handsome return for your capital outlay. Brighton, Lewes, Seaford and Newhaven markets are within easy distance, and London is only 58 miles from the Estate.

THE AIR is invigorating, health promoting, and you get the maximum of sunshine.

FREEHOLD LAND ON THE HARBOUR HEIGHTS ESTATE.

Freehold Land on the Harbour Heights Estate will treble and quadruple in value. Here you can secure, for £25, plots of building land absolutely Freehold, which is not less than 2,500 superficial feet in extent. Owing to its elevation the plots are particularly valuable on this Estate for building purposes, and command magnificent views over the Sea and Downs. You have maximum sunshine in one of the sunniest spots on the South Coast.

THE EXTENT OF PEACEHAVEN.

Although not yet three years old, the Peacehaven Estates extend over an area of nearly five square miles and have a frontage of almost five miles in length. They stretch from the right bank of the River Ouse, in the neighbourhood of Newhaven, up to the quaint old village of Rottingdean, close to Brighton. Peacehaven is the outcome of the greatest Seaside land development scheme ever undertaken in this country.

What SIR JOHN FOSTER FRASER says about PEACEHAVEN.

In a recent issue of the "Daily Chronicle" Sir John said:—" . . . It struck me that everything is done to retain the beauty of the Downs. The Bungalows are mostly detached, and rest contentedly on the uplands, with their bits of gardens, and in many cases with Cornish rustic slate, so that the colours seem to blend with the landscape. . . . Yes, Peacehaven, the garden city by the sea, is one of the most remarkable places in the world. . . . I found the Peacehaveners a happy, jolly community, very proud of their infant prodigy of a garden city."

UNPRECEDENTED OPPORTUNITY TO SECURE YOUR COMPLETE HOME ON YOUR OWN FREEHOLD LAND FOR A £50 CASH DEPOSIT. THE BALANCE CAN BE PAID AS RENT UNTIL YOUR PURCHASE IS COMPLETE. ONLY SIX HOUSES ARE AT PRESENT AVAILABLE UNDER THIS OFFER.

"Good Housekeeping" is intimately associated with the ideal home, because the latest labour-saving devices make it more easily possible under the best conditions.

Peacehaven abounds in such homes, which are so plentiful that the famous Garden City of the South Coast has come to be known as the Home of Ideal Homes.

Peacehaven homes are snug and cosy. They will all be supplied with Electric light and water by Peacehaven Companies, and are in very great demand. Standing on their own Freehold Land, some of these delightful Peacehaven homes are ready for immediate occupation, and, provided with modern conveniences, can be purchased for as low as £400 inclusive.

A £50 cash deposit will secure you one of the available charming Seaside Homes, and, if more convenient, you can pay the balance monthly according to arrangement, just as if you were paying rent, but with this difference, that the Home will be your own property all the time.

PEACEHAVEN'S POTENT POINTS.

1. **EXCELLENT SANITATION,** fulfilling all local Council Requirements.

2. **WONDERFUL CHALK CLIFFS** rise to a height of from 50 to 150 feet above sea-level.

3. **STEPS** have been cut through the great cliffs to the Beach, where there are caves and sands for bathing.

4. **MANY FACILITIES FOR SPORT** in the Parks, already provided, or in course of preparation. There are also Tennis Courts, and the Peacehaven Golf Course will shortly be available for play.

5. **BUSINESS OPPORTUNITIES** await enterprising tradesmen, business people, and all professional men.

HOTEL PEACEHAVEN.—During your visit stay at the Hotel Peacehaven, the loveliest hotel on the South Coast. Beautiful Italian Gardens, Excellent Cuisine. Fully licensed. Terms moderate.

HOW TO GET TO PEACEHAVEN.

1. Travel by train from Victoria or London Bridge to Brighton, and thence by bus from the Aquarium to Peacehaven: or

2. Travel by train from Victoria or London Bridge to Newhaven Town Station, where the Company's motor cars will meet you by request, or where you can take a bus to Peacehaven.

OUR FREE OFFER COUPON

To the SOUTH COAST LAND & RESORT CO., LTD., PEACEHAVEN, SUSSEX.

Forward me, Post Free, your attractively illustrated three-coloured brochure, telling the full story of Peacehaven.

NAME ....

ADDRESS ....

....

POST THIS COUPON TO-DAY

You can do so under a halfpenny stamp providing your envelope is marked "Printed Matter" and the flap is only tucked in. *Good Housekeeping, August.*

POST THIS COUPON TO:
The South Coast Land & Resort Co., Ltd., Peacehaven, SUSSEX

WORTH

CHANEL

Here is black chiffon
trimmed with black
silk fringes unusually
held by copper orna-
ment. The bow and
flower are of chiffon

Beaded Elegance

is Decreed for

Evening Occasions

This distinctive dinner
frock in a light red
crêpe de Chine is cut
very low at the back,
with the skirt quite
straight and simple

Catering for the Home

By

G. H. Donald, B.Sc.

Household and Social Science, King's College for Women, London

Familiar examples of body-building, and energy- and health-producing foods

QUESTIONS frequently asked are, "How much food should one allow per head?" And conjointly with this, "What does a person's food cost?" The solution to this problem can be found in studying the results at which housewives have arrived after long years of experience, or by calculating scientifically—rather in the way in which the fuel consumption and wear and tear of machinery is done—the quantities of protein, carbohydrate and fat which the body needs. It is common knowledge that all food consists either of body-building, heat- or energy-giving substances.

A Shopping Guide giving daily requirements of Ordinary Household Foods

	Per head	Four adults	Two adults, two young children
Butter . .	1½ oz.	6 oz.	4 oz.
Milk . .	1 pint	4 pints	4 pints
Bread . .	5½ oz.	⅔—2½ lb. loaf	½—2½ lb. loaf
Bacon . .	1 oz.	4 oz.	2 oz. *Bacon fat for children*
Meat (flesh) .	4 oz.—1 meal	1 lb.—1 meal	¾ lb.—1 meal
Chicken . .		3½ lb. as purchased	3 lb. as purchased
Fish (flesh) .	4 oz.—1 meal	1 lb.—1 meal	¾ lb.—1 meal
Brussels Sprouts	⅓ lb.	1½ lb.	1 lb.
Cauliflower .	¼ @ 5d.	5d.	4d.
Potatoes . .	1 lb.	4 lb.	3 lb.
Cabbage .	¼ @ 2d.	2d. or 3d.	2d.
Sugar . .	2 oz.	8 oz.	6 oz.
Apples for Pie .	⅓ lb.	1½ lb.	¾ lb. *8 oz. fruit for children*
Tea (twice) .	½ oz.	2 oz.	1 oz.
Coffee for breakfast . .	½ oz.	2 oz.	1 oz.
Jam . .	1 oz.	4 oz.	3 oz.
Marmalade .	1 oz.	4 oz.	3 oz.

During the war, the necessity for food restriction became so acute that a committee was formed to decide these factors. It agreed that for a man doing light work, the daily ration should be: protein 3½ oz. (approx.); fat 2⅛ oz.; carbohydrate 19⅜ oz.

Later, meat and other protein food became so scarce that the protein was decreased to 2½ oz. It is generally accepted that 1½ oz. of the protein eaten should be of animal and 2⅛ oz. of vegetable origin. If all the animal protein comes from one source, one might choose, say 15 oz. of loin of mutton, which contains 1½ oz. protein in addition to much fat and bone, or if the cost has to be considered carefully, a cheaper form such as 7¾ oz. herring (flesh, which only contains a little fat) and similarly with vegetable protein, fats and carbohydrates. But in practice this is never the case—one usually has, as in the menus given, 4 or 5 foods which contain protein.

There has been considerable controversy about the standard quantities required of the three great classes of food, American scientists tending towards a lower estimate than English investigators, but it is generally accepted that for a man doing light work the War Committee results are satisfactory.

At this stage the housekeeper may be thinking, "But my husband works in an office. Would the same apply to him, and what about myself and children?"

The above quantities are variable for occupation, sex, age, climate and the family resources. Thus, a man with an indoor occupation would require less; a woman, owing to her body's more economical use of food, requires rather more than three-quarters of a man's allowance; children's requirements vary according to their activities, but to give a general idea of the quantities allowed, a child of six should have about one-half the amount given to the average man, increasing to three-quarters at fourteen years of age. After this age, a boy needs the same quantities of the different foods as the average man and a girl as much as a woman.

In hotter climates the requirements are lower, and in colder correspondingly higher. In glancing through the typical menus included in this article, it will be noticed that compared to the War Committee figures the fats are high, and the carbohydrates low. Providing that these balance scientifically, this is satisfactory, but if economy has to be practised, fats which are a more expensive source of energy than carbohydrates should be decreased, and the latter increased as in the War Committee standard, in which the financial aspect had to be considered very carefully.

How is one to supply these proteins, fats and carbohydrates? Where does one find them? are the next problems to solve. If foods could be divided into groups and labelled as above, the answers would be easy, but unfortunately Nature has not been so kind to us.

Protein foods are generally associated with fat. Carbohydrate foods with the exception of sugar often contain fat or protein, sometimes both, e.g. cheese comes under protein and fat rations, and milk under the three, protein, fat and carbohydrate. Most vegetable proteins contain a large percentage of carbohydrate.

The menus given in this article were chosen as being fairly typical of an Englishman's daily fare. The cost in the more elaborate ones averages 14*s.* 2*d.* per head per week, but in the cheaper the items were chosen from among the less expensive forms of food, thus showing that the particular food value can be given, or even increased, more cheaply. The actual fat foods were decreased, but the resulting

What & How to Buy

quantity of fat (4½ oz.) happens to be now as high because a fat joint, i.e. loin of mutton, was included. Anyone who is interested in the calculations whereby the food value of these diets was arrived at, can obtain the information on application to Good Housekeeping Institute.

In order that the body may make full use of fats, a balance of carbohydrates must be consumed. If the former are increased beyond a limit and the latter decreased, feelings of malaise and headache, due to incomplete conversion of fatty foods into substances which the body requires, may result.

In criticising the first menu, it is noticeable that the proportion of animal proteins is high and vegetable proteins are lacking. These latter are satisfactorily obtained by using split peas, lentils and haricot beans in soups, or in nuts as dessert. The somewhat high cost of vegetables and fruit is justified by their vitamin, roughage, and mineral contents. All are necessary factors in maintaining the body in a state of health. It would improve these menus if fruit, fresh or stewed, were added for breakfast.

Any one of the protein foods below contains 1½ oz. of animal protein, which is sufficient for one person for one day

Different menus may be drawn up based on the two typical ones given, bearing in mind the following criticisms. If one could generalise about the average Englishman's diet—which one cannot—it would be safe to say that insufficient fruit and vegetables, both fresh and cooked, are included; that animal flesh could often be substituted by cheese dishes, lentils, haricot beans, nuts and other forms of protein with advantage to the health; that too much pastry and too many steamed suet puddings, though very satisfying, are unsuitable to any but those with healthy digestions owing to the slowness with which they are digested; and that insufficient vegetable soups, which supply the mineral salts and part of the daily quota of liquid which the body needs, are taken.

The thoughtful housewife will question herself as to the particular error, if any, which she makes when planning the menu and endeavour to rectify this.

It is often remarked that the inclusion of extra fruit and vegetables means increasing the daily cost; this is partly true, but if the quantity of meat, always an expensive item, is reduced as suggested above and replaced by cheaper forms of protein the cost is counterbalanced. When the housewife is anxious to calculate the daily cost of living, it is easier to total one ingredient at a time, such as ¾ pint of milk or 1¼ eggs for the day, rather than deal with it separately for breakfast, lunch and dinner.

It may appear at first sight that in this calculation of one's daily food unnecessary trouble is being taken, but when the economy involved, and the advantages to health which are gained, are considered, it is hardly possible that anyone—even unwilling mathematicians—will consider it a labour ill-spent.

Typical Menus for the Man Doing Light Work

No. I. 14*s.* 2*d.* per week

Breakfast	
Porridge, plateful containing 1 oz. oatmeal	1 oz.
Bacon, 2 thin slices	1 oz.
Egg	1
Butter	½ oz.
Milk for porridge and tea	⅓ pint
Tea	
Bread, 2 slices	3 ozs.
Marmalade, 1 level tablespoonful	1 oz.
Sugar in tea, 1 dessertspoonful	⅓ oz.
Lunch	
Stewed Steak (As purchased)	4 oz.
Boiled Potatoes (As purchased)	8 oz.
Carrots (As purchased)	4 oz.
Onion (English) (As purchased)	4 oz.
Apple Pie	
Tea	
Jam	1 oz.
Milk	⅛ pint
Bread 1 slice	1½ ozs.
Butter	½ oz.
Sponge Cake	1
Sugar in tea	¼ oz.
Dinner	
Roast Leg of Mutton	4 oz
Cauliflower (uncooked cost 5d.)	¼
2 Brown Potatoes	8 oz.
Steamed Chocolate Pudding	

No. II. 12*s.* 5*d.* per week

Breakfast	
Porridge	1 oz.
Grilled Herring	1
Butter	½ oz.
Milk for porridge and tea	¼ pint
Tea	
Bread 2 slices	3 oz.
Marmalade 1 tablespoonful	1 oz.
Sugar in tea 1 dessertspoonful	¼ oz.
Lunch	
Stewed Rabbit about	6 oz.
Potatoes	8 oz.
Cabbage ¼ at 2d.	
Rice Pudding	
Tea	
Syrup	1 oz.
Milk	¼ pint
Bread 2 slices	3 oz.
Butter	½ oz.
Rock Cake	1
Sugar in tea	¼ oz.
Dinner	
Lentil Soup	¼ pint
Loin of Mutton	5 oz.
Brussels Sprouts	⅓ lb.
2 Potatoes	8 oz.
Apple Charlotte	

Summary of Ingredients

Proteins		*Cost* s. d.
Bacon—uncooked	1 oz.	1¼
Beefsteak—uncooked	4 oz.	3½
Mutton—leg ,,	4 oz.	3
Egg—1¼	1¼	2½
Milk	¾ pint	2¼
		1 0½
Fats		
Butter for bread and pastry	2 oz.	2½
Dripping	¼ oz.	¼
		2¾
Carbohydrates		
Sugar	2½ oz.	½
Jam and Marmalade (Average)	2 oz.	1½
Flour	1¾ oz.	¼
Oatmeal	1 oz.	¼
Bread	5½ oz.	1
Chocolate	1 oz.	½
Potatoes (As purchased.)	1 lb.	1½
Carrots (As purchased.)	4 oz.	½
English Onions (As purchased.)	4 oz.	½
Cauliflower (As purchased.)	4 oz.	1¼
Apple (As purchased.)	5 oz.	1¼
		9
Proteins	3¼ oz.	1 0½
Fats	4½ oz.	2¾
Carbohydrates	14¼ oz.	9
		2 0¼

Proteins		*Cost* s. d.
Herring (As purchased)	1	1½
Rabbit (As purchased)	6 oz.	4
Loin of Mutton (N.Z.) (As purchased)	5 oz.	3¾
Milk	½ pint	1½
Lentils	¾ oz.	¼
		11
Fats		
Butter	1 oz.	1¼
Dripping	¼ oz.	¼
		1½
Carbohydrates		
Sugar	1 oz.	¼
Marmalade and Syrup	2 oz.	1
Oatmeal	1 oz.	¼
Bread	6 oz.	1¼
Potatoes (As purchased)	1 lb.	1½
Cabbage (As purchased)	4 oz.	½
Onions (As purchased)	4 oz.	½
Brussels Sprouts (As purchased)	⅓ lb.	1
Rice Pudding		1
Apple Charlotte		1
Rock Cake		½
		8¾
Proteins	4 oz.	11
Fats	4½ oz.	1½
Carbohydrates	15 oz.	8¾
		1 9¼

Illustration by

On
BREACH
of
Promise

FROM time to time our news-papers are enlivened by the reports of breach of promise cases; and in recent years it has happened that judges have used the occasions thus provided to express their opinions upon this class of action.

One High Court judge in summing up to a jury recently said that he had no doubt that the existence of actions for breach of promise often operated to compel a man to carry out a promise which his conscience and his heart told him he ought not to fulfil. No one could look round the world without seeing many cases of engagements hastily made, after which the man or woman might find that a mistake had been made. What was the man to do?

Was he to say to the girl: " All my affection is gone. I have grown almost to dislike you, but I will marry you rather than face a breach of promise action"; or was he to say, " No, I believe the right thing, and the honest thing, is not to marry you, and I will submit to the verdict of the jury."

His lordship added that he had for a long time felt that an action for breach of promise to marry was not an ordinary contract. It was wholly dif-ferent from the bargain that was made in the counting-house; it carried with it a sense of status; it was a life contract, and, according to the great

Churches, it was a contract which nothing but death could dissolve.

Therefore the consequences of a happy marriage were of vast im-portance to the whole community, and the conse-quences of an unhappy marriage were seen in the thousands of separations granted by magistrates and in the con-gested lists in the Divorce Division.

If the jury would reflect on the con-sequences of the unhappy marriage they would realise the gravity of the issues at stake—lifelong misery, frequently in-fidelity, the Divorce Court, and social ruin.

The breach of promise action was in many ways degrading for the woman, because she had to ask the jury to assess the commercial value of the man whose affections she had lost.

If the woman were to remain single for ever that would be one thing, but he would like the jury to consider the degrading features of these actions from the woman's point of view.

The phrase " breach of promise " carries with it an understood conclusion, namely, that it is a breach of promise to fulfil an engagement to marry. An

engagement to marry any person is in itself a contract. This point comes out much more strongly in Continental legal systems than it does in England, where we have largely dropped all the cere-monial adjuncts of a betrothal. Cen-turies ago the betrothal formed an integral part of the marriage; and it was under Canon Law of sufficient account to obtain a decree of nullity of marriage, if the bride or bridegroom had been pre-contracted before the mar-riage ceremony to some other person.

There was an interesting illustration of this in the history of England. King John was pre-contracted in marriage to a lady called Hawisa of Gloucester. Ignoring this, he carried off another

By

Helena
Normanton, B.A.

Is compensation on this score an Anachronism in these days of Emancipated Women?

These actions are nearly always brought by women . . . and are apt to be regarded as deserving occasions for the exercise of judicial wit

Breach of promise actions are nearly always brought in this country by women. That is, perhaps, one of the reasons why they are apt to be regarded as deserving occasions for the exercise of judicial rebuke and humour and of that lesser species of wit which flourishes among the Bar. I say lesser, because of course it is obvious that a barrister could not possibly make as funny a joke as a judge could. The fact that a woman is seeking compensation for wasted years of her life is intensely wit-provoking. Perhaps in real life the rupture of an engagement is not quite so laughable an affair as it sometimes seems in Court.

An engagement to marry is a contract made on a somewhat peculiar footing with regard to the time for its fulfilment. If Edwin proposes to Angelina on Monday, Angelina has not necessarily the right to require Edwin to marry her within a month or any other

fixed date. The only interpretation the law places upon a fulfilment of the contract is that it should be within a reasonable time. The reasonableness of the time is a matter to be settled by the surrounding circumstances. If Edwin is a sort of Dick Whittington, he may say: "I will marry you when I am Lord Mayor of London" and, if Angelina agrees to that, she has not much remedy if Edwin takes a good many years in reaching the mayoral chair.

I think in general practice anything from between three months and five years is taken as being a reasonable duration of an engagement, unless special circumstances have arisen: suppose a long war between two countries absolutely severs two loving hearts of different nationalities for a space of some seven years; then again the time is extended by *force majeure*. But there is something horribly pathetic about extremely long drawn out engagements. The young man who takes his weekly flowers and chocolates to the young lady for eight, nine, ten, eleven, twelve years, is very likely wasting both her time and his own; and if a woman lets things drift on and on, she has only herself to blame.

Candidates for marriage have not— unless I am greatly in error—the Chancery (Continued on page 104)

lady, Isabella of Angoulême, and married her, ignoring the fact that she also was pre-contracted to Hugh de Lusignan. His marriage was thus doubly open to dissolution. Nor did the powerful Pope, who then occupied the See of Peter, forget to remind him of the fact.

Nowadays, the breaking of one engagement to marry by the mere fact of contracting a marriage with a different person would have no legal effect upon the marriage. It might have very considerable effect upon the subsequent career of the bride or bridegroom in the Law Courts, when acting as defendant in an action for breach of promise.

On Breach of Promise

(*Continued from page* 103)

remedy of "specific performance." One cannot bring an action to compel the dilatory lover to buy the licence and the wedding ring and complete his share of the contract. But if after events make it sufficiently clear that the reluctant lover has broken his contract, then either party to the engagement may bring in an action for damages, that is to say, monetary compensation for the loss sustained by the non-attainment of the marriage.

As men in this country are twopence each and women two for three-ha'pence, the action has practically always been brought by women, because the supposition is that it is she who has been the loser by not becoming a wife. It is not legally impossible for a man to bring an action for breach of promise to marry; and now that it has become more and more a good economic proposition to marry some kinds of women, it is not improbable that the numbers of actions brought by men may show in the future a tendency to increase and may even in time have serious results in the shape of damages against a fickle lady. Suppose Madame Mantalini had not married Mr. Mantalini, would he not have been able to say and say very truthfully that a breach of promise on her part would have brought him nearer much earlier to the "demnition bow-wows"?

I can visualise some such a situation as this. Suppose that some woman of marked artistic genius has been brought forward by a man of great business capacity but little artistic skill himself: for example, let it be a film producer and a very lovely and fascinating film actress. Suppose that after a time they become engaged and that the engagement and his devotion to the production of the actress result in his passing by many another lucrative chance. After some years of engagement, let it be that the lady throws him over and marries somebody else, appointing him producer in the place of her first love. Has Number 1 any moral claim to some compensation? I should think so myself, but I am not at all sure how a jury predominantly masculine would regard it.

Let us assume for the moment that a breach of promise case is to be upon a human and a business footing and not conducted in the silly way in which it often is conducted. What are the arguments which can properly be urged for the plaintiff? Let us get rid of *Serjeant Buzfuz* and his countless imitators. The best thing a plaintiff can do is to rest her case upon the facts: the engagement to marry must be proved up to the hilt. Affectionate letters couched merely in the flaming language of love are not sufficient if they do not clearly indicate the fact that the faithless love at one time was set upon marriage with the plaintiff. Just sufficient letters to prove the engagement should be put in on the principle that enough is enough. When the plaintiff is being examined in the witness box her simple story ought in itself to be sufficient to engage the serious attention of judge and jury; and the less it is attempted to make the action a mode of punishment for the fickle defendant the better it will be.

If the case is conducted upon a dignified footing, the chief object will be to show the measure of damages which the plaintiff has sustained by the non-performance of the contract. One does not want to bring in an undue amount of sentiment into the whole business; and the woman who seeks to get damages from the Court on account of her blighted affections must think very seriously what the effect of such a line of

tactics will be before a mixed jury. It is not much use nowadays, as I remember one young lady plaintiff doing, wringing her handkerchief out in a basin of water before going into the Court. The great principle to be followed is to let the facts speak for themselves and then it is very likely in the vast majority of such cases that the element of pathos which will move the jury to be human will come out quite naturally from the very structure of the story.

One case which I have in mind, in which a jury awarded a poor girl £250 damages and costs some years ago, was based upon the following facts. The girl was a poor, pretty young creature who had become a waitress in a small restaurant. The proprietor seduced her under promise of marriage and in due course she had an unfortunate little baby. The poor little thing died almost literally of starvation, and the mother herself was not very far distant from meeting such a fate. The story was sad enough, but the point which perhaps weighed most with the jury was that the very day after this young man obtained possession of his fiancée's person he actually married another young woman. If that was not a proper case for the jury to award damages, it is hardly conceivable what could be; and if there is or was any occasion for humour in the story, it has quite escaped my comprehension.

One of our learned High Court judges has recently expressed himself as being out of sympathy with breach of promise actions, which he appears to regard as an anachronism in these days of the changed relationships of the sexes. He is not altogether wrong, because it is plain that if every time an engagement was broken by one party, the other followed that up shortly and sharply by an action for damages, then a great many unsuitable engagements too recklessly entered into would be persisted in through pure cowardice and even larger crops than we at present enjoy of unsuitable marriages would be the result. That is particularly the case when a young couple of about equal abilities, age, and prospects break off their engagement. In such cases it is very often doubtful what, if anything, the young woman has lost. A pretty, weeping plaintiff may perhaps move the sympathies of the jury; but, if they reflect for two minutes in such a case as that, it will be agreed that the prettier the girl the more likely she is to marry somebody else and therefore the less she needs compensation.

But until the day arrives when men and women have absolute economic equality in this country, there will endure the just causes for compensation when a woman has been made to lose the most golden years of her life for the sake of a man who, after years of devotion, discovers that he does not want her. Pure fickleness should not have its path made altogether easy; and, if a man does intend to change his mind, the least he can do is to do it quickly and not to precede it by the seduction of his fiancée. That occurrence, alas, is a very constant accompaniment of breach of promise cases; and to trick a woman into the surrender of her chastity under a promise of marriage is, even regarding it on its lowest commercial basis, just as dishonest as to trick a greengrocer out of money by promising good potatoes and then supplying him with diseased ones. The fact that it is accompanied with much more human suffering, not less, seems no adequate reason for considering the offence a lighter one.

For Embroidering Children's Clothes
Clark's "Anchor" Coton à Broder

Also :
"Anchor"
Stranded Cotton
"Anchor" Flox for
bold designs
"Anchor" Velveno
for crochet·hats
"Anchor" Filosheen
for mending
"Scintilla" & "Estella"
for knitting & fringing

For embroidery that will wear and wear—that can be boiled, rubbed, wrung out and still come up gay and fresh as the day it was new—use Clark's "Anchor" Coton a Broder. It is a cotton thread with a delightfully glossy finish. It is made in an amazing range of exquisite shades, guaranteed fast. Use Coton à Broder to give charm to children's clothes, lingerie, tub frocks, table linen. Also for crochet. Obtainable in skeins in various "grists" or grades of thickness.

Remember always that whatever your requirements for needlework—embroidery thread, every kind of fancy sewing or crochet cotton, artificial silk—you make sure of getting the best possible article if you look for the famous names of Clark and Coats.

Clark's

Threads Embroideries Cottons

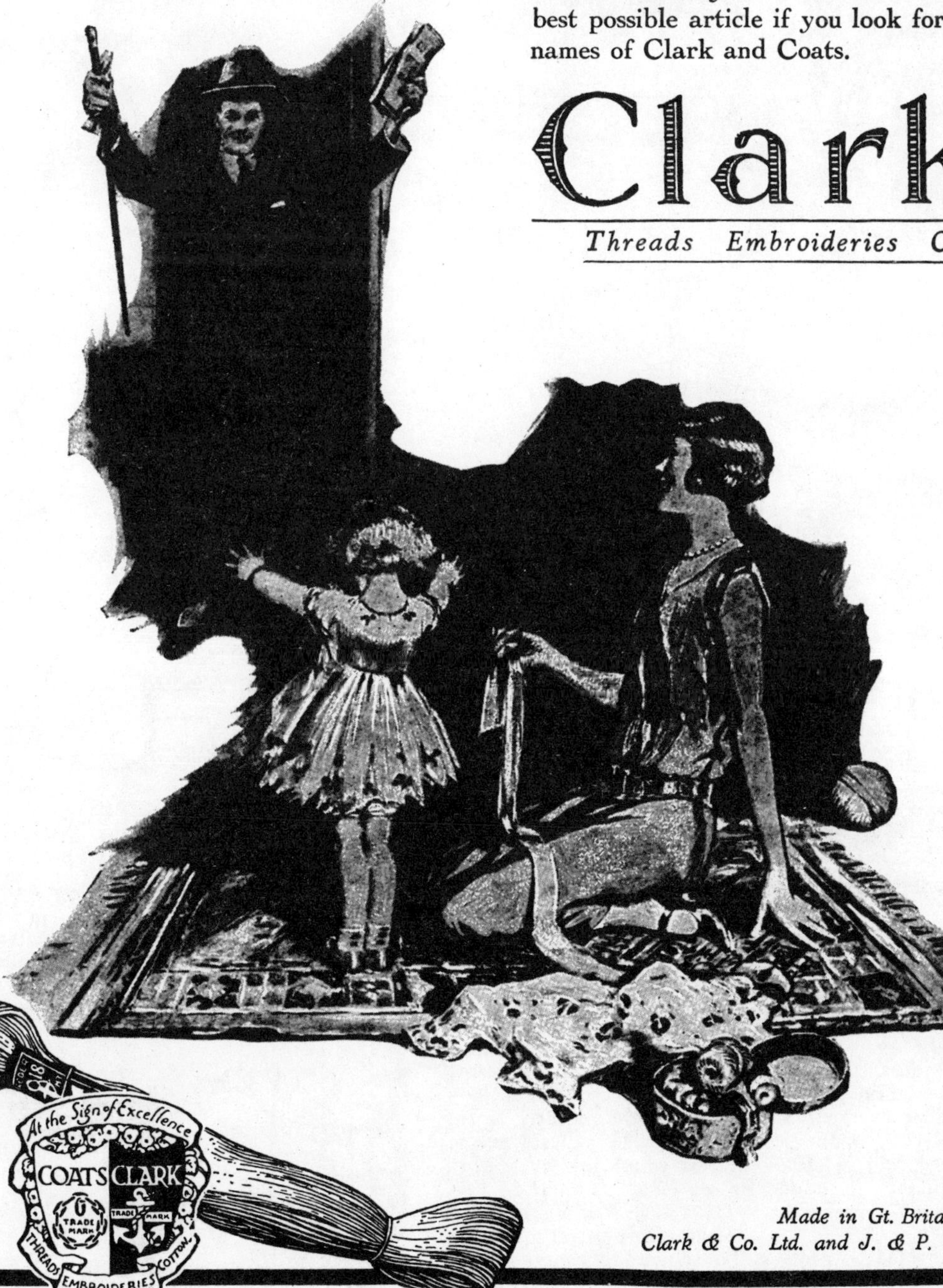

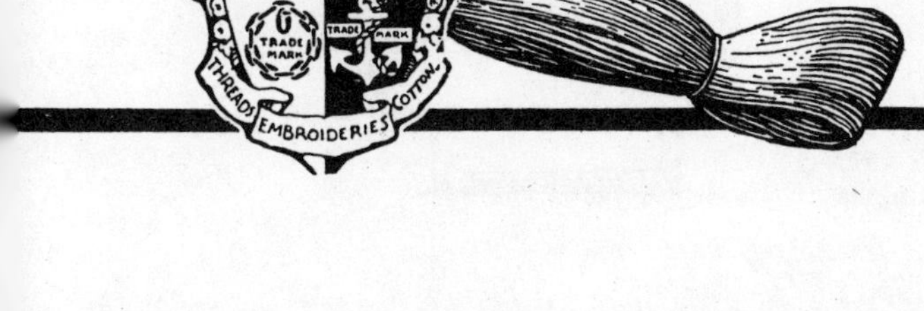

Made in Gt. Britain
Clark & Co. Ltd. and J. & P. Coats Ltd. Paisley

C 91

Built-in cupboard to lower recess on landing

The Thousand

By Alan Fort

THE problem of the £1000 house to suit the needs of the cultured individual, and at the same time attain to the highest demands for efficiency, general practicability, and domestic economics, is still only partly solved, and in spite of the great advance in this direction during recent years, the real solution is still to be attained.

The £1000 figure is quoted as probably representing the limit of expenditure contemplated by the majority of people whose ambition it is to possess a complete and modest home, situated in suburban areas, within easy travelling distance of the working centres of our large towns, where land is expensive and restricted in area.

Architects are frequently being accused of failing to tackle in an adequate and suitable manner this problem of well-designed houses. Up to comparatively recent years this accusation might have had a measure of justification. Now, however, it is felt to be somewhat laboured in view of the many outstanding examples of efficient and tasteful work of this character which have been brought recently to the notice of the general public, and of which the house illustrated is an example.

It is true that a proportion of the effort towards solving the house question is at present confined more to literary treatises on the subject than to executed examples of really efficient work, but it must be borne in mind that the supply of such work must of necessity be governed by the demand for such homes. Although most people are capable of appreciating good design in preference

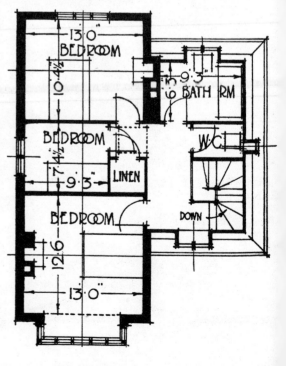

Pound House

escue, A.R.I.B.A.

to bad, they do not always trouble to seek out the authors of the better schemes, who almost invariably prove to be architects who have made this class of work their special study.

Why do the majority of people, while complaining of the badly planned house full of dirt-traps, badly lighted, and overloaded with commonplace detail, still

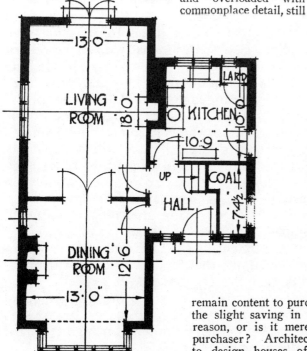

Folding doors from dining-room, and drawing-room fireplace

The Director of Housing answers readers' queries addressed to him c/o Good Housekeeping, 153 Queen Victoria Street, London, E.C.4. A stamped, addressed envelope should always be enclosed

unable to give tangible assistance until commissioned to do so. The public must realise that the house it demands (embodying the virtues of comfort, labour-saving, installation of up-to-date methods of heating, ventilation, etc.) can at present best be obtained by the individual thought and attention of an architect and not by the more popular methods of speculation often adopted.

In these days much is heard of the "modern" house, and without being in any way desirous of appearing in a reactionary rôle, it may safely be said that too much adventure into "the realms of future needs" when designing homes may actually defeat the object in view.

remain content to purchase such houses? Is the slight saving in initial outlay the sole reason, or is it merely the apathy of the purchaser? Architects capable and ready to design houses of the right kind are

The 1930's

The optimism of the early Twenties faded into the depression and mass unemployment of the Thirties. This was heightened by the threatening rumblings from the continent which were eventually to lead to another great war at the end of the decade.

These were the days when middle-class women bobbed their hair and painted their nails red for the first time; when a businessman with two children lived comfortably on £1,000 pa (*Budgeting the Income*, page 122); when a telephone call placed between 2 pm and 7 am cost 6d, regardless of distance (*Do You Use the Telephone to Full Advantage?* page 128) and when the telephone was described thus: 'There is perhaps no public service more consistently criticised than this of the telephone' (plus ça change!).

Nowhere is the mood of the post-war generation expressed so movingly as in *Why Are We Failing the Dead?* by Godfrey Winn (page 132), a piece which chronicles this much-maligned generation's seeming excesses, and excuses them as attempts to dull conscience and ward off guilt. 'They died that you might live . . . Yes, but as they died . . . they did not realise . . . what a difference, what a gulf, there was destined to be between their England of 1914 and ours of today. Had they been able to foresee the changes that would occur, the series of economic crises that were to cripple us and delay indefinitely our return to prosperity, perhaps they would not have gone so cheerfully to their death; perhaps they would not have been so willing to believe that their incredible sacrifice was to make the world a better and a happier and a safer place in the future.'

The dire economic situation seems to have been the preoccupation of many of the brilliant young writers of the Thirties. Beverley Nichols in *A Study in Black* (page 140) paints a picture which is strikingly relevant even today. 'My reading of contemporary history tells me that the whole of western civilization as we know it is a sinking ship.' Nichols portrays a future when Mr Henry Ford will have no more markets in which to sell his cars because all the markets will be saturated; and foreshadows the butter mountains and wine lakes of today when he writes about a situation where the coffee growers of Brazil throw tons of coffee into their harbour while in New York men don't even have enough money to buy one cup of coffee, of Canadian farmers who burn their wheat, of English farmers who let their potatoes rot in the soil, of Australian farmers who allow whole orchards of fruit to fall to the ground and perish, when the world is filled with people who cannot afford to buy bread, potatoes or a single apple.

Relationships between the sexes, too, had changed dramatically due to the war. As Godfrey Winn acknowledges in *What Has Happened to the Femme Fatale?* (page 164): 'What man could not be a god and what woman would not remain an enchanted figure of mystery so long as the couple in question only addressed each other in the language of love? So it went on for centuries and might indeed have gone on for ever . . . had not the war come and driven nail after nail into the coffin of this so carefully nurtured romantic approach of the sexes. Men were suddenly forced to realise that women were people as well as playthings; women found that men made charming friends and companions as well as husbands and lovers.'

But anticipating the buzz word of the Seventies, he admits that he is worried by the possibility that the Thirties lady is expected to be a superwoman. 'Surely too much is expected of the modern women. Urged on by my sex, she has set herself an impossibly high standard of all-round excellence.'

On a lighter front, the shopping service continued to provide reasonably priced clothes for readers with little access to London stores. You could send off for an evening coattee for 52s 6d or an afternoon gown for 37s 6d. At least today, one outfit can get a woman through her day and often into the evening as well. And mothers could take advantage of *Good Housekeeping's* children's patterns and make up a red riding hood cape for just 9d or an Empire dress for just 1s (*Party Clothes for the Younger Set*, page 163).

As war approached, rationing and the new crisis facing Britain were uppermost in the minds of *Good Housekeeping* readers. The staff of *Good Housekeeping* moved to Wales in 1939 (*Editing Good Housekeeping in Wales*, page 192) and by 1940, due to the paper shortage, began producing issues which were much smaller than the normal size.

As we move into the Thirties, there are obvious changes in the styles of advertisements, with copy generally shorter and much cleaner and slicker art-work. For the first time in *Good Housekeeping*, white space is used for its own sake. The ads reflect the fact that advertising was burgeoning in this decade with the growth of advertising agencies and the increasing recognition of the role of the art director in creating advertisements.

In the Twenties, copy was often ponderous and prolix, in contrast to the Thirties where an economy of writing style becomes evident. The use of drawings was still widespread, even in the selling of motor cars and petrol, and cartoon figures and visual jests were frequent, as seen in the splendid series by Shell. Strip stories, personified by Horlicks, were popular with some series running for several years.

Among the plethora of advertising for toothpaste, the ubiquitous constipation remedies, the indigestion cures, petrol and oil, the new man-made fibres, cars and furniture, a new product category emerged. This was the refrigerator, possibly the decade's status symbol for the affluent family, and the electric vacuum cleaner, which could be yours for ten shillings down, was steadily replacing the carpet sweeper. The occasional colour page advertisement appeared in the magazines as did the rare sighting of the double page spread. Most advertisers, however, were content (or financially constrained) to peddle their wares within the confines of half or two-thirds pages – even the big names of the period such as Bisto, Oxo, Bovril, Eno's, MacLeans, Colgate and Ovaltine.

Like the editorial, the advertisements are a great reflector of social change and development. Housemaids, so often portrayed in the Twenties, disappear altogether. Even the apple-cheeked home helps become sparser as the decade progresses. The cars become progressively cheaper – Ford had achieved the £100 family model – and the HP terms more tempting. The families in the advertisements reflect the economic climate of the decade – the only child was the norm.

But life was becoming more convenient, more comfortable for the affluent family man on £1,000 a year. Life had style and the advertisements seemed eager to reflect and encourage the attainable good life – before September 1939 shattered the dreams and lives of everybody, including those families who had been attracted to one of the new houses which were advertised for £700 freehold.

NOËLLE WALSH
BRIAN BRAITHWAITE

Streaming down the Great West Road
—TWO THOUSAND CARS AN HOUR!

Over roads like this the Vauxhall, built for to-day's crowded thoroughfares, carries you safely and comfortably at marvellous *high average speed*

AT THE RATE of two thousand cars an hour, traffic pours down the Great West Road during the week-end rush! To-day there are nearly a million and a half cars on Britain's roads.

That is why it takes a car of *exceptionally high average speed*, built expressly for crowded roads, to avoid delays and hold-ups in the press of to-day's traffic — such a car as Vauxhall engineers have produced in the 1930 Vauxhall.

Wherever you drive, the Vauxhall maintains a higher average speed with greater safety and comfort than many other cars costing far more.

For the Vauxhall will, without hesitation, throttle down while in top gear to a walking pace, and yet from this pace get away again through the gears to a speed

On sharp bends the long, soft springing, well-balanced steering and low centre of gravity make the Vauxhall particularly stable. If you are compelled to slow up on a bend it is usually because you cannot see round it, never because the Vauxhall would fail to hold the road.

of 40 m.p.h. in under 15 seconds; it is so well sprung and stable that it can corner at speeds that would be unsafe in many other cars; its four speeds and suitable gear ratios give it fast climbing on very steep, long hills.

And, once in the open, it can wipe out distance with its 70 miles an hour or more

of *safe* speed — safe because it is perfectly controlled by the famous Vauxhall brakes (far more powerfully efficient and more costly than ordinary brakes).

And everything is designed for greater convenience and comfort. The pressure of the driver's foot on a pedal lubricates 28 points of the chassis at once. Brakes, steering, gear-change, and controls are so finely adjusted that driving is sheer joy.

The great beauty of line and finish of the new Vauxhall models (built throughout by British workmen, from 97 per cent. British materials) places them in the forefront among fine cars. There are six models, costing from £495 to £695. All are obtainable by the G.M.A.C. plan of convenient payments.

See the new Vauxhalls! The nearest Vauxhall dealer will gladly lend you one to drive. Or write for particulars to Vauxhall Sales Department, General Motors Limited, Hendon, London, N.W.9. Complete range of models on view at 174-182 Gt. Portland St., London, W.1.

THE RICHMOND SALOON, £530
(Sliding roof, £15 extra)

V A U X H A L L

LELONG

EARLY WINTER REVELATIONS

BY ELAINE NEAL

The bolero holds its ground, as shown in this elegantly cut formal frock of navy marocain trimmed with ermine

THE collection season in Paris is not a commercial event, at least not on the surface. It is a ceremony and a tradition. Twice a year full-sized collections are shown to the press and to the buyers, and after that, all over the world, feminine fashions take their cue from these openings. The big collections are in February and August. In between, in April and November, small collections are shown, but these, as a rule, are simply follow-ups of the former season, or tentative attempts towards a new idea.

The season of 1929 was as epoch-making as any since the war. Fashions, as I have so often said, follow a general

JANE
REGNY

Jane Règny stresses plaids in her collection. Above is an excellent all-round suit of blue and green plaid woollen material, worn with a white handkerchief blouse. The three-quarter coat is typical of the new season

cycle, and for ten years after 1919 we followed the silhouette of short skirts, long waists, and extreme simplicity of line. We modified it, lowered skirts a bit, or raised them, without actually changing the feeling or inspiration, until last year. By that time, simplicity and youth and the sports feeling had been used to the fullest extent of their elasticity, and a change was inevitable. With a suddenness and a thoroughness that was unbelievable what we still call " the new silhouette " crashed in. Now we are again completely settled into another cycle, which at first created much controversy, but which looks to be as deeply embedded in the feminine consciousness as was its predecessor.

As this goes to press, a great many of the most important houses have not yet shown their collections, but we are able to get some advance sketches, and we have seen enough to know what the trend is. We know that the evolution of the present line has reached a certain perfection, and what may have seemed impractical at first, has been made wearable and graceful.

The sports silhouette has changed practically not at all. Skirts to the middle of the calf, normal waists, rough woollens or tweeds, short jackets, sum it up. The same may be said of street clothes in general. Here also the skirt is not exaggeratedly long, and many classic *tailleurs* are used for the morning. There is also the street costume with the three-quarter coat, that is (Continued on page 114)

BROADCLOTH, VELVET,

SILK CRÊPE AND

WOOL CRÊPE LEAD

IN THE DAYTIME

NICOLE
GROULT

WORTH

Left: one of the very popular short jacket suits for medium weather, of brown marocain stitched diagonally with fuzzy hat "beaver" felt. Above: an afternoon gown showing the moulded silhouette and becoming short sleeve

THE COIFFURE

IN CURLS

THE MOOD OF THE

In spite of predictions to the contrary, there is a strong element in favour of keeping the hair short— even although "short" means longer than formerly

(*Continued from page* 112)

slightly more dressy and usually completed by a very feminine type of blouse, which is worn either in the belt or as a tunic.

It is when we approach the afternoon costume that skirts are longer. All frocks of silk or crêpe georgette are almost to the ankles, and these are completed with long slim coats, often of broadcloth, that hug the figure snugly and flare a bit at the bottom. The newest ones either tie or are fastened tightly at the waistline on the side, wrapping closely around the front. No more holding one's coat together in the front, thank goodness!

In the way of afternoon gowns for tea in the house or for cocktail parties, there is even greater softness and elaboration, often no sleeves, but the upper arm covered with little capes or a fichu of the bertha type. And the materials are chiffon, lace, and the lovely soft lamés so good this year. In fact, the lamés give almost the only pattern among the season's fabrics. They are seen in discreet designs for afternoon wear, and in gorgeous ones for evening; they have quite taken the place of last winter's printed velvets and satins. Velvets of all varieties are good too, but without patterns. One sees panne, Lyons velvet, and transparent velvet, used for both afternoon and evening. One also sees much heavy crêpe marocain and crêpe georgette, proving that dull materials are better than shiny.

For the formal evening gown I have seen two sorts of skirt silhouettes: the very tight skirt with the fullness beginning at the very bottom, and the skirt with the fullness from just below the hips. I must confess that I prefer the latter, but the very tight sheath skirt as an indication is not

SEEKS INSPIRATION

TO SUIT

NEW SILHOUETTE

to be ignored. Bodices are simple, to the rather high waist line, with square or oval *décolletage* and tiny shoulder straps, but almost every model has some sort of little cape to complete it, which is sufficient to make the gown less formal if one keeps it on.

Trains are seen at many collections, and the skirt that grazes the floor all round is general. A gown to the ankles at once looks like an afternoon gown. Flowers are reappearing on evening gowns on the shoulders or at the back of the neckline, and white *boutonnières* are once more being worn with the tailored coat and skirt. The off-the-shoulder effect, or bertha neck for evening gowns is very important and a becoming style for anyone tall enough to wear it. It has a tendency to shorten, however, and should be chosen with care.

Obviously the main materials for daytime are broadcloth, velvet, wool crêpes, and silk crêpes, and instead of tweeds rough or bouclette woollens. For evening again velvets and lamés and chiffons and lace. Also many crêpe georgettes and satin. As to colours, the outstanding ones are very dark browns, reds, and greens, but these are so dark as to approach black. All white and all black remain good for evening, and I notice a great deal of light blue.

The street frock trimmed with ermine from Lelong, on page 61, demonstrates the continuation of the bolero, and the suit from Règny on page 62 is an excellent example of the use of plaid. The Worth evening gown on page 64, and the model from Chantal on page 64, show graceful handlings of the short train that hangs independently of the skirt. Molyneux' charming black and pink lace

All the same one cannot help wondering whether, the mode being on very pre-war lines, the hair will not revert to the elaborate puffs and curls of 1912?

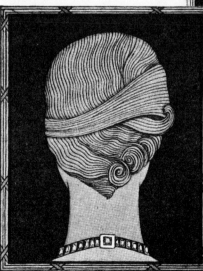

Mrs. John Buchan

after reading a recent new novel deplores

THE BRIGHT YOUNG PEOPLE

I HAVE often been very sorry about the increasing number of my years, but when I read Mr. Evelyn Waugh's *Vile Bodies,* and I realised how terrible it is to be young, I was comforted.

The life of some young people of to-day, as depicted by Mr. Waugh, is a revelation of tragic futility. According to him, they move in a kind of twilight of debts and quarrels, always suffering from either embarrassment or sickness, for "too shy-making," "too shaming," "too sick-making" are words always on the lips of his Bright Young People.

Their only means of making money seems to be by writing highly innocuous news to the society papers about their friends' engagements, preferences in clothes, and presence or absence at such and such a point-to-point or race meeting. Apparently this pursuit, though lucrative, and blameless except in taste, is not a very safe one, as mistakes about people may lead to libel actions and instant dismissal of the gossip-writers from the journal to whose staff they are attached.

Owing to my sex I never had to go through the ordeal of life at a preparatory school, but I have frequently been assured that the years at a private school are the part of a man's life which he looks back to with least satisfaction. Any man who reads *Vile Bodies* will be, I should imagine, painfully reminded of his private school by the type of jokes and stories which pass between the bright young men and maidens, the "sickness," and the general atmosphere of rather meaningless mischief. Sickness is, to use his well-worn phrase, a complex of Mr. Waugh's. His book begins with a painfully accurate account of a Channel crossing, and sickness haunts the whole book, till finally, someone has the cruelty to give a party in a captive airship, and of course all the guests are sicker than ever.

With real ability, and knowledge of how to present a story, Mr. Waugh sets up his little puppet show before us. One would suppose that he bitterly dislikes his puppets, as all the time he gives them savage tweaks which reveal their aimlessness and hollowness. There is something oddly eighteenth century about the world he shows us. We are reminded of the more sordid memoirs of those days, when the out-at-elbows gentry lived by their wits in an atmosphere of debt and quarrels and makeshifts in sordid bedrooms and second-class hostelries. There are some excellent scenes in the book—the revival meeting, when the effect of the preacher's words is completely shattered by a dowager remarking, "with a resounding snort of disapproval, 'What a damned impudent woman!'"—the arrival in the Prime Minister's study of the young person in Hawaiian undress!

Mr. Waugh has also a vivid sense of nomenclature. Mrs. Melrose Ape, the Honourable Miles Malpractice, and Margot Metroland are all excellent names. He is able to make his queer little crowd dance at his bidding, rush about to their parties, peddle news about society, even die in nursing homes under morphia, and, though we may be repelled and disgusted, we are also amused. But when the curtain goes down, I would venture to prophesy that no one will stand to attention when the "Funeral March of the Marionette" is played, or even breathe a sigh of regret when Mr. Waugh packs his puppets into their bags and carries them away in his suitcase.

One glimpse into the desperately joyless world of the "Bright Young People," where the careless pleasures of youth seem to have been bartered for a withered sophistication, is enough to last us for a lifetime. We ought to be more shocked, perhaps, but the tragedy of an apathetic post-War world is that no one is much shocked by anything.

When in doubt, it is always a help to blame the Great War for everything. Perhaps in this case it is justified. These people, prominent in the gossip columns of the press, but without minds, morals, standards or occupations, with no kind of stake in any country, are, let us hope, figments of Mr. Waugh's fertile brain. If not, their childish activities are part of the confusion resulting from the most monstrous upheaval the world has ever known.

The Home Laundry

Instruction in all branches of laundrywork may be obtained from our Service Folios I and II. The first contains detailed information on blueing, starching, drying, and bleaching, whilst the second deals with the laundering of silks and woollens, the treatment of lace, stains and their removal, home dyeing and ironing. Price, post free, 7½d. each, or both 1s. 2d., from Good Housekeeping Institute, 49 Wellington Street, Strand, London, W.C.2

When he asks you

"WHAT WOULD YOU LIKE FOR XMAS?"

—stand boldly up to the opportunity and say you'd like a Triplex Grate!

And if he says, "What's a Triplex Grate?" just tell him it's the grate that does such beautiful cooking!... that gives hot water galore for baths and everything else!... that makes the kitchen fit to look at and to live in!... that cuts down fuel costs by fully one-half! You can add, too, that over 120,000 other wives have Triplex Grates, and that you don't like to feel "out of it."

Ask him to imagine how much nicer and roomier the kitchen would be with a neat Triplex fireplace in lieu of that unsightly stove ... how much lighter your work would become ... how much better for everyone to have wholesome coal-fire cooking instead of fumes-tainted food ... and what a lot you could do with the money a Triplex Grate would save you!

That is the way to win a Triplex Grate. . . .

Put yourself in readiness by writing now for the Triplex Free Booklet. So helpful to be able to show him full colour pictures of the various Triplex models.

The
TRIPLEX
GRATE

TRIPLEX
FOUNDRY LTD.

GREAT BRIDGE,
STAFFORDSHIRE

Showrooms :

LONDON :
12 Newman Street, W.1

BIRMINGHAM :
3 Stephenson Place

MANCHESTER :
33 Princess Street

A Gift that every good wife deserves

Do Women to

THIS is an old and vexed and unsettled question. Some men, feeling impregnable in their masculine conceit, assert without a quaver or a blush that a woman never puts a hat on her head without wondering what effect it will have upon the men she may meet, while others, less sure of themselves and perhaps a trifle acid on that account, declare that the only thought in her head is a hope that she may throw all her women friends into a state of anger and envy. I doubt myself if there is much in either of these theories, although I would not deny that there is something. I believe that the average woman, when she buys a hat or any other article of dress or adornment, thinks only of its effect on herself, and is not greatly interested in its effect on other people. "Do I look nice in this hat? Does this dress make me feel nice?" Such are the questions that a woman, consciously or subconsciously, puts to herself when she buys a hat or puts on a new frock. I am very certain that women could not possibly wear some of the astonishing things they do wear or keep the habits that some of them have, if their first or only thought were of pleasing men. If that were their first or only thought, then women must be the world's worst psychologists, for many of them have habits that are not merely displeasing to men, but positively revolting to them.

Let me take the small instance of nails: human nails, not iron nails. Many women, especially those who devote much time to the culture of their bodies, have their nails trimmed to a long, sharp point and reddened with varnish. I have never met a man who was not utterly disgusted by this horrible habit. I have met men who cannot bear to look at long, sharp, red nails, which, they roughly and rudely assert, remind them of bloody talons. "They look

like claws dripping with blood!" is what a man once said of them in my presence. I believe that if a canvass of men's opinions on this subject were taken, not one man would be found to say that he admired long, sharpened, reddened nails on women: I am certain that all men would proclaim their loathing for them. Yet a remarkable number of women are addicted to this fashionable habit. They cannot be trying to please men with it. Whom, then, are they trying to please? Do they think that nails trimmed into that shape and stained to the colour of blood are beautiful? Their sense of beauty must be queer if they do. Men believe, and I think rightly believe, that the delicate

pink natural colour of the human nail is very lovely, and they are totally unable to understand why women smear their finger tips with varnish which, at best, makes them look dirty and, at worst, suggests association with a slaughter-house. I know a lady who stains her nails with gold-leaf, and I have heard that manicurists were lately offering to paint their clients' nails green! Evidently there is some intention in the people who do this sort of thing, but what? No man knows.

I think it well to say, lest there should be any misunderstanding on the point, that this

What do men really think of the dress and habits of the modern woman—her paint and powder, her reddened nails, short skirts and plucked eyebrows? St. John Ervine uncompromisingly reveals the feelings of his own sex when he says, "I greatly doubt if many women realise how deeply men are revolted by some of their habits. . . . If women dress to please men, they must be the world's worst psychologists." And that is that!

article is not intended to be a denunciation of the use of cosmetics. Only village prigs and suburban sourfaces complain of their use, although all men strongly dislike their unskilful or overuse. A man likes to see a bit of colour in his girl's face, and if nature has given her a pale or sallow complexion, he thinks she does well to repair nature's defects. He knows, too, that the use of powder in a modern, sooty city is obligatory on a woman who does not wish her face to be roughened and spoiled by smuts. He knows, too, that women have been addicted to cosmetics ever since life began, and is too much of a philosopher to imagine that an ancient and universal

Dress Please Men ?

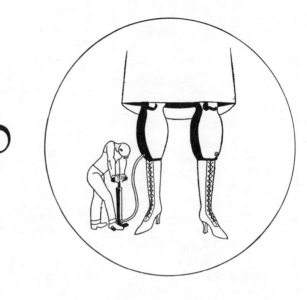

Sketches by Eric Fraser

custom is likely to be abolished in five minutes because he announces his dislike of it. What he hates like poison is to see lip-salve stuck on a girl's lips as if a house painter had been busy with a big brush, slapping the paint about in a careless and slovenly manner. In America, where the use of cosmetics is excessive, and even children of ten have their rougepots and lipsticks, I have seen women with lips so reddened with moist-looking paint that I fully appreciated the horrified exclamation of a man who, on seeing a woman decorated in that style, said aloud, " She looks like a butcher's shop ! " This, then, is not a Puritanical article, demanding that women shall neglect their looks. It is strictly an enquiry into the cause of certain habits of dress and decoration that women have. Why do they do and wear some of the things that they do do and wear ?

Why, for example, do so many women endure the agony of having their eyebrows plucked? This is an ancient enough habit, but its ancientry does not explain it. I have yet to meet the man who likes to see a woman with plucked eyebrows, and I conclude, therefore, that the women who undergo this painful process do so for some occult reason of their own. They certainly do not please men by it, as I lately proved to myself when I suggested to a theatre-manager that he should see an actress who, I thought, might be suitable for a part in a play by me. He saw her, but disapproved of her. " Why ? " I enquired. " I can't stick her plucked eyebrows ! " he replied. " She looks horrible ! " Yet she is accounted, in the women's papers, a beautiful actress and is supposed to be full of that queer quality which is called sex-appeal. She *was* very beautiful when I first knew her, but she has so disfigured herself with pluckings and grotesque paintings that she now disgusts men whom she formerly attracted. This, from her point of view, is very serious, for she may lose work through the fact that managers are beginning to believe that she is physically revolting. Clearly, she is a proof, if any were needed, that whatever may be the reason why women indulge in some of their odd cosmetical habits, it is not the desire to allure and please the male. I greatly doubt, indeed, if many women realise how deeply men are revolted by some of these habits. Even those men who like to see colour on a woman's lips are put off when they see the red stain spreading from the lips to the teeth, and I have known more than one man who was turned against his food by seeing a woman put down a cigarette whose tip was stained with lip-salve. " Looked as if she were bleeding ! " is what one of them said afterwards.

The majority of men like bobbed hair, even when they have a sentimental affection for long tresses, but no man can abide the contemporary habit of combing the hair in public, especially at a dinner table, nor does any man like to see a woman lipsticking herself in public. They have a name for these women. " She's a Lipsticker ! " they say when they see one of them at their unpleasant business. The sensations a man feels when a woman begins to comb her hair all over her food would startle her if she (Continued on page 120)

119

Let us be frank about Obscene Books

Public opinion, powerful, even resistless when fully aroused, might with incalculable benefit be aroused now, so that this pernicious and defiling flood might be stemmed and prevented from doing further ill. Whose job is it? Everybody's job. Surely there are enough of us left who care for things honest, and lovely, and of good report?

Well, what can we do about it?

(The other side of this question—the reviewers' side—will be taken next month by Frank Swinnerton)

Do Women Dress to Please Men?

(Continued from page 119)

were to know of them. I recollect one night in a famous London restaurant seeing a young woman frequently take out a mirror and comb from her vanity-bag and gaze at herself and tidy her hair. The young man who was her host, bore with her in patience that was sublime. Compared with him Job was fretful and fussy. But at last his temper snapped, when for the fifteenth time she opened her vanity-bag, and he suddenly snapped at her, "For heaven's sake, stop looking at yourself. Your face is still there! And if you want to comb your hair, go to the cloakroom and do it!" The silly wench looked surprised at his outburst, but no one within earshot of them felt any surprise at it. What did surprise them was that he had borne with her toilet habits so long.

I have heard men say that the custom of wearing long, sharpened and reddened nails is a sign of a cruel and sadistic nature, but I am not satisfied by that attempt to explain it, which, in itself, is a proof of the bewilderment men feel about it.

The very brief skirt was intensely disliked by men, partly because it embarrassed them by its impropriety, but chiefly because it revealed the pitiable ugliness of so many feminine legs. Actresses were specially trained in the proper way in which to sit down in very brief skirts so that they should not cause embarrassment and giggles in the audience, but even they were not always able to accomplish the feat without difficulty. Women off the stage seemed to have no understanding of the exhibitions they sometimes gave, and men found themselves obliged to look anywhere but at their women friends. There was a time when a man, on suddenly looking up, would catch sight of one woman winking and grimacing and looking very meaningly at another woman who would then clutch wildly at her skirts! . . . Oh, a most embarrassing and ridiculous business, and one that was not at all pleasing to men, who are less allured by the display of underwear than some women imagine. When one thinks of the match-stick legs and the roly-poly legs and the legs that seemed to be suffering from elephantiasis which were lavishly revealed by the too, too abbreviated skirt, it can scarcely be maintained that this garment was invented for the delight of man. The average man thinks that the right length for a skirt is one that leaves the hem hovering about midway between the ankle and the knee. He loathes the knee-length skirt or the skirt that ends above the knee, and he insists that it is usually worn by aged females who are vain enough to believe that their faces will seem young and smooth if their legs are excessively exhibited. Not many women are so indifferent to their appearance as to wear boots with short skirts, but some do—they are commoner on the Continent than they are in England— and a dreadful sight they are. They do not consider men's feelings when they boot themselves, and allow two or three inches of bulging calf to be seen between the top of the boot and the hem of the skirt. Men

dislike the sleeveless dress, for reasons that need not be detailed here—they are obvious —but thousands of women wear dresses that not only have no sleeves but have large holes through which the arms are thrust!

It is very doubtful if any woman has ever seriously dressed herself to please men. The crinoline was a continual annoyance to the males of its time. They had to perform acrobatic feats to keep in step with their young ladies and were always crushed into corners, especially in cabs, so that there might be room for the mass of wire which made the crinoline. Can anyone believe that *that* was pleasing to men? The crinoline looks very pretty on the stage, but those who admire it there forget that the stage drawing-room is much bigger than the drawing-room of life, and that men have space in which to move about it, even if the place *is* cluttered with crinolines. When a man peeps into the dismal museums in which women's cast-off fashions are preserved, he is appalled and puzzled by what he sees there. Did women wear those things? If so, why? The bustle, for example . . . but what man can think of the bustle without wishing to shriek with laughter? A portrait of Queen Elizabeth, arrayed in all her glory, makes a man realise instantly why she was a Virgin Queen. Who could possibly have wished to marry that mass of machinery? Look at her pinched-in waist, her swelling skirts that covered a multiplicity of petticoats, her general appearance of being in a strait-jacket, and then inquire of yourself, could any man in this world have thought that her style was handsome or have wished to spend his life with a lady so devoid of sense that she allowed herself to be constructed in the Elizabethan fashion?

Men, so far from being delighted with most of the habits and clothes of women have spent much time in deriding them. The masculine papers—there are, alas, few of them left!—are full of male derision of women's wear and ways. A survey of the pages of *Punch* throughout the period of its publication proves that men, when they have not been revolted by feminine fashions, have made fun of them. I daresay that the fashions of men often seem absurd to women, but no fashion of men can ever seem so absurd to women as all women's fashions seem to men. I end, then as I started, with the assertion that women do not behave or dress to please men. What I want to know is, for whom do they dress and behave?

They may, of course, reply that their clothes are designed by men and that therefore, men must accept responsibility for them, but to that feeble answer, one may retort that women are not under any obligation to wear what fashions are ordered for them. Think of the hobble skirt which threw women to the ground when they attempted to move at a greater speed than a crawl. Think, too, of the fiasco at Ascot in 1930 when the rain fell on the long organdie skirt. For whose comfort and delight were those absurdities designed

'I wish you wouldn't use so much make-up, Mary!'

How hateful husbands are when they make remarks like that! thought Mary. And then John made it worse by adding, "Look at Hilda—she hardly makes up at all—and she's got a lovely complexion."

"Well, she doesn't have wretched spots to cover up as I do!" snapped Mary.

"But make-up doesn't hide them!" said John, with the devastating frankness of husbands.

Mary felt furious, but John's criticism went home. And a few days later, when she met Hilda, she put her pride in her pocket and said:

"My dear, John's been admiring your complexion. Do tell me what you do to keep it so beautiful."

"Well," said Hilda smiling, "I put it down to taking Eno's 'Fruit Salt' every morning. A doctor once told me that self-neglect caused more ugliness than age and worry put together! I've always remembered it.

And I've taken Eno ever since."

How Mary blessed Hilda for that hint! For sure enough, when she began taking Eno, her blemishes gradually vanished. You see, inner cleanliness was what she lacked. And Eno was what she needed to purify her system. Now, day by day, Eno washes away all harmful poisons—sends pure, vigorous blood to feed her skin and keep it clear and fresh. How lovely she looks now! How fit she feels! There's never a word from John about too much make-up!

But what a lot of women are like Mary—trying to hide defects instead of getting rid of the cause of them! Take a refreshing glass of Eno every morning. Eno acts quite naturally. It forms no habit. Contains no harsh aperients to upset you. And it will give you the only perfect foundation for clever make-up—a clear, healthy skin.

Budget

The need for careful accounts was never more urgent than it is at present. " Good Housekeeping Diary and Household Account Book " will be found ideal for the purpose, as it enables the housewife to see at a glance how the money is going

BALANCING one's home budget is as much a controversial subject as balancing the national budget year by year. Details of expenditure are so much a personal question, and to some extent a matter of temperament, that even given the same income and similar circumstances no two individual householders would probably agree as to how it should be spent to the best advantage.

It is quite impracticable to lay down hard and fast rules for home budgeting; not only do tastes differ considerably, but the cost of commodities and services vary appreciably in different parts of the country, so that what, for example, would be an ample allowance for fuel in the vicinity of the coal pits would be far from sufficient where coal has to be transported some distance.

It is not suggested from these remarks that home budgeting should be dispensed with, but that each individual should work out a general if not a detailed plan of expected expenditure during the coming year, remembering to allow a reasonable margin for unexpected contingencies. Conditions may, of course, make it necessary to modify this during the year, but in most cases the basis of the scheme will remain.

While everyone is hoping that the coming year will show an improvement as regards finance and matters generally, the majority of people in the country are faced to a greater or lesser extent with increased taxation, and many also

with a reduced incom conditions bound involve a certai amount of hardshi It is not general realised that th year's prices compa very favourably wi those of a year or tv back. Although by means stabilised at t time of writing, t cost of living ind figure published September 1st, 193 shows a reduction 12 per cent. compar with the same mon in 1930. Still, there no doubt that in t forthcoming mont it will be found nece sary to make adju ments to meet ne living standards, a in order that the may be wisely ma the past year's e penditure should carefully reviewed that any cuts nece sary may be made to the best advantag This need not entail the keeping of ve elaborate account books, an almost ir possible ideal for many people wl possess neither the time nor the i clination for detailed book-keeping. is for such people that the *Good Hous keeping Diary and Account Book* h been devised, for the main items household expenditure are arrang under headings, and the amounts spe day by day and week by week can quickly and easily entered in the corre spaces.

Economies being the order of the da possible means whereby they may effected will be considered first. It obvious that unless drastic retrenchme is demanded luxuries or semi-luxuri

By P. L. Garbutt, A.I.C.

*First Class Diploma King's College
of Household and Social Science;
late Staff, Battersea Polytechnic*

The
1930's
1931

ing the Income

*Readers who have had to readjust
their income during the last few
months will find this article particularly helpful to meet 1932 expenses*

...ust bear the brunt of
...his. It may be that the
...ost of upkeep of the
...ar is running away with
... larger proportion of the
...ncome than it should, or
...ossibly subscriptions to
...port or social clubs will
...e the expenses upon
...hich the "axe" must
...all. It may be neces-
...ary for entertaining to
...e on a simpler scale, or
...isits to the theatre or
...icture house either made
...ss frequently or less
...xpensive seats taken.
...conomies of this de-
...cription may not be
...ltogether agreeable in
...rospect, but reductions
...f standing expenses
...uch as rent, rates, edu-
...ation, etc., are much
...ore difficult to bring
...bout, and are often un-
...ise for what may be only a more or
...ss temporary "tightening up."

...Reduction of expenditure on food
...elow a certain point, provided there is
...o waste and only simple meals are
...erved, is also an unwise economy, for
...here can be no doubt that the health
...f the entire family depends to a tre-
...endous extent on a liberal and varied
...iet, including in particular plenty of
...airy produce and fresh fruit and
...egetables. It is impossible to give any
...ard and fast rule as to what consti-
...tes a fair food allowance, for much
...epends on the size of the family, larger
...umbers being catered for relatively
...ore economically, the type of meal
...rved, the amount of entertaining, and
...hether any considerable amount of
...uit and vegetable produce is grown
... the garden. In a middle-class house-
...ld from 12s. 6d. to £1 per head per
...eek should be sufficient to provide
... adequate diet, greater variety and

How are *You* Economising?

*In order to stimulate interest among readers
who are having to give careful thought to
the business of ways and means, the Editor
has decided to run an Economy Competition.*

A Cheque for £10

*will be awarded to the sender of the best letter
of not more than a thousand words on the subject
"How I am economising." Several other money
prizes will be awarded for the next best letters.
Full details of prizes and entry will be found*

On page 188

interest being of course available for
the larger sum.

At the time of writing this article an
endeavour was made to gain some idea
of the comparative costs of food at the
present time and a year or two back.
The index figures published by the
Ministry of Labour month by month
give some indication of this, those for
food on September 1st, 1930 and 1931,
being 44 per cent. and 28 per cent. re-
spectively, in excess of that in August
1914, the last being 16 per cent. less
than that of a year previously. This
figure is based on the basic foods such
as beef, mutton, bacon, fish, flour, bread,
potatoes, tea, sugar, milk, butter, margarine, cheese and eggs. These appear regularly in the menu, and it has
been calculated that normally they account for about three-quarters of the
average working class expenditure on
food. Every housewife realises that
this figure applied with modifications to

the middle-class budget,
indicates very clearly
that food prices in
general are considerably
less than they were even
a year or two ago.

Economists have from
time to time endeavoured
to state the proportion
of the income which
should be spent on food,
but obviously it is pos-
sible only to give a representative figure applicable
to a few incomes within
a limited range. Thus, a
l a r g e r proportion is
necessarily spent on all
essentials including food
when the income is small
than when it is larger
and more elastic. It has,
however, been calculated
by Professor Mottram—
a world authority on
m a t t e r s of diet—
that it is possible at the average
prices prevailing for food this year to
provide an adequate, although necessarily a very simple diet for one shilling
per head per day.

It is impossible to predict in detail
how housekeeping prices will be affected
by recent political events, but it seems
clear that food will be no cheaper, if it
does not become actually dearer. It would
therefore probably still be true to say
that should expenditure fall beneath the
daily sum of about one shilling it is
doubtful whether a healthful diet can
be supplied unless there are compensat-
ing factors such as a plentiful supply
of garden produce at little or no cost
to the housekeeping purse.

Insurance and saving are other items
of the home budget which most people
will very wisely hesitate to raid, while
medical and dental expenses are as a
rule largely beyond control, although
if a more or (*Continued on page* 124)

The 1930's

1931

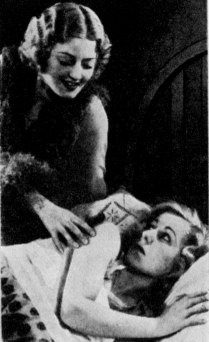

WHO ARE THE GIRLS WHO MARRY?

Wake Up, You Girls, and Realise the Priceless Secret Of Happy Matrimony

Beauty alone will lure few men to the altar. The sterner sex is interested in the physically-fit woman rather than the pretty-pretty girl. Nice features must always be accompanied by vivaciousness, vitality, and personality. The greatest of these is the vitality born of rich red blood coursing through the veins, which is the real giver of the bloom of youth. By taking Bile Beans at bedtime you can acquire a clear, soft complexion, sweet breath, and sparkling health.

These nice oval pills—so easy to swallow—perform the valuable service of gently clearing out of the system those bodily impurities which are the root cause of feminine unattractiveness.

If food-waste is allowed to remain in the body, toxins or poisons are given off, passed into the blood, thereby producing bad complexion, facial blemishes, halitosis, and a generally lowered vitality. Start taking Bile Beans to-night and they will give you new buoyant health which will increase your personal attractiveness.

The Bile Bean girl is the girl who is clean and healthy inside, and with her vivacity she has the world at her feet. She's the girl who has the looks and the sweet temper with which to win and keep the best husband.

Adornments for the Evening

Approximate Prices of Beads, Leaves, and Flowers

Autumn Glory

Flat Cedar Flowers	.	8d. doz.
Small Cedar Flowers	.	5d. „
Large Leaves	. .	1½d. each
Small Leaves	. .	9d. doz.
Wire	. . .	3d. coil

Moonlight

Blue Bells	. . .	8d. doz.
Blue Berry Beads	. ..	4d. „
Blue Leaves	. .	9d. „
Blue Fairy Flowers	.	4d. „
Wire	. . .	3d. coil

Magpie

Crystal Leaves	.	4d. doz.
Black Berry Beads	.	4d. „
Crystal Beads	.	6d. „
Crystal Fairy Flowers	.	4d. „

Beads for the centres of flowers 4d. per bunch.

The above materials can be bought at most large bead shops or stores, or can be supplied through an address which we will be pleased to give on application. Complete materials can be supplied at an inclusive charge of 6s. 6d. each for " Autumn Glory " and " Moonlight," 4s. 6d. for " Magpie," and 2s. each for brooches.

Budgeting the Income

(*Continued from page* 123)

less definite sum is allowed yearly anything unspent should be put aside to accumulate so that it is available for what may be termed " a rainy year."

In addition to the cuts on more or less luxury expenses, a certain amount of reduction can often be made with little inconvenience on dress as well as other personal expenditure. Other economies may be managed merely by being a little strict with oneself regarding small, often more or less, unconsidered purchases. If accounts be kept of these it will be very apparent that they are often responsible for a much larger annual sum than would have been believed possible.

The price of clothing is on the whole considerably less than it was a year or two ago. Enquiry of the merchandise manager of a leading store in London indicated that in the case of articles where the cost of production is made up largely of raw materials such as cotton, wool, etc., the prices show a fairly considerable decline. On the other hand, where there is much workmanship and therefore cost of labour to be covered in a particular article, prices have not been reduced to the same extent, wages not having fallen. A few instances will suffice to illustrate this point. Thus, as regards dress materials, the price of similar quality crêpe de Chine sold at 8s. 11d. per yard not more than a year ago has been reduced in the particular store referred to, to 6s. 11d. per yard, while marocain, previously selling at 12s. 9d., is now priced at 6s. 9d. Wool stockinette, previously 6s. 11d., is 4s. 11d., or silk stockings which a few months ago were 8s. 11d., are now 6s. 11d., 4s. 11d. chiffon lisle stockings being 2s. 11d. The number of instances that could be given are innumerable, but the above are typical, and will probably suffice to show quite clearly that prices have been very appreciably reduced.

In addition to the reduction of personal expenditure, which the above figures indicate, much can also be done by careful supervision of the household and the maids in particular. While many modern maids are doubtless incompetent, there are still others who are efficient workers, and who would gladly co-operate with their mistress in reducing unnecessary waste if the real need for this is pointed out to them. Switching off electric light or gas in unused rooms, turning off gas cooking burners when not required and having them so adjusted that the flames do not lick the sides of the pans, avoidance of banking up the fire last thing at night unless it is of the slow-combustion type, and is to be kept in until morning, avoidance of waste of food, possibly arranging to undertake some of the laundry work at home, all these are

means whereby household expenses can be cut down so as to cause little or no inconvenience.

Those who are interested in the budgeting of moderate incomes ranging from £400 to £700 will probably be glad to know that suggestions for apportioning these in households consisting of two adults and also of two adults and two children are given in *Good Housekeeping Diary and Account Book,* of which details are printed on a later page.

Not long ago, as a result of a broadcast on Home Budgeting, listeners were invited to contribute details of their annual expenditure. Although most of the budgets sent in related to working-class households, middle-class householders were also represented.

Analysis of these budgets and also of those sent in by readers of GOOD HOUSE-KEEPING MAGAZINE from time to time is of great interest, and reveals very clearly how diverse are the conditions and views of expenditure held by different people. A few specimen budgets illustrating this point are given below:

Research Chemist (4 in family, including one child of school age and one grown-up daughter).

Earned Income of £500	£
Income tax (old rate) . . .	1?
Rent, property tax and rates . .	8?
Household expenses, including food, wages, laundry, light and fuel .	21?
Education	1?
Clothing, personal allowances and charity	9?
Holidays, amusements . . .	3?
Insurance, saving	3?
Incidental expenses, including doctor and dentist, etc. . . .	2?
	£50?

Electrical Engineer (5 in family; 3 children—2 of school age).

Earned Income of £410	£
Income tax (old rate) . . .	—
Rent, property tax, rates . . .	8?
Household expenses, including food, wages, laundry, light and fuel .	15?
Education	3?
Clothing, personal allowances and charity	6?
Holidays, amusements, or upkeep of car	3?
Insurance, saving	3?
Incidental expenses, including doctor and dentist, etc.	1?
	£41?

Budgeting the Income

Four in household, 2 adults and 2 children (15 and 10 years of age).

Earned Income of £550

	£
Income tax (old rate) . . .	12
Rates and income tax on house . .	35
Household expenses, including food, wages, laundry, light and fuel .	186
Education	112
Clothing, personal allowances, charity	70
Holidays, amusements, or car . .	40
Insurance, saving	60
Incidental expenses, including doctor and dentist, etc.	35
	£550

Business Man (2 adults and 2 grown-up daughters; 1 at college. One maid kept).

Earned Income of £1,000

	£
Income tax (old rate) . . .	106
Rates and property tax . . .	120
Household expenses, to include food, wages, laundry, light and fuel .	326
Education	100
Clothing, personal allowances, charity	170
Holidays, amusements, and car . .	130
Insurance (saving unnecessary) .	25
Incidental expenses, to include doctor and dentist, etc. . . .	23
	£1,000

Unearned Income of £1,250
(2 adults and 2 maids kept)

	£
Income tax (old rate) . . .	199
Rent, property tax, rates . .	140
Household expenses, to include food, wages, laundry, light and fuel .	440
Education	—
Clothing, personal allowances, charity	180
Holidays, amusements, and car . .	170
Insurance, saving . . .	100
Incidental expenses, to include doctor, dentist, etc.	21
	£1,250

All the above budgets could no doubt be criticised on one point or another, for one householder spends what appears an undue portion on education and another very little on this item, and so on. It would, however, be hard to find an individual budget more open to criticism than that of a Dispensary Doctor in a country district with a total income of £315. Out of this, force of circumstances makes it imperative for him to spend as much as £100 per year on the upkeep of his car. This is obviously exceedingly high in proportion to the income, but as he points out, it is accounted for by the very bad state of the roads, involving much expense in tyre renewal as well as other spare parts. Further, it is necessary to put something aside each year towards the purchase of a new car. Against this excessive expenditure, his rent on the other hand is particularly low, the yearly outlay being covered by £15.

While the variations demanded from any standard budget may be comparatively large because of exceptional circumstances or individual ideas, all that finally matters is that " both ends should meet," and preferably show a balance. The means whereby this is accomplished are not of such material importance provided due attention has been paid to ensure the provisions of all essentials to the health and well-being of the household, including, in particular, a well-balanced, adequate diet.

It is hoped that all our readers—men and women—will enter for the competition announced in this issue and write to us about the ways in which they are effecting economies at the present time. The information collected will be of interest and assistance to a great number of people when published later in the magazine and the incentive of money prizes adds a spice of excitement to an occupation which, if not very pleasant in subject, is at least pleasant to do! The closing date for letters intended for the competition is December 31st.

Enter to-day for our
GRAND CHRISTMAS ECONOMY COMPETITION

Write a letter to the Editor (not more than 1,000 words) about the ways you are economising to meet increased prices and taxation. The form and topics of your letter are in no way restricted, but each entry should be accompanied by the form below correctly filled in, and must be received at 153 Queen Victoria Street, E.C.4, by December 1st, 1931. Mark your envelope " Economy Competition." No letters can be returned or correspondence entered into and the Editor's decision is final. Prizes will be awarded as follows:

First Prize: £10
Two Second Prizes: £5 each
For each letter published in full: £2

The result of the competition, with the winning letters, will be published in the March number.

ECONOMY COMPETITION

Mr.
Mrs. }...
Miss
Address ....
....
....

To the Editor: Good Housekeeping, 153 Queen Victoria Street, London, E.C.4

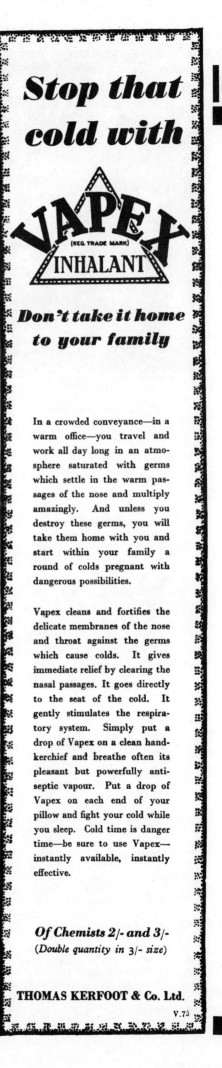

" Incongruously . . . an old, grey country church."

Illustrations by Robin Tanner

To all who know or dream of the glamour of London we commend this finely etched word picture of London River, first in a gallery of scenes made vividly alive by the brilliant pen of

VIRGINIA WOOLF

"WHITHER, O splendid ship," the poet asked as he lay on the shore and watched the great sailing ship pass away on the horizon. Perhaps, as he imagined, it was making for some port in the Pacific; but one day almost certainly it must have heard an irresistible call and come past the North Foreland and the Reculvers, and entered the narrow waters of the Port of London, sailed past the low banks of Gravesend and Northfleet and Tilbury, up Erith Reach and Barking Reach and Gallion's Reach, past the gas works and the sewage works till it found, for all the world like a car on a parking ground, a space reserved for it in the deep waters of the Docks. There it furled its sails and dropped anchor.

However romantic and free and fitful they may seem, there is scarcely a ship on the seas that does not come to anchor in the Port of London in time. From a launch in midstream one can see them swimming up the river with all the marks of their voyage still on them. Liners come, high-decked, with their galleries and their awnings and their passengers grasping their bags and leaning over the rail, while the lascars tumble and scurry below—home they come, a thousand of these big ships every week of the year to anchor in the docks of London. They take their way

" Greenwich Hospital . . . comes down in perfect symmetry to the water's edge."

majestically through a crowd of tramp steamers, and colliers and barges heaped with coal and swaying red sailed boats, which, amateurish though they look, are bringing bricks from Harwich or cement from Colchester—for all is business; there are no pleasure boats on this river. Drawn by some irresistible current, they come from the storms and calms of the sea, its silence and loneliness to their allotted anchorage. The engines stop; the sails are furled; and suddenly the gaudy funnels and the tall masts show up incongruously against a row of workmen's houses, against the black walls of huge warehouses. A curious change takes place. They have no longer the proper perspective of sea and sky behind them, and no longer the proper space in which to stretch their limbs. They lie captive, like soaring and winged creatures who

have got themselves caught by the leg and lie tethered on dry land.

With the sea blowing its salt into our nostrils, nothing can be more stimulating than to watch the ships coming up the Thames—the big ships and the little ships, the battered and the splendid ships from India, from Russia, from South America, ships from Australia coming from silence and danger and loneliness past us, home to harbour. But once they drop anchor, once the cranes begin their dipping and their swinging, it seems as if all romance were over. If we turn and go past the anchored ships towards London, we see surely the most dismal prospect in the world. The banks of the river are lined with dingy, decrepit-looking warehouses. They huddle on land that has become flat and slimy mud. The same air of decrepitude and of being run u

"There is scarcely a ship on the seas that does not come to anchor in the Port of London in time."

The Docks of LONDON

provisionally stamps them all. If a window is broken, broken it remains. A fire that has lately blackened and blistered one of them seems to have left it no more forlorn and joyless than its neighbours. Behind the masts and funnels lies a sinister dwarf city of workmen's houses. In the foreground cranes and warehouses, scaffolding and gasometers line the banks with a skeleton architecture.

When, suddenly, after acres and acres of this desolation one floats past an old stone house standing in a real field, with real trees growing in clumps, the sight is disconcerting. Can it be possible that there is earth, that there once were fields and crops beneath this desolation and disorder? Trees and fields seem to survive incongruously like a sample of another civilisation among the wall-paper factories and soap factories that have stamped out old lawns and terraces. Still more incongruously one passes an old grey country church which still rings its bells, and keeps its churchyard green as if country people were still coming across the fields to service. Further down, an inn with swelling bow windows still wears a strange air of dissipation and pleasure making. In the middle years of the nineteenth century it was a favourite resort of pleasure makers, and figured in some of the most famous divorce cases of the time. Now pleasure has gone and

labour has come; and it stands derelict like some beauty in her midnight finery looking out over mud flats and candle works, while malodorous mounds of earth, upon which trucks are perpetually tipping fresh heaps, have entirely consumed the fields where, a hundred years ago, lovers wandered and picked violets.

As we go on steaming up the river to London we meet its refuse coming down. Barges heaped with old buckets, razor blades, fish tails, newspapers and ashes—whatever we leave on our plates

"Barrels of wine . . . laid on their sides in cool vaults."

and throw into our dust bins—are discharging their cargoes upon the most desolate land in the world. The long mounds have been fuming and smoking and harbouring innumerable rats and growing a rank coarse grass and giving off a gritty, acrid air for fifty years. The dumps get higher and higher, and thicker and thicker, their sides more precipitous with tin cans, their pinnacles more angular with ashes year by year. But then, past all this sordidity, sweeps indifferently a great liner, bound for India. She takes her way through rubbish barges, and sewage barges, and dredgers out to sea: A little further, on the left hand, we are suddenly surprised—the sight upsets all our proportions once more—by what appear to be the stateliest buildings ever raised by the hand of man. Greenwich Hospital with all its columns and domes comes down in perfect symmetry to the water's edge, and makes the river again a stately waterway where the nobility of England once walked at their ease on green lawns, or descended stone steps to their pleasure barges. As we come closer to the Tower Bridge the authority of the city begins to assert itself. The buildings thicken and heap themselves higher. The sky seems laden with heavier, purpler clouds. Domes swell; church spires, white with age, mingle with the tapering, pencil-shaped chimneys of factories.

Do you use
to full

By

N. L. Gall

An example of the new hand combination
set. This model, in ivory, is designed for
use in provincial districts, where it is
only necessary to dial the number

Alexander Graham Bell, the inventor
of the telephone. An interesting point
about this photograph is the fact that
the original was transmitted from San
Francisco to New York (3,305 miles) over
a telephone wire in under eight minutes

IF everyone studied the intro-
ductory pages of the telephone
directory, much of this article
would have no excuse for having
been written.

But who studies these pages? Who
knows, among many other and more important things, that he or she, like the
telephone operator, is requested as a
"useful precaution" against being misunderstood, to say " fife " and not five,
or that for the same excellent reason a
short pause should be made between the
hundreds and tens when asking for a
number? These particular remarks
apply, of course, to the users of the
manual telephone and not to those of
the automatic system which is gradually
superseding it.

The preface to the telephone directory
is a veritable mine of useful information. It should be studied by the competent telephone user in much the same
manner as the competent cook studies
her book of recipes, knowing full well
that neither can obtain the best results
for her efforts by mere guesswork, and
that without such study much will be
left undone through lack of knowledge.

The telephone system is now a
colossal organisation and, at the time
of writing, plans are being made for
a huge advertising campaign still
further to increase its popularity.

Its present magnitude may be grasped
to some extent by the fact that there
are 2,000,000 telephones in this country
and 34,000,000 all over the world.

There are more than 4,760 telephone
exchanges in this country, 1,252,000
miles of overhead wire and 7,587,000
miles of underground wire. Approximately 33,350 call offices and
kiosks are also in existence.

In London the cost of the telephone is 2s. 6d. per week, in Manchester, Liverpool, Birmingham and
Glasgow 2s. 4d. per week, and in all
other places 2s. 1½d. Business
premises have an additional charge
made of 7s. 6d. per quarter. Local
calls cost one penny each, others
according to distance, and the time
at which the call is made.

Reduced charges are in force for
distance calls between 2 p.m. and
7 p.m., while between 7 p.m. and
7 a.m. the charge for a three-minute
call is generally half that for the morning period.

There is perhaps no public service
more consistently criticised than this of
the telephone, but, as the opening words
of that excellent preface are careful to
tell you, " There are three parties
to a telephone call: yourself, the exchange, the distant subscriber "; is it
not possible that blame for faulty operation should sometimes attach itself to
any one of the parties mentioned, and
not invariably and of indisputable
necessity to one only?

It must not be thought that these or
any following remarks are an attempt
to whitewash the Post Office in connection with its telephone service, or are

sponsored by instigators of a " telephon
more " or any similar campaign. The
are merely intended to remind the sub
scriber of the ways in which he ca
assist efficient service, and obtain th
full facilities available.

Much of the annoyance felt toward
the telephone service by the manu
telephone user is caused by " wron
numbers " both received and give
There can be no doubt that this diff
culty would be overcome to a larg
extent if each subscriber were mo
careful to give the number required i
the right way, i.e. to give figures whic
are liable to become blurred or mistake
for others the pronunciation recom
mended by the Post Office and

the *TELEPHONE* advantage ?

Many subscribers may not be aware of all the facilities that the telephone service offers and will be glad to have the points in this article brought to their notice

A telephone table designed to fit over the arm of a chair enables dial telephoning to be accomplished in comfort

A general view of one of the newest automatic exchanges : these eliminate the use of telephone operators as an electric current finds the number

divided burr-burr of the " ringing tone," when the number required is being rung. These tones are again entirely different from the buzzing noises which indicate that the number is engaged or unobtainable.

The actual dialling requires nothing beyond a little practice to obtain speed, and the knowledge that the first three letters only of the exchange required (which are printed in heavy type in the directory) must be dialled, followed by the numerals.

Full instructions on these and all other points connected with the automatic telephone are given in the directory preface, and if carefully followed little or no trouble should be experienced.

It is very doubtful if all telephone users are aware of the extent to which they can employ their telephone. The personal call service is one of the most recent facilities. It enables a trunk, toll or international call to be booked to a specified person or his substitute, or if preferred two numbers may be given, at either of which the person desired may be found. Such personal calls are only connected when the person to whom it is desired to speak (or his specified substitute) is obtained. The extra charge for this service is from *1s.* to *2s.*, according to distance, from 7 a.m. to 2 p.m.; and *6d.*, regardless of distance, between 2 p.m. and 7 a.m.

separate the hundreds and tens as already mentioned. The word " double " —that bane of so many telephone users— should be employed when the double figure comes before or after the dividing pause, and not when it occurs in the middle of the number, *i.e.* 6662 should be referred to as double six, six two; not six double six two.

When trouble is experienced in making any particular word clear the various letters or any one of them can be readily understood by such analogy as G for George, U for uncle, etc. These simple methods will often avoid misunderstanding or irritation through delay caused by wrong numbers. Time should also invariably be saved if that

most popular of all answers to the telephone bell, " Hullo," were dropped in favour of the name of the subscriber or business house concerned.

The coming of the automatic system seems to be unnecessarily dreaded by many telephone users. Their particular fear appears to be that they will not be able to distinguish the various audible signals called " tones," which are used in place of the information previously given by the exchange operator. There is, however, nothing formidable or confusing about these tones once they are heard and remembered. The continuous burr-rr-rr of the " dialling tone," indicating that dialling may be commenced, is quite distinct from the

Which do you like best—cat or dog? The majority

Sketches by
J. H. Dowd

I'd rather

by

I HAVE often wondered why so many people invariably refer to a cat as "she." Perhaps because, like a woman, a cat is so frequently misunderstood. To begin with, our name for the strange, graceful little creature who honours our households with his (or her!) presence can only be justified as a convenient label, for the so-called domestic cat is not really domesticated at all. Puss accepts the comforts of a human household simply because it suits him to do so, but he is quite capable of reverting to type.

Turn a cat loose in the woods and he can fend for himself as readily as his primitive ancestors. He retains nearly all the racial instincts and characteristics which preserve his species. His scrupulous cleanliness, for example, especially after eating, is almost certainly due to an instinctive impulse to remove from his mouth, paws and fur all traces of his meal, so that he in turn shall not be tracked to his lair and devoured by some more powerful inhabitant of the jungle.

The cat is unique in the preservation of his independence after three thousand years of association with mankind. Yet, curiously enough, puss has become a symbol of home. A tramp once told me he avoided any house if he heard a dog bark, but he was pretty sure of hospitality if greeted by a cat sunning himself on the doorstep. What budding Royal Academician would paint a cottage fireside without a cat coiled asleep beside it? An ironic destiny for the cat, to whom independence is sacred and frequent solitude a pleasure!

It is a tribute to the cat's pertinacity and charm that his place is secure under the family roof. There are people, it is true, who keep cats to catch mice, but for the majority of us that useful habit is merely a sideline for use in emergencies, if our cat will condescend when required. Shakespeare summed up the average Englishman's attitude when he wrote "the harmless, necessary cat." What ignorance lies beneath that casual dismissal!

For a long time, indeed, cats were decidedly unpopular in this country. The mediæval association of cats with witches and sorcery still lingers in nursery tales and folklore. Some people, who mistrust on principle what they do not understand, are emphatic in their dislike of the cat. (I do not mean genuine ælurophobes, who are relatively few.) It must be admitted that the cat makes no effort to win popularity. Canine flattery is contemptible to him. Sometimes I tease my favourite cat by offering sweets to my wife's wirehaired terrier, Peter. Now Peter has a sweet tooth and will go into slobbery ecstasies at the rustling of a paper bag. So I toss him a chocolate now and then just for the fun of watching my cat's supercilious and disdainful expression. Nor can cats generally be credited with a companionable nature. Many of my cats (I have had over a hundred in my time) have been waywardly affectionate, but I have never known a cat who could be relied upon to display affection when required. On the contrary cats are amusingly perverse in their indifference to human blandishments and in their deliberate preference for people who have no use for them. Beyond all doubt cats have their own sense of humour.

It is not surprising that so self-contained, perverse, often unsociable a creature should not be widely popular. Yet there are many indications that the cat is becoming fashionable. The legend of the cat's wit and resource has been revived no doubt by the immortal Felix. Cat shows and clubs are multiplying in number all over the country; every day newspaper space is given to photographs of cats and news items about cats, famous and otherwise. Above all, the decorative value of the cat is appreciated as never before. There is perhaps something which appeals to a civilised society in the barbaric grace and exquisite poise which is the heritage of all cats.

This revival of interest in the cat will doubtless leave him as unperturbed as ever, but to the true cat lover it is a little disturbing. How many people know anything of the animal they profess to admire? Already there must be thousands of kind and worthy people who habitually ill-treat their cats because they know no better.

of people seem to prefer dogs but here's someone who says

have a CAT

MICHAEL JOSEPH

Because the cat is singularly clever in looking after himself it is often thought that he needs no attention beyond a regular saucer of milk and an occasional caress. The truth is that the cat is an exceptionally sensitive animal, and will respond only to sympathetic understanding of his requirements, which, although simple, are important. Milk is not a substitute for fresh water; and, while cats vary extraordinarily in their food preferences, all of them need variety in their diet and cannot eat in comfort unless their food is fresh and clean. Even a hungry cat will reject stale food and I have known many cats who refuse to eat from a dirty plate. Fastidious? Yes, but the cat is fastidious by nature.

No one who has had any experience of cats would attempt to fix a diet to suit these creatures of such individual palates; and only for the guidance of others would I suggest that some cats at any rate flourish on raw meat or fresh fish (bones removed) once a day, milk, vegetables, dry, plain biscuit or biscuit soaked in broth, liver (lightly boiled) occasionally, and of course plenty of fresh water. Cats eat extraordinary things: olives, beetroot, cucumber, cheese, fruit, asparagus—such are the eccentric appetites of their kind.

Although the question of food is important, cats usually manage to survive by the simple process of refusing what they do not want (and cats are far wiser than human beings in knowing what is not good for them) and by obtaining somehow or other what they need for sustenance and the satisfaction of their palates.

Which brings me to a common accusation against cats. Most cats steal food when they can. To a cat good food is obviously meant to be taken if the opportunity comes his way and it is absurd to expect a cat to conform to human standards of morality. Dogs learn to obey, perhaps not because they are intelligent, as is commonly supposed, but because they are capable of obedience. In the same way a dog will readily perform tricks, fetch and carry, and follow at his master's heels. The cat applies his intelligence to his own uses and cannot be persuaded or coerced into performing—to him—senseless antics for the gratification of his owner.

To treat a cat as one would a dog is entirely unreasonable. They have nothing in common beyond four legs and a tail and a liking for a warm, cosy resting-place. We humans must seem queer, irresponsible, prejudiced beings in the eyes of a cat. Cats know instinctively how to keep themselves clean and in perfect health; they are not greedy, or untidy, or noisy (except on auspicious, nocturnal occasions!); they understand the secret of relaxation; they will defend themselves fiercely—usually with success—against the attacks of dogs three times their size and weight; and they go serenely on their own way, neither causing nor inviting interference.

Yet people will persist in shouting at cats, trying to reason with cats (who, from choice, I suspect, understand no language but their own) and hurting their sensitive bodies by rough handling. Few people know how to pick up a cat; it should be done with care, not by the nape of the neck, but by placing one hand under the forelegs, at the same time raising the hind legs with the other hand, so that the weight of the body is evenly supported. The most sensitive parts of a cat are his whiskers, and his tail, which is connected to the brain and consequently should never be pulled. The only cat I have ever had who plainly enjoys a rough-and-tumble is my Siamese, but Siamese are notably different from other cats in many ways, being almost like dogs in their loyalty, clumsiness and good spirits.

To my mind the cat is well worth the attention and understanding which are necessary if one is to gain his respect. There is no more restful companion (when he is in the mood) and none more graceful or intelligent. A cat does not bestow his friendship lightly, but it is a friendship well worth having.

J.H.D.

Why are we

IN a way, I'm rather frightened of writing this article; frightened to think what may emerge in the course of it. Fears only half sensed before, will stare at me in cold reality from the page, ghosts will point accusing, reproachful fingers. And yet, perversely, I am glad to be given the opportunity of writing it. For I can say so much that I have wanted to say, but have never been allowed to because of the conventional attitude towards youth as being always gay and carefree and optimistic, and to the young men who write as always gay and carefree and optimistic too.

Most of us, of course, have to be, although there are exceptions. Two of them were the subject of a recent article written by Mr. St. John Ervine in this magazine. I refer to Noel Coward and Beverley Nichols. They are in the lucky position of being able to write always only what they want to write and what they really feel and in consequence, as Mr. St. John Ervine remarked in his article, their work is suffused with despair and despondency and disillusionment.

At this he expressed—at first—extreme surprise. Have not these two young men, he asked, everything to make them happy? Success and wealth, good looks and health and popularity. Why, therefore, do they despair? But looking deeper he found a reason, a very good reason. He recalled how these two young men belong to the generation that was still only children in 1914. The years of their adolescence, those sensitive, acutely perceptive years, when the nerves lie too close to the surface and strange emotions harry and torment one, were spent in an atmosphere of acute strain, a horrible, unnatural, topsy-turvy atmosphere, when tears and laughter followed each other with a bewildering rapidity and conversation universally smacked of death.

It is not surprising, therefore, that the unceasing horror of those years should have been so impressed upon our minds and so engraved upon our hearts as to colour and depress our lives ever since. And it is thus that Mr. Ervine accounts for our present condition. Nor will anyone deny that he is right in his hypothesis, *as far as it goes*, but I cannot help feeling that it does not go nearly far enough. One must dig deeper, if one wishes to realise to the full the tragic position in which my generation finds itself to-day.

It seems to me that it is not so much our memories and even experiences of the war itself that cause us to adopt so gloomy an attitude towards life, as the realities of the aftermath, the terrible happenings, the bitter circumstances of this post-war

Photo: Tanqueray

era. Cradled in one world, a world of peace and plen[ty] ease and security and happiness, we have grown up [in] another, a world of stress and torment, poverty a[nd] transition and disillusionment, a world, moreover, f[or] which we find ourselves suddenly, unexpectedly held [re]sponsible.

It is that responsibility that brings us so often ne[ar] to despair; that responsibility that makes us pessimi[sts] instead of optimists, old men almost before we have be[en] young. "They died that you might live. Carry on. . .

Failing
the Dead?

The CRY of

the

younger generation

—of those

who were children

in the days of

the "War to end War"

echoed despairingly

in his

twenty-fifth

year

By

GODFREY
WINN

Author of " The
Unequal Conflict "
Etc.

us and delay indefinitely our return to prosperity, perhaps they would not have gone so cheerfully to their death; perhaps they would not have been so willing to believe that their incredible sacrifice was to make the world a better and a happier and a safer place in the future.

Doubtless in their hearts they carried a picture of post-war England that was identical in every respect with their own memories of the prosperous, contented state of things in being in August 1914. Once the enemy were finally routed, the order given to "Cease Fire," it would start all over again exactly and absolutely the same. They would return, those who were left of them, to their work and their play, their homes and their clubs and their golf links, they would catch the same train every morning and go to the same place for their annual holiday, and smoke the same brand of cigar and send their sons to the same public school as themselves. In short, they would pick up the threads of their own life, in a moment at peace again in their former prosperity and security.

There is no need for me to expatiate upon the tragic disillusionment that followed their return. You know as well as I do what they felt, are still feeling, as the months lengthened into years, and so far from things improving, the situation went from bad to worse.

There is nothing that I can say that

has not already been said about the tragedy of the war generation and I only draw attention to it again in this article, because that tragedy is so closely linked up with that of my own generation. How closely, or even what our tragedy is exactly, I do not think the majority of people realise—for the simple reason that my generation are not very good, for the most part, in giving expression to feelings. We wear masks to the world, and in regard to our emotions, our deep and instinctive emotions, we either maintain a cold and secretive silence or else we cover them up with layer upon layer of insincere, unreal talk.

In consequence, you think that we are hard and casual and ungrateful. You think that we spend our nights—and often our days, too—in a round of idle amusement—*Dance, Dance, Little Lady* . . . —because we like doing so, because that is the only kind of life that we really enjoy. It isn't. I promise you, it isn't. We only do it, because the constant repetition, the unceasing physical activity drowns our thoughts, deadens, for the moment, the prickings of our conscience, lifts from our shoulders the weight of despair.

"But why does despair possess you?" I hear someone protesting. "You are young and strong, life is still before you, there is plenty of time for you to build up a new world on the ashes of the old." I know. I thought that, too, once. Ten years ago, five even, I used to remind myself with a sense of tingling pride that here was my opportunity to prove to the dead and those survivors of the war who were left by it either physically maimed or mentally crippled, that the sacrifice that they had made on our behalf had not been made in vain. Together with the rest of my generation, I would dedicate my life to reconstruction.

And honestly we have tried to do so. That we seem to have failed is surely not our fault, but rather the fault of the present economic situation that stultifies

(Continued on page 134)

s, but as they died, flinging from ir nerveless grasp the torch that we re to bear aloft henceforth in their ad, they did not realise (how could y realise?) what a difference, what ulf, there was destined to be between ir England of 1914 and ours of day. Had they been able to forsee changes that would occur, the series economic crises that were to cripple

Reduce your kitchen fuel bill to £1 per quarter with an

AGA COOKER

(Registered Trade Mark)

More labour-saving

than gas . . . . as clean

as electricity—

Independent of both

Independent of Gas and Electricity. Burns small coke or anthracite. Two large ovens (one roasting, one slow). Two Hot-Plates (one boiling, one simmering). Dimensions : 3 ft. 3 in. wide, 2 ft. 4 in. deep, 2 ft. 10 in. high. Ten-gallon hot-water tank. Draught controlled by thermostat. Automatic fuel filler. Fixed fuel consumption. Insulated throughout with Bell's Asbestos in such a way as to keep the kitchen comfortably warm—no more.

The All-British Aga, made in England, now shows many distinct improvements, such as better enamel finish, Chromium Plated exterior metal parts, etc.

Your Aga Cooker can be installed for a first payment of £5 : 10 : 0.

PETER has ordered an Aga Cooker. Peter is " in the City " and has worked out that by cutting his fuel bill from £6 a quarter to £1, the Aga will pay him about 26 per cent. ! There is the added advantage of knowing exactly what cooking will cost him—for the fuel consumption of the Aga is constant —25 cwt. of coke or anthracite a year. Peter has investigated that claim and is satisfied that it is literally true. Why don't you ?

PATRICIA is looking forward to her Aga because Peter adores good cooking and she knows how well the Aga cooks. What's more, Cook was getting a bit grumpy. Pat took her to see the Aga and now she's all smiles. No wonder ! For the Aga will do all she wants it to more easily than any gas or electric stove—it is cool, clean and compact, and need be refilled only once and riddled only twice every 24 hours. Cook's an Aga "fan."

We would like to send you our 16-Page Fully-Illustrated Booklet. The Aga Cooker is really rather a wonderful invention—but in the compass of our advertisement it is impossible to tell you as much about it as you would probably like to know. Please address your card or letter to—

BELL'S HEAT APPLIANCES LTD.

(Associated with Bell's Asbestos and Engineering Supplies Ltd.)

85 BESTOBELL WORKS, SLOUGH, BUCKS

(Telephone : Slough 830)

London Office and Showrooms : 157, Queen Victoria St., E.C.4. (Tel. : Central 6281)

BRITISH MADE AND INSULATED WITH BELL'S ASBESTOS

Advertised Goods are Good Goods.

Why are we Failing the Dead ?

(Continued from page 133)

industry, blockades enterprise, minimises opportunity. Twice only since the war have we been able to prove our ability to "carry on." Once in 1926 when the general strike gave us the chance of showing that we were not the degenerate weaklings our critics called us ; again more recently in the General Election, it was largely due to the enthusiastic support of the younger generation that the National Party were returned with such a sweeping majority. On both these occasions we proved that we were willing to work hard and work overtime, cheerfully and competently. We are still willing to do so, but in nine cases out of ten, the chance is lacking ; work, the right kind of work, does not come our way. In consequence, we cannot free our consciences from the reproach, either deserved or not, that we are failing the dead, and then despair creeps over us like a winter sea.

A great deal is written about the unemployment among the lower classes, while the prevalence of that evil among the middle and upper classes is completely ignored. There are hundreds of young men like myself who have had a good education and who before the war would have easily obtained for themselves positions of trust and responsibility : positions, that is to say, that would have given them the power to do good, creating and renewing, but who to-day are either completely idle, kicking their heels sullenly against the wall of depression, or else find themselves sitting on an office stool, earning a pittance, out of sympathy with their work, the slaves of a routine that is slowly but surely sapping their vitality and destroying their initiative. No wonder they despair, when they think of the future, wondering what is going to happen to them in the future, or look back upon the past, "the good old days," and compare it with their dreary present. No wonder that they seek relief in pleasure and still more pleasure. Do not blame them. Pity us rather that we have no prospects, no proper background, no real security.

I do not want to exaggerate, I do not want you to think that all my generation are poor, all slaves ; that, of course, is not true. I am free to do the work I want to do, and I earn enough to keep myself in moderate comfort. *But only myself.* That is to say, not a wife as well. And I want a wife. We all want wives and we cannot afford them. The income that our parents married on would scarcely pay our rent to-day. We daren't take the risk. The future is too unsettled. And so we drift from one love affair to another, obtaining no real happiness, no lasting satisfaction from any of them, chiefly because our parental instinct remains unfulfilled.

I have left this point to the last, because I think in a way it is almost the most important one I have to make. The generation who preceded us were practically without exception, at our age, already parents.

But that parental pride, which is probably the most satisfying of all emotions, that desire for parenthood, that instinct for perpetuating one's kind which is as natural as one's desire for food and drink and sleep, and as necessary, is denied us through no fault of ours. It is suppressed and bottled up, hidden away in the deep recesses of our heart. And because it looks as if it must remain there indefinitely, my generation are in despair. Do you understand now ?

The Big Idea..!

As modern luxury gains on us, chairs and settees seem to grow larger and larger and more and more visible. Choosing covers for them is rather like dress-designing for elephants. An over-bold pattern gives them the air of fat men in checks. A dull material turns them into huge nonentities. But how adroitly you can hit the happy medium with Sundour fabrics! The patterns neither shout too much nor have too little to say. The charming colours delight the eye, but never dazzle it. When you want new loose-covers for your chairs, you really must go and see the Sundour range. It's the shortest and most certain way to an artistic—and domestic triumph!

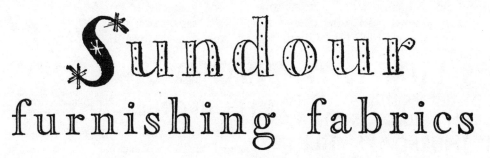

Sundour furnishing fabrics

USEFUL DRESSES
FOR THE MORNING

Designed by Caroline Gray

OUR IMPROVED PATTERN SERVICE
includes a detailed cutting chart and instructions for making up the garment with each pattern. The latter are hand-cut and very reliable. Of the four patterns this month N5 and N6 are in sizes 36–44, N7 and N8 sizes 34–42, rising 2 in. between each size. N5, N6, and N7 cost 1s. 6d. each post free. N8 is 1s. 3d. for the skirt, 1s. 3d. for the jumper-coat or 2s. inclusive (all post free). Send orders, with number, size, your name and address in block letters, and correct amount in stamps, cheque, or postal order, to Good Housekeeping Pattern Service, 153 Queen Victoria Street, E.C.4.

N5   N6

THESE four suggestions for day dresses, to be made up in light-weight woollen materials (or heavy silk for afternoon wear) will commend themselves to the amateur dress-maker at the present season. The two above are especially suitable for the not-so-young woman and are obtainable in bust sizes up to 44 in. with hips to correspond.

Numbers N5 and N6 could be made up for morning or afternoon, and wool crêpe, stockinette wool, silk marocain and crêpe de Chine are possible fabrics. A georgette jabot finishes the cross-over front of N5, and a collar of self-material comes up fairly high at the back of the neck. Flared panels are inset at either side of the flared skirt. Frock No. 6 derives its skirt fullness from a number of gores and the original crossed bodice fastens with a buckle at the back of the waist. An outline of contrasting colour is a pretty finish to the front.

Number N7 is attractively cut with the panel pleats back and front and a hip-yoke which fastens at the back. A long plaid scarf forms the collar and gives the cross-over front of the slightly bloused bodice, ending in a loose end beneath the hip-yoke. The latter also fastens at the back, as can be seen from the small sketch.

The jumper-coat and skirt, N8 (worn with or without a blouse) is a very practical style and very easy to make. Choose woollen fabrics of the same or different weights, the heavier one for the skirt, in shades of the same colour or in any of the smart colour combinations now in fashion. Belt the coat with the skirt material. The latter is made on a hip-yoke, with a belt to fasten at the waist.

N7   N8

THE LONDON SCENE II

Oxford Street

All the colour and fascination of London's most garish, impermanent, rolling ribbon of a street are in this brilliant word picture: and in the beautiful precision of its language and thought it reveals the name of its distinguished author—

VIRGINIA WOOLF

DOWN in the docks one sees things in their crudity, their bulk, their enormity. Here in Oxford Street they have been refined and transformed. The huge barrels of damp tobacco have been rolled into innumerable neat cigarettes laid in silver paper. The corpulent bales of wool have been spun into thin vests and soft stockings. The grease of sheep's thick wool has become scented cream for delicate skins. And those who buy and those who sell have suffered the same city change. Tripping, mincing, in black coats, in satin dresses, the human form has adapted itself no less than the animal product. Instead of hauling and heaving, it deftly opens drawers, rolls out silk on counters, measures and snips with yard sticks and scissors.

Oxford Street, it goes without saying, is not London's most distinguished thoroughfare. Moralists have been known to point the finger of scorn at those who buy there, and they have the support of the dandies. Fashion has secret crannies off Hanover Square, round about Bond Street, to which it withdraws discreetly to perform its more sublime rites. In Oxford Street there are too many bargains, too many sales, too many goods marked down to one and eleven three that only last week cost two and six. The buying and selling is too blatant and raucous. But as one saunters towards the sunset—and what with artificial light and mounds of silk and gleaming omnibuses, a perpetual sunset seems to brood over the Marble Arch—the garishness and gaudiness of the great rolling ribbon of Oxford Street has its fascination. It is like the pebbly bed of a river whose stones are for ever washed by a bright stream. Everything glitters and twinkles. The first spring day brings out barrows frilled with tulips, violets, daffodils in brilliant layers. The frail vessels eddy vaguely across the stream of the traffic. At one corner seedy magicians are making slips of coloured paper expand in magic tumblers into bristling forests of splendidly tinted flora—a subaqueous flower garden. At another, tortoises repose on litters of grass. The slowest and most contemplative of creatures display their mild activities on a foot or two of pavement, jealously guarded from passing feet. One infers that the desire of man for the tortoise, like the desire of the moth for the star, is a constant element in human nature. Nevertheless, to see a woman stop and add a tortoise to her string of parcels is perhaps the rarest sight that human eyes can look upon.

Taking all this into account—the auctions, the barrows, the cheapness, the glitter—it cannot be said that the character of Oxford Street is refined. It is a breeding ground, a forcing house of sensation. The pavement seems to sprout horrid tragedies; the divorces of actresses, the suicides of millionaires occur here with a frequency that is unknown in the more austere pavements of the residential districts. News changes quicker than in any other part of London. The press of people passing seems to lick the ink off the placards and to consume more of them and to demand fresh supplies of later editions faster than elsewhere. The mind becomes a glutinous slab that takes impressions and Oxford Street rolls off upon it a perpetual ribbon of changing sights, sounds and movement. Parcels slap and hit; motor omnibuses graze the kerb; the blare of a whole brass band in full tongue dwindles to a thin reed of sound. Buses, vans, cars, barrows stream past like the fragments of a picture puzzle; a white arm rises; the puzzle runs thick, coagulates, stops; the white arm sinks, and away it streams again, streaked, twisted, higgledy-piggledy, in perpetual race and disorder. The puzzle never fits itself together, however long we look.

On the banks of this river of turning wheels our modern aristocrats have built palaces just as in ancient days the Dukes of Somerset and Northumberland, the Earls of Dorset and Salisbury lined the Strand with their stately mansions. The different houses of the great firms testify to the courage, initiative, the audacity of their creators much as the great houses of Cavendish and Percy testify to such qualities in some faraway shire. From the loins of our merchants will spring the Cavendishes and the Percys of the future. Indeed, the great Lords of Oxford Street are as magnanimous as any Duke or Earl who scattered gold or doled out loaves to the poor at his gates. Only their largesse takes a different form. It takes the form of excitement, of display, of entertainment, of windows lit up by night, of banners flaunting by day. They give us the latest news for nothing. Music streams from their banqueting rooms free. You need not spend more than one and eleven three to enjoy all the shelter that high and airy halls provide; and the soft pile of carpets, and the luxury of lifts, and the glow of fabrics, and carpets and silver. Percy and Cavendish could give no more. These gifts of course have an object—to entice the shilling and eleven pennies as freely from our pockets as possible; but the Percys and the Cavendishes were not munificent either without hope of some return, whether it was a dedication from a poet or a vote from a farmer. And both the old lords and the new added considerably to the decoration and entertainment of human life.

But it cannot be denied that these Oxford Street palaces are rather flimsy abodes—perching grounds rather than dwelling places. One is conscious that one is walking on a strip of wood laid upon steel girders, and that the outer wall, for all its florid stone ornamentation, is only thick enough to withstand the force of the wind. A vigorous prod with an umbrella point might well inflict irreparable damage upon the fabric. Many a country cottage built to house farmer or miller when Queen Elizabeth was on the throne will live to see these palaces fall into the dust. The old cottage walls, with their oak beams and their layers of honest brick soundly cemented together still put up a stout resistance to the drills and bores that attempt to introduce the modern blessing of electricity. But any day of the week one may see Oxford Street vanishing at the tap of a workman's pick as he stands perilously balanced on a dusty pinnacle knocking down walls and façades as lightly as if they were made of yellow cardboard and sugar icing.

And again the moralists point the finger of scorn. For such thinness, such papery stone and powdery brick reflect, they say, the levity, the ostenta-

TIDE

Illustrations by

S. G. Hulme Beaman

"Oxford Street is not London's most distinguished thoroughfare"

tion, the haste and irresponsibility of our age. Yet perhaps they are as much out in their scorn as we should be if we asked of the lily that it should be cast in bronze, or of the daisy that it should have petals of imperishable enamel. The charm of modern London is that it is not built to last; it is built to pass. Its glassiness, its transparency, its surging waves of coloured plaster give a different pleasure and achieve a different end from that which was desired and attempted by the old builders and their patrons, the nobility of England. Their pride required the illusion of permanence. Ours, on the contrary, seems to delight in proving that we can make stone and brick as transitory as our own desires. We do not build for our descendants, who may live up in the clouds or down in the earth, but for ourselves and our own needs. We knock down and rebuild as we expect to be knocked down and rebuilt. It is an impulse that makes for creation and fertility. Discovery is stimulated and invention on the alert.

The palaces of Oxford Street ignore what seemed good to the Greeks, to the Elizaethan, to the eighteenth-century nobleman; they

are overwhelmingly conscious that unless they can devise an architecture that shows off the dressing-case, the Paris frock, the cheap stockings, and the jar of bath salts to perfection, their palaces, their mansions and motor-cars and the little villas out at Croydon and Surbiton where their shop assistants live, not so badly after all, with a gramophone and wireless, and money to spend at the movies—all this will be swept to ruin. Hence they stretch stone fantastically; crush together in one wild confusion the

"Seedy men with tortoises"

styles of Greece, Egypt, Italy, America; and boldly attempt an air of lavishness, opulence, in their effort to persuade the multitude that here unending beauty, ever fresh, ever new, very cheap and within the reach of everybody, bubbles up every day of the week from an inexhaustible well. The mere thought of age, of solidity, of lasting for ever is abhorrent to Oxford Street.

Therefore if the moralist chooses to take his afternoon walk along this particular thoroughfare, he must tune his strain so that it receives into it some queer, incongruous voices. Above the racket of van and omnibus we can hear them crying. God knows, says the man who sells tortoises, that my arm aches; my chance of selling a tortoise is small; but courage! there may come along a

buyer; my bed to-night depends on it; so on I must go, as slowly as the police allow, wheeling tortoises down Oxford Street from dawn till dusk. True, says the great merchant, I am not thinking of educating the mass to a higher standard of æsthetic sensibility. It taxes all my wits to think how I can display my goods with the minimum of waste and the maximum of effectiveness. Green dragons on the top of Corinthian columns may help; let us try. I grant, says the middle-class woman, that I linger and look and barter and cheapen and turn over basket after basket of remnants hour by hour. My eyes glisten unseemlily I know, and I grab and pounce with disgusting greed. But my husband is a small clerk in a bank; I have only fifteen pounds a year to dress on; so here I come, to linger and loiter and look, if I can, as well dressed as my neighbours.

139

Because under the cloak of civilisation man continues to hide instincts of bestial cruelty, I see to-day's world as

B Y the time these words appear in print it is quite possible that the world may be bathed, once more, in a rosy glow of optimism. Trade may have improved. The pound sterling may be back at par. The unemployment figures may have dropped. The Nations of the world, driven by desperate necessity, may have been stampeded into a sullen but effective form of co-operation. They may even be lowering a few of their tariff walls, turning a few of their swords into motor-tractors, and a few of their poison gas factories into perfumery works.

I think it highly improbable that any such transformation will have been effected. However, even if it has, the title of this article will still apply. I shall still be a black pessimist with regard to the affairs of the world, of this country, and of my life.

Mr. St. John Ervine, in a recent article in this journal, commented upon the respective mentalities of Mr. Noel Coward and myself. It seemed to him paradoxical that two men, who were still fairly young, whose lives had been not unsuccessful, who were not, moreover, suffering from a violent form of indigestion or any social ostracism, should yet see life in such an unsatisfactory light. Some of Mr. Coward's more acid lyrics were quoted—lyrics which are like a high and windy echo of a lunatic's laugh. And some reference was made to an article I wrote in which I apparently observed that human existence was "a profoundly boring and stupid and miserable state."

Mr. St. John Ervine wants to know the reason for this pessimism in the face of personal prosperity. I cannot speak for Mr. Coward. But I can speak very plainly for myself.

My own pessimism is not a "temperamental" affair. It is not due to any psychological kink, nor does it arise from any disorders of the blood or fevers of the brain. It is the result of honest observation and cold reason. To put it generally, my reading of contemporary history tells me that the whole of Western civilisation as we know it, is a sinking ship. And I don't happen to like the sensation. As Aristotle observed, " Man is a political animal." I take this to mean that man cannot lead a full, useful, or happy life except in the society of his fellows. Some sort of social organisation is necessary.

I think that the social organisation, as we know it, has broken down for good and all. And again Aristotle may be quoted. He was of the opinion that the only logical basis for a state is slavery. It is a perfectly correct opinion. We may fool ourselves with all sorts of polite references to " democracy," but the fact remains that Western civilisation is based on slavery, and on nothing else.

And now the slaves have revolted for good and all.

I do not see how this statement can be contradicted. Consider it in two periods, before and after the industrial revolutions. How were the fine and permanent things of civilisation created, before the industrial revolution? Who built the Pyramids? Who was really responsible for the " grandeur that was Rome? " What was the state of Russia, until only a few decades ago? What were the English Factory Acts, but an emancipation of slaves? On what did the fine fabric of French civilisation repose? What was the patronage system in Italy?

To ask these questions is to answer them automatically.

Of course, the conventional answer to this sort of argument is that machinery will eventually take the place of slavery. In Bloomsbury and Moscow and Greenwich Village you will find plenty of idealists who, after a glass of gin or its equivalent, will sketch for you a charming picture of the future state of the world. As far as I can gather, we shall spend most of our time reclining in public parks in the shade of immense but very hygienic factories, talking with brilliant intelligence to ladies who wear smocks but no corsets. If I thought that there was any possibility of this rapturous conception being fulfilled, I should instantly leap into the dirty but kindly waters of the Thames. However, I fear that no such solution to our difficulty is likely.

Let us reiterate the situation as I see it. Western civilisation is based upon slavery. (England's wealth, for example, is largely due to her possession of India. Which is, of course, permanently and irretrievably lost to her.) About a hundred years ago the industrial revolution confused the issue by enormously adding to the number of the slaves. And yet, you will still find to-day numbers of fatuous optimists who attempt to bamboozle the public by drawing comforting analogies between 1832 and 1932.

I have read at least a
(*Continued on page* 142)

A Study in Black

Declares BEVERLEY NICHOLS

This is a most extraordinary article. Its completely pessimistic views on modern conditions and philosophy will probably arouse readers to wrathful disagreement, but at the same time they will be interested in such a trenchant argument from one of the most brilliant writers of the younger generation

*Photography by
Logan (London) Ltd.*

A Study in Black

(*Continued from page* 140)

dozen articles, by persons who should know better, comparing the state of the world to-day with its state in the period succeeding the Napoleonic wars. "The same despair, the same unemployment, the same financial morass . . ." that is the theme of these optimists.

Such comparisons are ill-formed and utterly misleading. *There is no comparison between* 1932 *and any other year which has ever dawned on the world.* Unless you admit this, you are living in a fool's paradise. History has no lessons to teach us. The past, for all we can learn from it, might as well be a blank page. We stand on the threshold of a dark, uncharted land, and for me that land is icy and forlorn, and swept with bitter winds of despair.

I must not take refuge in rhetoric. I have no need of it. The facts are tragic enough. What *are* the facts about these facile comparisons with the past, which are supposed to comfort us?

Well, in 1832 it took almost as long for the Duke of Wellington to go from London to Edinburgh as it would have taken Julius Cæsar. In 1832 telephones, telegrams, motors, aeroplanes—the whole mechanical world in which we live—was non-existent. The difference is so vast and immeasurable that it need not be dwelt upon. The wonder is that any sane man can comfort himself by comparing the two eras. The capitalist system is a modern creation and it has broken down. Please do not let us mince words about that. It is not merely functioning imperfectly for the moment. It has completely and finally collapsed.

If you deny that collapse, will you kindly ask me what you think of a system which causes the coffee growers of Brazil to throw tons of coffee into their harbours at the very moment when the streets of New York are lined with men who have not enough money to buy a cup of coffee? What do you think of a system that forces the farmers of Canada to burn wheat, the farmers of England to let their potatoes rot in the ground, the farmers of Australia to let whole orchards of fruit fall to the ground and perish, when every capital in the world is filled with people who cannot buy bread or potatoes or a single apple? Is that a sane system?

You may reply, " But this is only a *temporary* crisis. There is plenty for everybody in the world. All that is needed is more international co-operation."

Quite. Well, do you think you will get it? I don't. I am hopelessly pessimistic about greater international co-operation. It is conceivable that we might get it in Europe . . . that is to say, in the small and comparatively unimportant part of Europe which remains when you exclude Russia. It is even conceivable that Europe might co-operate with America. It is not beyond the dreams of fancy that the white men of the world might eventually league themselves together. (It is beyond the dreams of *my* fancy, but I am quite prepared to admit that a man could entertain such an idea without laying himself open to the accusation of insanity).

However, even if you got such a league you would be only at the start of your difficulties. What about the coloured races? We occasionally read, in newspapers, discreet references to the Colour Problem. However, if there is one thing which is clear to the imaginative historian, it is this, that we have not even begun to envisage the eventual difficulties of the colour problem.

As the economic machine grows more and more complicated, it is forced by the very nature of its construction to expand. To take a very practical example: Mr. Henry Ford, having discovered that the American market for his cars is "saturated," comes to Europe to develop his business here. The European market is reaching "saturation" point. What is Mr. Ford therefore doing? He is casting his eye upon the coloured races. They are the only market left. Well, one day, that market will be "saturated" too. What will happen then? The only thing that I can think of is an industrial exploitation of the moon.

If the economic machine includes, as it is including to a larger and larger extent, the coloured races (viz. the independent cotton industry of India) those races will eventually become powerful, cunning and independent. The example of Japan, which sixty years ago was a completely medieval state, shows that these awkward transformations have a habit of happening somewhat quickly. However, just as they are becoming independent, the white men will be crying for co-operation. "The whole world *must* be an economic unit, or we shall perish by starvation." They will wail . . . just as they are wailing to-day that the British Empire must be an economic unit. "It must also be a political unit, or we shall die a horrible death from war," they will also wail.

They will be quite right. But you cannot have world political unity—which is the only thing that will ever save the world—unless you also have spiritual unity. And this I maintain is utterly impossible, in view of the wild chaos of races which inhabits this tortured planet. I do not mean by "spiritual" unity a uniformity of creed. I mean a certain common basis of character. It is difficult enough to get an Englishman and a Frenchman to agree, but at least they do not feel any *basic* antipathy . . . they are not different animals . . . they respond, on the whole, to the same emotions . . . they have much the same hates and loves. The white man and the black man are fundamentally hostile.

Do you like Indians? I don't. I think it would be blatant hypocrisy to pretend that I did. During the recent Round Table Conference in London, when one used to meet stray Maharajahs at dinner parties, I felt hot and embarrassed. I believe that most other white people felt hot and embarrassed too. Yet, the only chance for the whites, in the future, will be to accept a position of equality with, or even subservience to, the blacks and the yellows.

" Old scares !" you may tell me. " People have been prophesying this sort of peril for generations." Quite. But the world is now moving so quickly that a week-end to-day is as prolific in change as a century of the past.

Unless you realise the hideous acceleration of modern mechanical civilisation—which is like a motor-car dashing down the side of a precipice—you cannot possibly visualise the unspeakable horror of the next war.

I am for peace at any price. Yes . . at any price. Why? Because I am firmly convinced that another war would not only destroy such civilisation as still remains but might quite possibly put an end to all life, human and animal, on the entire planet. And in spite of the general folly of existence, I do not like to think of this earth as a scarred and blackened globe spinning empty through space.

Yet . . . is it not possible that this may

(*Continued on page* 145

IN THE PUBLIC EYE

that keep slim and trim

on Vita-Weat

THE SOCIETY HOSTESS If there's one eye she fears, it is her dressmaker's. It is a regular tape-measure of an eye. At one accusing glance it will bring to light that new half-inch of girth that certainly was not there last time.

If only for this reason, therefore, she employs every wise measure to keep her figure down ; and the wisest of all her measures is the substitution of Vita-Weat for ordinary bread or toast. Because Vita-Weat is free from unconverted starch she finds that it arrests the advance of unwanted fat; and because it contains all the nourishment of the whole wheat grain it gives her the energy and staying-power her strenuous social round demands.

You too will benefit by making Vita-Weat your daily bread. Your digestion will improve, your system will run more regularly and efficiently, your teeth will grow healthier, you will experience a new sense of buoyancy and of youth. And how you will love its "crunchiness" and its ripe-corn flavour !

The British Whole-wheat

Crispbread

In cartons 1/6 and 10d. Packets 6d. and 2d.

MADE BY
PEEK FREAN
MAKERS OF FAMOUS BISCUITS

Immediate HEAT

A gas fire you can carry to any room, plug in, and in a few minutes, have the place cosy and warm. It weighs less than 20lbs., is made of pressed steel, and is beautifully finished. It requires no permanent fixing, but sits in front of the ordinary coal grate and connects up to the gas supply by a safety "plug-in" connection.

What a boon on chilly mornings . . . in the autumn evenings . . . when you are using a room for just a few minutes ! How conveniently you can carry it about the house, upstairs and downstairs— one gas fire for a whole house !

There can be no discomfort from cold in the house that has a " Mainscreen."

Please see the "Mainscreen" demonstrated at your local gas showrooms, or send coupon for illustrated folder.

Mainscreen
PORTABLE GAS FIRE

POST THIS COUPON TO-DAY

A Study in Black

(*Continued from page* **142**)

happen, sooner than we imagine? The next war will make the last war look like a storm in a tea-cup. But the last war nearly destroyed Europe! For example, if the Germans had held back their first gas attack until they could use it simultaneously along the whole front, many millions of men would have died, overnight, in indescribable agony. The weapons of destruction have been highly polished since the famous Treaty of Versailles—(that grotesque Witch's Sabbath in which the yells of sadistic statesmen triumphed over the groans of the dying). Very prettily and delicately have they flavoured their gases since then. Very brightly have they polished their guns. They are at it, night and day. If you doubt it, take a cursory glance at the budgets of the various nations, and compare the expenditure on armaments before and after the "Great" War.

Guns are made to be fired. Gases are made to suffocate. These things are not being produced because of their decorative value.

"Well," you may say, "if things are so desperate, surely mankind will devise a way out? Surely, if it is a question of Peace or Death, of Unity or Starvation, of Sacrifice or Extinction, we shall choose Peace and Unity and Sacrifice? After all, there *are* great brains in the world," etc., etc.

Dance, dance, dance little optimist! Who told you those charming fables? I have no such polite illusions about mankind. Like H. G. Wells, I see all too clearly the "red teeth of Neanderthal man" gleaming behind the polite mask of the twentieth century gentleman. However gaily the band may be playing, however softly the lamps are lit, I see those red teeth gleaming . . . in all their ghastly cruelty. I believe that I myself am as kind and as generous as the average man. I think I've given rather more than I've got, have turned the other cheek reasonably, have made an adequate number of "soft answers." Yet, I have horrible instincts. Strange, latent impulses, deep down in me, are frightening. I am still

half ape. So are you. That is not an encouraging thought in a world of shrill machines. A lot of apes, tinkering with the wheels of a factory.

"And so," says the saint, "there is nothing left but God. You admit that man has failed. You agree that the structure that he has raised is crazy and rotten. There is still one refuge . . . Nature. Go into the fields, bend your knee, receive absolution in the peace of heaven."

I could tear the paper before me, with angry fingers, at such an epitome of folly. Nature! Pardon me while I laugh, as the Americans say, when they are very angry. How dare you parade that bloodstained and lascivious image before me?

I live in a world of hideous cruelty. The cries of tortured men and women, the screams of frightened animals . . . they assail me. I hear them. God apparently doesn't. You may tell me that it is all ' part of a plan." Is it? Who told you that? And why should you be more right than I am?

Stay with me for a moment, and look over in the corner of the room. A cat is playing with a mouse. Part of a plan, isn't it? Yes . . . part of the plan that the mouse should stagger away, dazed, with half its leg hanging off . . . be drawn back into the circle of the cat's hot breath . . . receive another moment's freedom . . . drag its tortured little body once more to the shadows in a pitiful effort to die alone . . . be dragged back again . . . you tell me that it is part of a plan? Indeed. I congratulate you. I prefer to kill the mouse and stroke the cat, which is just as much a victim as you or I.

Now, perhaps, you will realise why I do not always greet the morning with a smile. Although I am fairly young, and fairly prosperous, and fairly successful. For the fairies at my christening gave me a certain gift, which is really a curse . . . decreed that I should occasionally tell the truth, when other men are telling lies. And it is terribly monotonous to have to spend one's life describing the grinning of a skull.

Dog Tickets on the L.M.S. Railway

AS a wrong impression seems to have been caused by a quotation from a reader's letter included in the article on "Railway Menus" in the January issue, the Director of the Institute wishes to draw attention to the following extract from a letter sent by the Scottish Divisional Passenger Manager of the L.M.S. Railway and regrets any misunderstanding that may have arisen.

"In this article reference is made to the charge for the conveyance of dogs accompanying passengers between Ballachulish and Oban.

"I would like to point out that the statement made in this article is not quite correct, as return dog tickets are issued at single rate for the double journey, under circumstances such as stated by your correspondent. Further, the charge for the

conveyance of dogs accompanying passengers is exactly the same between places in Scotland as between places in England, and your correspondent has not therefore been correctly informed.

"Between any pair of stations in Scotland or England dogs accompanying passengers making single journeys only not exceeding 10 miles are charged 3d. per dog, while return tickets are issued covering return journeys between any two stations for dogs accompanying passengers at the ordinary single rate for the double journey. These return tickets for dogs are available for the return journey on the day of issue or within the period of availability of week-end tickets.

"Passengers taking out walking tour tickets are also permitted to take their dogs with them at the charge of single rate for the double journey."

Autum

FORTNUM & MASON

*Navy felt with a crown folded lengthways
and a white and navy grosgrain band.*

ADELE

*Peau d'ange velvet cap, a deep
russet brown, with upstanding
fluted frill and a band of shaded
beige and brown minoche pads*

*One of the new bérets in black, pin-
tucked velvet. It shows most of the
hair at the back and is flat as a pan-
cake in front and pulled well forward*

DEBENHAM & FREEBODY

*Left, a collarless shirt of washing silk with wide revers and
buttoned down the front and at the cuffs. The Celes tailored
shirt is in a pale colour stitched with a vivid contrast. The
triangular machined sections behind the buttons are interesting*

*The top of Scott's tweed fe
hat is brown and beige, th
under brim is plain dar
brown, also the jaunty quil
The lady holds a Bembaro
bag in brown calf as thic
as a novel and claspe
with nickel and brown galalit*

Original lines

on blouses and hats from the

early collections

SCOTT'S

Accessories from London Shops

MARSHALL & SNELGROVE

MARSHALL & SNELGROVE

VIYELLA

JOHN LEWIS

Oyster coloured crêpe de Chine blouse, elaborately hand veined, with a scalloped frill worn like a fichu and also on the sleeves

A pale rose pink georgette blouse has panels of minute tucking, and fine hemstitching round the neck and the immense bow. Both are bound with satin

The tailored sports shirt in sunflower yellow Viyella is checked with white and fastens down the front with white pearl buttons

The powder blue flamisol blouse above has a scarf knotted loosely in front and three rows of attractive stitching on the heart-shaped yoke

JOHN LEWIS

Mushroom satin sleeveless blouse with beautiful hand-worked fagoting round the neck, which forms a design something like a scarab

SCOTT'S

Country felt hat in a pinky beige banded with dark brown. The crown is tucked inside so that the stitches show on the outside in a neat fancy pattern. The brown soutache calf bag from Bembaron has a semi-circular nickel frame and opens out flat

The
QUEEN'S

*" The Queen and the Prince Consort were partaking
The Queen asked for some cherry tart . . .*

The Queen went to the Mansion House
In a gown of blue.
The kind Lord Mayor asked her to lunch.
He asked Prince Albert too.

They sat about the groaning board
And gobbled up their fish.
They gobbled up their chicken,
As much as they could wish.

The Queen told little stories
Of her childhood days.
The table rocked with laughter
At her comic ways.

" She's happy," said the butler,
" You can see it in her look."
" She's happy," said the footman,
And then he told the cook.

The cook ground up the coffee,
So pleased at his success.
He even kissed the kitchen-maid,
Whose Christian name was Bess.

" The Queen's enjoyed her chicken! "
" The Queen enjoyed her meat! "
The news rang round the Mansion House
And reached the London street.

The porter told the cabman,
The cabman told his horse.
It was the talk of London,
As far as Charing Cross.

When her plate was empty,
The Queen gave all a start.
She said, " Well now, let's see what's next?
I fancy *cherry tart.*"

The butler told the footman,
The footman told the cook.
The Lord Mayor pulled his whiskers
And gave his wife a look.

She blushed and turned magenta,
She clutched her beating heart.
" Dear me, what shall I do? " said she,
" She thinks it's *à la carte.*

" I suppose I was mistaken,
I should have sent a note,
To tell such splendid people
'Twas only *table d'hôte.*"

By HECTOR

TACT

of the Chief Magistrate of the City's hospitality.
there was none." (The Private Life of the Queen.)

The cook swooned on the table.
The footman brought him to.
" Oh dear," he said, " I'm ruined,
Whatever shall I do?

" There's cranberry and mulberry,
And greengage, bless my heart!
How could I know that she would ask
A slice of *cherry* tart? "

The cook became so flustered,
He simply lost his head.
The butler saved the moment,
He served her *plum* instead.

The Queen was very clever,
She saw the Lord Mayor's face.
She helped herself to plum tart
With quite exquisite grace.

" I hope it is not cherry,
'Tis a fruit I never take.
I know that's what I ordered,
But only by mistake."

Thus charmingly she soothed them,
The Lord Mayor smiled once more.
The butler told the footman,
As he passed through the door.

The footman sought the kitchen,
And found a dreadful scene.
The cook was crying woefully
Into a soup tureen.

The footman soothed him gently,
" Don't look so down and glum,
Her Majesty seems quite content
With a slice of *plum*."

They dried the poor cook's eyelids
With a chamois leather.
Then they joined up, arm in arm,
And danced about together.

*   *   *

Prince Albert and the Queen drove home
In their stately carriage,
The people smiled as they went past,
For such a happy marriage.

'Tis in such kindly acts as these,
Great people rule a nation,
By exercising royal tact
In an awkward situation.

*Illustrations
by
Douglas
England*

BOLITHO

Christmas and the

" I decided the leaden saucer was for cat's milk, so I filled it with same. But the cat gave the Thing a nasty look and a wide berth . . . "

YOU are either " pro " or " con " Christmas. There can be no half-way measures about it.

Those who are " pro " are those who love children, and the " patter " (though I think it should be called " wollop ") of little feet. If these people cannot surround themselves, on the happy day, with yards and yards of children, theirs or anybody else's, they wilt and take to drink. They also wilt and take to drink when they *have* surrounded themselves, all day, with the little patterers. But that is a cynical reflection unsuited to this fragrant topic.

Those who are " pro " are also those who are so heartily sick of little feet that they palm them off at Christmas on female relations who, for reasons best known to themselves, are footless, I mean, childless. These depraved parents are very " pro " Christmas indeed. They think it is much too short.

I have no feelings one way or another about children. True, I think that babies should never be looked at with the naked eye. Babies should wear veils, and even then, should only be observed, by the sensitive, through smoked glasses. That vacant grin! That awful feeling that it has either just dribbled or is just about to dribble! That sense that it is a sort of human bomb—touch it, and it will explode in all directions. No, you will agree with me that babies are a grave mistake. They should be abolished at once.

Still, as I say, I have no feelings, one way or another, about children, even at Christmas. Small girls, of course, should be destroyed *en masse*. An agreeable holocaust might also be made of all small boys. But I don't feel strongly about it. As long as they are just all wiped off the face of the earth, I shall not complain.

I have suddenly observed, with astonishment, that the title they have put on this article is " Christmas and the Gardener." May I, as politely as possible, ask why they did that? Can *you* tell me? It is extremely provoking, in the middle of these delicate reflections upon Our Little Ones, to have such a topic thrust upon one. I do not in the least desire to write about Christmas and

" I think babies should wear veils . . . That vacant grin ! That awful feeling that it is a sort of human bomb . . . "

gardeners. I absolutely refuse to do so. No . . . it is no use entreating me. Not even a little line? About the first snowdrop popping up through the trembling whatnots? No. Not even a little line.

But stay . . . I *will* write a little line, which does concern Christmas and does concern gardeners, and what happens to them at Christmas.

They are given presents. And they are always given gardening presents.

I speak with particular feeling about this because, a year or two ago, I wrote a book about gardening, which, for some reason or other, has induced everybody who read it to write to me, and not only to write to me, but to send me presents.

Now this was charming when it began, but as the flood of presents grew (and it shows no sign of receding), it became a little worrying.

For one thing, it is wearing out the carpet in the hall. In case this sounds obscure, I should explain that most of the parcels contain earth, and many of them drip, so that as my servant carries them from the front door to my study (registering a hauteur that is worthy of Jeeves), a trail of mud is deposited on the carpet which has to be brushed off every day. Therefore, I should like to drop a gentle hint that instead of sending me any more roots of *hysterica corpulosa* (which don't " do " in my garden, anyway), somebody should send me a new carpet.

At Christmas the flood of gardening presents becomes quite overwhelming. The presents may be divided into three classes:

1. The literary and pictorial.

There will be, for example, thirty-seven copies of the works of Mrs. Marion Cran. There always are.

There will be, roughly, 365 gardening calendars. These are embellished with charming moral mottoes telling me to make my life as beautiful as a herbaceous border. I am not quite sure that I like the thought of 365 people suggesting that my life may *not* be as beautiful as a herbaceous border, but we will let that pass.

There will also be a sheaf of letters containing snapshots of other people's gardens. Nearly all these snapshots appear to have been taken in a deep fog, but this does not deter the

Illustrations by W. Heath Robinson

Gardener

A
not-to-be-taken-seriously
article by

BEVERLEY NICHOLS

" People never send me anything useful. They send things like scarecrows which disclose a cocktail set "

senders from asking me all sorts of gay little questions about them. This sort of thing.

"Don't you think that the clematis over the third arch is marvellous? And is not this a topping picture of my dog? I call him Mr. Wu, and he is a *rogue* among the antirrhinums! That is me, behind the hollyhocks. Of course, you can't tell from a snapshot, can you, but would it be terrible of me to ask you what you thought of me? I shan't tell anyone! I have a few enlargements, and if you'd care, I *could* send you one. But only if you *really* cared. Please forgive this foolish letter, but I've never written to an author before! But I *do* feel that all gardeners ought to be friends, don't you?"

If you think that is exaggerated, I can assure you that it is same compared with the average.

Class number 2 of gardening presents is a little more mysterious. I can best explain what I mean by telling you a story.

Last year, a Thing of paralysing ugliness arrived which, for a long time, we stood in the hall. We thought it was some sort of hatrack - cum - umbrella - stand, and as it was obviously very expensive we decided that we would bear its presence for, at any rate, a week or so, in case the anonymous donor called and asked what we had done with it.

Gradually the Thing, which was made of

" It usually happens that a perpetual simulation of a mysterious complaint makes it tactless of donors to force their presence into my garden "

wickerwork and covered with knobs in the most unexpected places, began to exercise a morbid attraction on us. What *was* it? What the blazes *was* it? If you tried to hang a hat on it, the hat fell off. The holes were too large for umbrellas. There was a sort of leaden saucer at the bottom which, in a bright moment, I decided was for cat's milk, so I filled it with same. But the cat gave the Thing a nasty look and a wide berth, and all the milk oozed through a hole on to the floor.

A few weeks later the problem was solved. Walking down Piccadilly I met a charming creature muffled to the eyebrows in mink. "Oh!" she said, drawing down a slab of mink from her face

for a moment, and then hastily replacing it . . . "it's *you*!" Even beneath the mink there was a tone of husky indignation which made me ask what was the matter. It transpired that it was she who had sent the Thing.

"But why didn't you let me know? I can't *tell* you how useful it's been! If *only* I'd known it was from you . . ."

The mink was lowered again. "Has it really been useful? I'm so happy. But I can't understand. I put in a card with the tools."

"The what?"

"The tools, in the other parcel. Didn't you get another parcel?"

"No."

The mink began to rise up again. "Then may I ask *what* you've been using the tool-stand for?"

I blinked. Light began to dawn. So the Thing was meant to hang garden tools on! That was why it had those sinister little wheels at the bottom which made us think it might be a go-cart for a peculiarly depraved sort of baby. And that was why it had those pieces of bass on each knob.

And that was why I had to buy something very expensive, that morning, for a charming creature in mink.

Now, if people really feel impelled to send me presents of this nature, may I make a courteous suggestion that what every gardener wants is an endless supply of clippers of every description? Clippers for hedges, clippers for cutting off stray branches, clippers of all sizes and shapes. Gardeners also need large, sharp and expensive spades. Nor do they despise trowels, watering cans and the like. But people never send me anything useful like that. They always send—well, all I can call them is . . . Things. Things like miniature wheelbarrows fitted with a wireless.

What Price

These budgets may offer a
in which expenditure
should be

THE TOWN-DWELLER. *This is the expenditure which we think should be normal for a woman who spends an average amount of money and care on her appearance.*

	Per annum £	s.	d.
Skin Treatment and Make-up			
Three times a year, a good "facial"	1	2	6
Cleansing cream, 4 jars		8	0
Foundation lotion, 3 bottles . .		12	0
Powder, 2 boxes . . .		6	0
Rouge, 3 compacts . . .		3	9
Lipsticks, 2		9	0
Hair			
Twice a year, a permanent wave .	3	3	0
Cut, shampoo and set once fortnightly, at 4s. and 6d. tip .	5	17	0
Occasional set, for special occasions	1	4	0
1 bottle brilliantine . . .		1	6
1 hairbrush		10	0
Bath Preparations			
Mostly gifts ; but allow 1 large box dusting powder . . .		5	0
Manicure			
A good manicure, 3 times a year .		10	6
2 bottles liquid varnish . .		3	0
1 bottle cuticle oil . . .		1	6
1 bottle cuticle remover . .		1	6
2 bottles hand cream . .		3	0
	£15	**1**	**3**

MISS BROWN, *age 18. Typist in a provincial town. Earns twenty-five shillings a week.*

	Per annum £	s.	d.
Hair			
One iron wave every fortnight, at 1s. 6d.	1	19	0
Camomile shampoos for home use fortnightly, at 3d. . . .		6	6
Eau de Cologne for home hairsets, 4 bottles at 6d. . . .		2	0
2 packets of hair curlers . .			6
Make-up			
2 boxes of face powder, 1/- . .		2	0
2 tubes of vanishing cream . .		2	0
(Lipstick, one at 3d., bought two years ago and still only half used)			
Manicure			
3 bottles of nail varnish . .		1	6
Bath			
A 2d. bath cube once a week .		8	8

Special Note.—Attributes her really lovely roseleaf complexion to two causes. She never eats between meals, but she does eat two to four apples a day.

| | **£3** | **2** | **2** |

Decoration
by
Bowyer

MRS. GREEN, *age 27. Wife of a soldier in the Indian Army ; six months of the year in Calcutta, six in the hills. Personal allowance, £2 weekly.*

	Per annum £	s.	d.
Hair			
Shampoo once weekly in Calcutta .	4	0	0
(In the hills it is washed at home)			
Brilliantine, 1 bottle . . .		1	0
Make-up			
Face powder, 5 small boxes . .		11	3
Vanishing cream, 3 jars . .		4	6
Lipsticks, 2 for day and 2 for evening		11	6
White lipsalve		1	0
Rouge, 1 compact . . .		3	0
Skin Care			
Cold cream, 5 jars . . .		7	0
Cleansing tissues, 3 large packets .		5	0
Astringent lotion, 5 bottles . .		16	10
Cotton wool, 3 small packets .		1	2
Manicure			
Cuticle remover, 1 bottle . .		1	9
Nail polish and remover, 3 bottles .		7	0
Bath			
Talcum powder (cheap variety, lavishly used for the feet) . .		3	6
Better quality, 3 tins . . .		5	0

Special Note.—Ice is the great beauty secret, small cubes rubbed over the face in a handkerchief.

| | **£7** | **19** | **6** |

Town Dweller

Wife of soldier in Indian Army

Provincial Typist

W HAT, indeed, is the price of beauty? Poets have set it above (variously) the gold of the stars, the song of the lark, the red of the summer rose; but our calculations are more prosaic. How much solid cash does the average woman spend upon her looks? What is the price, in money and time, of her beauty?

The answer seems to be a multiple one. There are almost as many answers as there are women. In this matter the average woman simply does not exist, and the typical budget is incredibly hard to find. The budget shown here can make only one claim: to give food for thought. The beauty-

Beauty?

*few suggestions for the way
on one's appearance
apportioned*

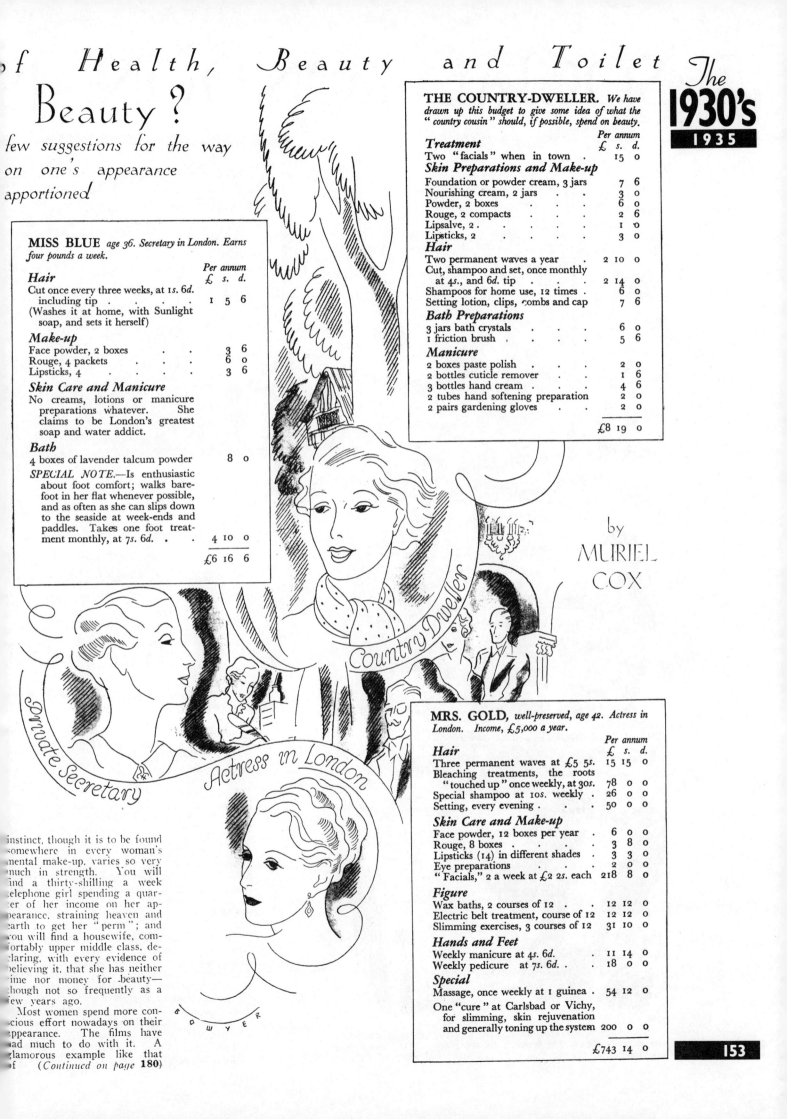

MISS BLUE *age 36. Secretary in London. Earns four pounds a week.*

	Per annum		
	£	s.	d.
Hair			
Cut once every three weeks, at 1s. 6d. including tip . . .	1	5	6
(Washes it at home, with Sunlight soap, and sets it herself)			
Make-up			
Face powder, 2 boxes . .	3	6
Rouge, 4 packets . . .	6	0
Lipsticks, 4	3	6
Skin Care and Manicure			
No creams, lotions or manicure preparations whatever. She claims to be London's greatest soap and water addict.			
Bath			
4 boxes of lavender talcum powder	8	0
SPECIAL NOTE.—Is enthusiastic about foot comfort; walks barefoot in her flat whenever possible, and as often as she can slips down to the seaside at week-ends and paddles. Takes one foot treatment monthly, at 7s. 6d. .	4	10	0
	£6	**16**	**6**

THE COUNTRY-DWELLER. *We have drawn up this budget to give some idea of what the "country cousin" should, if possible, spend on beauty.*

	Per annum		
	£	s.	d.
Treatment			
Two "facials" when in town .	15	0
Skin Preparations and Make-up			
Foundation or powder cream, 3 jars	7	6
Nourishing cream, 2 jars . .	3	0
Powder, 2 boxes . . .	6	0
Rouge, 2 compacts . . .	2	6
Lipsalve, 2	1	0
Lipsticks, 2	3	0
Hair			
Two permanent waves a year .	2	10	0
Cut, shampoo and set, once monthly at 4s., and 6d. tip .	2	14	0
Shampoos for home use, 12 times .	6	0
Setting lotion, clips, combs and cap	7	6
Bath Preparations			
3 jars bath crystals . . .	6	0
1 friction brush . . .	5	6
Manicure			
2 boxes paste polish . . .	2	0
2 bottles cuticle remover . .	1	6
3 bottles hand cream . . .	4	6
2 tubes hand softening preparation	2	0
2 pairs gardening gloves . .	2	0
	£8	**19**	**0**

by
MURIEL
COX

Country Dweller

Private Secretary

Actress in London

DWYER

instinct, though it is to be found somewhere in every woman's mental make-up, varies so very much in strength. You will find a thirty-shilling a week telephone girl spending a quarter of her income on her appearance, straining heaven and earth to get her "perm"; and you will find a housewife, comfortably upper middle class, declaring, with every evidence of believing it, that she has neither time nor money for beauty—though not so frequently as a few years ago.

Most women spend more conscious effort nowadays on their appearance. The films have had much to do with it. A glamorous example like that of (*Continued on page* 180)

MRS. GOLD, *well-preserved, age 42. Actress in London. Income, £5,000 a year.*

	Per annum		
	£	s.	d.
Hair			
Three permanent waves at £5 5s.	15	15	0
Bleaching treatments, the roots "touched up" once weekly, at 30s.	78	0	0
Special shampoo at 10s. weekly .	26	0	0
Setting, every evening . .	50	0	0
Skin Care and Make-up			
Face powder, 12 boxes per year .	6	0	0
Rouge, 8 boxes . . .	3	8	0
Lipsticks (14) in different shades .	3	3	0
Eye preparations . . .	2	0	0
"Facials," 2 a week at £2 2s. each	218	8	0
Figure			
Wax baths, 2 courses of 12 . .	12	12	0
Electric belt treatment, course of 12	12	12	0
Slimming exercises, 3 courses of 12	31	10	0
Hands and Feet			
Weekly manicure at 4s. 6d. .	11	14	0
Weekly pedicure at 7s. 6d. . .	18	0	0
Special			
Massage, once weekly at 1 guinea .	54	12	0
One "cure" at Carlsbad or Vichy, for slimming, skin rejuvenation and generally toning up the system	200	0	0
	£743	**14**	**0**

Illustrated by Treyer Evans

Vienna is derelict, Pa
Moscow a morgue. On
old traditions of Socie
fashionable than ever

says Rober

WE were discussing London and changes of the last thirty years.

"I remember a dinner party given Apsley House, I think it was in 1908," said well-known politician, the *enfant terrible* of Tory Party in pre-War days. "Seventy of most distinguished people in London we gathered in the dining-room. They included King and Queen and the leading figures of Cabinet and Opposition. Imagine a dinner pa now that included Baldwin and Lansbu Churchill and Cripps. It was another world.'

"Yes, and do you remember the fancy-dre ball at Devonshire House in '97?" asked famous social leader of Edwardian da "There were people, then, who seriously co sidered suicide when they found that they h not been invited. There is no society to-day we knew it. It has vanished as completely Devonshire House."

"And with it all formality in manners a dress," said a third. "Those were the da when one could not dine at one's club in Season, unless one wore 'tails'; and after a da one was expected to call on one's hostess a arrayed in a frock-coat, to balance a tea-cup Sunday afternoons in Mayfair drawing-room

An elderly man interrupted the flow of re niscence. "You do not know the meaning change," he said. "Fashions have altered, course, but there has been no real revoluti

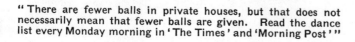

"There are fewer balls in private houses, but that does not necessarily mean that fewer balls are given. Read the dance list every Monday morning in 'The Times' and 'Morning Post'"

STILL PRE-WAR

*...rovincial, Berlin dull, and
...ondon keeps up the
...nd Season, more gay and
...his year of Jubilee*

...Bernays, M.P.

...he essential structure of London Society—your
...ourt, your London Season, your Ascot and
...ord's, your dinner parties and your talent for
...ntertaining on the grand scale, remain substan-
...ally unchanged. London is pre-War, and it is
...e only city in the world of which that can be
...id."

...He spoke with a slightly foreign accent and I
...rned to my neighbour to ask who he was.
..."Count Mensdorf," she whispered. "He was
...ustrian Ambassador before the War and a tre-
...endous figure in the London of 1913."

...I had just returned from Vienna and could
...nderstand his point of view. Compared with
...ienna, London was indeed unchanged.   In
...ustria everything has gone—Emperor, Court,
...overning classes, that positively eighteenth-
...ntury social exclusiveness, musical comedy
...niforms, even Madame Sacher, of the famous
...acher hotel, for so long the last surviving
...ndezvous of the aristocracy.   The great
...laces are silent and empty and decaying. The
...ienna of the early twentieth century has
...nished as completely as the Versailles of the
...te eighteenth century.

..."London is still pre-War."   I have often
...ought of that remark of Count Mensdorf as I
...ve watched the clatter and glitter of this
...bilee season. Is it so very different from
...e past?

...Of course there (*Continued on page* 156)

" The Royal Enclosure in Ascot Week is still a dream of fair women,
and there are few sights more lovely than Lord's when a hot summer
afternoon and the Eton and Harrow cricket match meet together "

155

SOCIAL LONDON IS STILL PRE-WAR
(Continued from page 155)

have been changes. It is difficult to imagine now the Speaker of the House of Commons giving a ball and the Terrace of the House being decked with striped awnings and fairy lights as a sitting-out place for Mayfair's rank and fashion. Yet that happened in the last days of July, 1914. One who was there has told me, that as the sun rose over Westminster Bridge, the junior members of the Cabinet drifted in from emergency all-night sittings, with the latest news of the German crisis.

Many of the great houses have gone. Devonshire House is a motor emporium, and luxury flats now stand where once was the Duke of Westminster's Park Lane palace. The great mansions of Grosvenor Place are clubs or offices. The motor-car has revolutionised the aspect of Hyde Park. I would give much to bring back for an hour or two the carriage parade of a glorious summer afternoon in the year of the Diamond Jubilee, when "Queen's weather" had set in—the slow pageant of trotting horses, the resplendent footmen and coachmen on the box, and behind them the Society women in their huge hats, bowing to friends or cutting them (for it was a generation that knew how to use the Cut Direct), and stopping to chat to top-hatted young men on the side-walks. How I would like to watch just once the operation of that delicate and complicated machinery by which it was instantly known that the Queen was taking her drive and to see the whole gay cavalcade, suddenly brought to a respectful standstill, as the little old lady, with her terrifying dignity, passed down in her "victoria"! It is not surprising that those who can recall the elegance of the carriage days and compare it now to the bustling vulgarity of the petrol age, believe in the existence of a Social Revolution. Hispano-Suizas cannot compete with the glory of a pair of well-matched chestnuts. Streamline is no compensation for the vanished barouche.

But most of these changes are only on the surface. They are like the illusion of speed. Motor-cars are constructed to travel at 60 miles an hour, but in London it is good going if they do more than average ten. The late Lord Salisbury used to allow twenty minutes to drive in the family barouche from his house in Arlington Street to King's Cross, and part of the journey was done at full gallop. Even admitting that the road was cleared for him, not even a modern Prime Minister in his motor-car with a special police pass could beat that time. Mr. Lloyd George

once told me that he used to reckon a quarter of an hour sufficient time to get from the House of Commons to Euston in a hansom cab. In his Rolls-Royce it takes him twenty minutes.

Much of the alterations in Society can be accounted for by a change of habit. Society no longer eddies round the Achilles statue after church on Sunday mornings, but then Society no longer goes to church. The West End churches that were once a Society parade present nowadays a desert of empty pews. Only those like St. Michael's, Chester Square, or St. Martin's-in-the-Fields, where men of the calibre of Canon Elliot and Mr. McCormick are the magnets, can boast of crowded congregations.

But London Society has not vanished. It has just sought fresh pastures—very literally, for most of it is on the golf-links nearest to the week-end party. So it is with the change in the place of entertaining. There are fewer balls in private houses, but that does not necessarily mean that fewer balls are given. Read the dance list every Monday morning in the Social columns of *The Times* and *Morning Post*. It is lengthy and the names are quite as impressive as ever they were in pre-War days. Watch the scene in Sunderland House, that can be hired for the night at 84 guineas, or any of the other ball-rooms. There are the same platoons of lovely girls in their Poiret gowns, and smooth-faced young men from Eton and the Guards; the same rows of tired-eyed chaperons; the same warm champagne, and tiaras on the heads of majestic Peeresses. Even the thrills and the tragedies for a girl in her first season have not really altered. If she is successful, life for three delicious months is one long whirl of charity ball committees and lunch parties and dances five nights a week. If she has not got "allure" or "sex-appeal" or "it," or whatever is the popular word at the moment for charm, then it is one long purgatory. No man, not even at an old-fashioned public school, has to endure a humiliation comparable to an empty dance programme. The wretched girl has to stand by ball-room walls waiting hopelessly for aggressive young cubs to ask her for a dance; she sees them pass her by, chatting to her friends, who may have twice her looks, but probably do not possess half her brains; she disappears to powder her nose and talks miserably to the cloak-room attendant; returns to the ball-room, perhaps has an occasional dance with some old friend of the family's and then joins her mother on a chaperon's sofa. Bravely they pretend that it is all being the greatest fun and in their hearts they know that it is a miserable failure. E. F. Benson's *Dodo* knew it all, and she captivated London more than forty years ago.

In spite of all the new opportunities for girls to earn their own living, the Season is still a marriage racket. Parents cast their bread upon the waters and hope it will return to them after not so many days in the engagement columns of *The Times*. A house is taken in Mayfair for the Season, a ball is given, and the girl is launched on the giddy round. If all goes well, it ends in wedding-bells. The only difference from pre-War days is that by some odd change of fashion, they more often nowadays ring from St. Margaret's, Westminster, than from St. George's, Hanover Square. But the alteration cannot be said to be fundamental.

Nor have the manners of youth changed nearly as much as is often supposed. "The bright young things" of 1926 belong to another age as much as the "Souls" of 1886. I know young men who before they go to bed on the morning after the Ball never fail to sit down and write a letter of thanks to their hostess. The gate-crasher is no more and the carpets on the grand staircases are not a mass of holes burnt by cigarette ends; and complete social ostracism would be the fate of a girl who had been careless about the mixing of her drinks.

Society, of course, is less exclusive nowadays. It is open to any girl whose mother has given a ball, and to any young man with a public-school accent and a well-fitting suit of dress-clothes. The jokes of Oscar Wilde's social comedies about those who are "in" Society and those who are not, and the "right" and the "wrong" side of Belgrave Square are quite meaningless to-day. But Society has its codes, and on the whole it keeps to them. It may be Vanity Fair, but it is not without its charm and elegance. It is certainly a grand pageant. The Royal Enclosure in Ascot week is still a dream of fair women, and there are few sights more lovely than Lord's in the luncheon interval when a hot summer's day and the Eton and Harrow match meet together.

Perhaps I am unduly obsessed with contrast between London and foreign capitals. No one who has visited them can fail to be struck by the staggering gulf that separates them. Berlin, though it has returned to the old pre-War militarism, has not returned to the pre-War social grandeurs. The Jews whom the Kaiser encouraged to race yachts at Kiel in imitation of Cowes, are in exile: the great houses on the Tiergartenstrasse are falling into decay, and the Prussian nobility that lived in them are in a state of hopeless insolvency on their estates in East Prussia, or on the edge of starvation in one-roomed tenement flats. There is nothing but Embassy entertaining and even Grand Opera is a drab affair of brown shirts and lounge suits. Moscow is a morgue and Paris is just provincial. A first night is about as smart as a suburban dance-hall. New York is just mass production and noisy vulgarity. In contrast with these, social life in London remains miraculously untouched by the hand of time. It may be that we are even here at the end of an epoch, that we shall look back to this great Jubilee season as the high-water mark of post-War social life, as we now remember the death of the old Queen as the turning point of the Empire's unchallenged supremacy. But whether the old social world is in its sunset or not, the substance of it is still with us and however much we would welcome a greater simplicity and a more even distribution of the good things of life, while it remains, it is very fair to see.

Who says Women are the Weaker Sex?

"*Tell it to the Marines*" *says*

ERIC LINKLATER

IT is a pretty training in fancy to botanise on a city pavement. To prove that Bacon wrote Shakespeare is no more than jog-trotting for any lively imagination. A moderate invention will easily stretch itself to describe the enjoyment of fish out of water, the humanity of munition manufacturers, and the stark snow-whiteness of ebony. These are simple exercises, and deserve but small attention.

You tell me the Atlantic is all dry land, and the Sahara is a puddle? I could maintain such opinions, had I time to think about them. You say the earth is flat, and the moon made of green cheese? I see no great difficulty there. But here's a statement, shouted in chorus by an army of little, round-shouldered, short-sighted, chalk-boned male romantics, that makes my wit despair, that drives me to the wall, that beats me to defeated knees. They say, these little men with newspapers in their hands and fear in their hearts, that All Women suffer from an Inferiority Complex. And now, as I have said, I admit defeat. I can prove, if you want me to, that summer days are dark and midnight has a golden hue. I shall show

" If there were thirty handsome women in the Diplomatic Service, the world would have a healthier prospect of peace "

how a mermaid may ride a bicycle the lion lie down with the lamb. But maintain what the little men believe, women are the Weaker Sex and harb a knowledge of their inferiority, is bey my power.

The belief, I admit, is widespread, it is perhaps a useful belief. But former times, when there was no n for it, it did not exist. It came slo into being as the progress of our pres civilisation interfered with the nat functions of women and modified hardships that women had previously dured. For centuries, all over the wo a woman's life had consisted of a li love and a lot of children, a minimum food and a maximum of hard work. A women had survived this toilsome ex

"All primitive men knew that women were the stronger sex, and kept them in a state of manageable weakness by beatings and long hours of work"

"Did Sir Walter Raleigh, more indulgent in dress than any woman, put a fortune on his back because he was aware of his inferiority to other courtiers?"

Are women weak because they pay attention to dress? Or because they can't read a time-table or abide by traffic lights? Of course they're not, says the witty author of "Juan in America," "Magnus Merriman," "Ripeness is All," etc., and in this amusing article he debunks, with characteristic gusto, the critics of femininity

Illustrations by L. G. Illingworth

nce, and no one ever suspected they were weaker than men. How could they be, when so indefatigably they bore and gave suck, carried wood and cooked pease-puddings, healed their wounded husbands and taught their daughters? Inferior? They were the stronger sex, and all men knew it, and kept them in a state of manageable weakness by incessant child-bearing, poor food, recurrent beating, and long hours of work. An All-seeing Creator —or biological accident, or Creative Evolution, or whatever you please to call it—had designed woman as one might design an unbreakable motor-car. And so long as sufficient burdens were piled upon her, there was no suggestion of her weakness or inferiority.

But times change, and we change with them. By some means or other— there is no need to discuss that here —pregnancy ceased to be the inevitable and ceaseless condition of a married woman, and the growing humanitarianism of the world permitted her to eat better food, refused to let her be beaten, and diminished her hours of physical labour. The result was that women discovered a huge surplus of energy, a great reservoir of strength, and men were stricken with fear. Some capitulated at once, and proclaimed themselves Feminists. Others, the little, weak-kneed but hopeful romantics, comforted themselves with an ingenious fiction: they saw that women still suffered various physical disabilities, that

women teachers, women shop-assistants, and business women were paid lower wages than men, and naturally resented this discrimination: and they construed this resentment and those disabilities —ignoring woman's power to overcome them—as admissions and symptoms of inferiority. Ostriches also, seeing what they fear or dislike, will bury their heads in the sand.

Among the many fatuities, offered with varying degrees of amiability as critical observations on female nature, there has been an ever-recurrent gibing, snarling, or complacent sneering at women's love of finery and changing attire. Male shoulders have been shrugged and scornful fingers pointed at bonnets (*Continued on page* 160)

Something for the Whole Family —A New AUSTIN

TEN-FOUR
LICHFIELD SALOON

My Lady's choice....

When my lady chooses for herself or the family, the preference is for an Austin; so easy to drive with its simple controls, so dependable with its certainty of many thousands of miles with but routine attention. Whether she desires a new or used model, there are five floors of Austin cars on view at the exclusive Austin Showrooms of the Car Mart, all the 1935 models and a wide selection of used cars, at prices to suit all. When in town, see this fine exhibition of Austin cars.

Prices of New Austins
'Sevens' from £100
'Ten-four' from £152
'Light Twelve-four' from £172.10.0
'Twelve' from £275
'Sixteen & Eighteen' from £318
'Twenty' from £595

THE WORLD'S LARGEST AUSTIN DISTRIBUTORS

Exclusive Austin Depot:
297-9 Euston Road, London, N.W.1.
Museum 4641

146-150 Park Lane,
London, W.1.
Grosvenor 3434

Stanhope House,
320-4 Euston Road, N.W.1
Museum 2000

ROLL'S COFFEE
"H.R." brand in Vacuum Sealed Tins 3/- lb.
EMPIRE „ „ „ „ „ 2/7 lb.
COFFEE AND CHICORY MIXTURES 1/8 lb.
The Coffee for Connoisseurs

HENRY ROLL & CO. LTD.
66 Stork's Road, S.E.16

WHO SAYS WOMEN ARE THE WEAKER SEX?

(*Continued from page* 159)

and mantles; at frocks of taffeta and figured silk and a cloudy drift of underwear; at hoops and crinolines and hobble-skirts; at paradise plumes and patterned velvet; at the bold exposure of a back and the lovely fenestration of a bosom in the whimsical architecture of satins and Chinese silk; at all the unnumbered adornments and fashions of infinite variety with which women have drawn attention to their beauty or distracted a questing eye from their lack of it. The little romantic men, and large bull-fronted boorish men, and penny-wise meagre-fisted men, have loudly declared that all this attention to finery and parade of costume are signs of inferiority and a woman's desperate attempt to compensate herself for the knowledge of her weakness!

One of His Majesty's judges, a man otherwise sagacious, learned, subtle in understanding, and profound in wisdom—the late Mr. Justice McCardie, who should have known better—said once (and often thought, presumably) that the dressmaker's art was "one of Nature's solaces for a constant and insuperable handicap. A reasonable indulgence in dress," he said, "is needed to counterbalance what I may call the inferiority complex of women."

What gravel-blind tomfoolery is this! Did Sir Walter Raleigh, more indulgent in dress than any woman, put a fortune on his back, hang jewels in his ear, and wear a silver breastplate because subconsciously he was aware of his inferiority to other courtiers? When pride was more rampant, wit more abundant, energy more explosive, and masculinity more indisputable than at any other period in our history—in the reigning-time of Queen Elizabeth and the Scots King James, that is—men canvassed fashion and dressed themselves with richer and more luxuriant fancy than ever before or since. So huge and so extravagant was their desire for new finery, their hunger for slashed hose and leg-of-mutton sleeves and vaster ruffs and jewellery of a novel shape, that fashion itself was beggared, and a man's own invention became his only arbiter in dress. And this was the time of desperate voyages and fantastic valour, of poetry that circled the earth more often than their ships, and struck the very stars with a sound like the clashing of swords.

Love of gay costume and ever-changing hats a sign of inferiority? Thrice-clotted nonsense, I say, and indurated folly. If any fashion of our time betrays a sense of weakness and degeneration it is man's most dismal suitings, our poor twin cylinders of unimaginative trousers, the bare utility of our coats, and the poorhouse queue of our waistcoat buttons. We, the men of our time, let our tailors dress us as though we were crabs on the seashore or small deer in the desert, creatures eager only to escape observation. The dull hues of our raiment and their meagre outline blend with and dissolve into the grimy background of our mercantile age, and make us indistinguishable from our dull surroundings. Women only, proud and unquelled by circumstance, proclaim their individuality in lovely and self-chosen clothes, and so assert, above the clamour of machines and the drone of a mechanised existence, their indefeasible humanity.

Had I the courage of my convictions I would never pass a well-dressed woman without raising my hat to her (if it were not that impersonal admiration is too likely to be misunderstood), for in the conscious gallantry of her attire I recognise, not compensation for inferiority, but a delighted and delighting boast of her invincible individuality. In an age when liberty is threatened on every hand, and half the world is dressed in some wretched sort of uniform, women stoutly—or slenderly, or in any shape at all—maintain their freedom to wear what they please, and change it as they like. They are the Old Guard of liberty, and by their suits you shall know them.

Now it may be said, by some inveterate pursuer of pin-pricking argument or dialectical nettle-grower, that women are plainly and patently inferior to men in the arrangement of many small matters of merely quotidian importance. Such a one will triumphantly recall his wife's inability to read a time-table, his daughters' indifference to traffic lights, his mother's incomprehension of current politics. No one can deny that there is a vast concourse of women who blandly ignore and implicitly deny the importance of much that seems, to a male intelligence, of vital moment. But is this necessarily a sign of inferior cerebration? Is it not rather the sign of an instinctively trained selective faculty? For the essential function of woman—of which many women are still aware—is the creation and nurture of life itself, and being engrossed by this central aspect of existence, she may be excused some lack of attention to the accidental occurrences or conventions on the periphery of life. What are time-tables when compared with the seasons of the year, or traffic lights when set beside the glad affirmative of her ductless glands? That many women are imperfectly adapted to the exigencies of our penny-in-the-slot civilisation is an indictment of civilisation, not of them.

But the Practical Man is still unanswered. The Practical Man—that large straw-stuffed creature who sees little and understands little and is successful in some little chosen way because he can neither smell nor hear the difficulties that appal more sensitive organisms—the Practical Man will say he knows, beyond all argument, that women are inferior creatures, because they all defer to him. They meet his wishes, they applaud his judgment, they

are grateful for his gifts. Therefore they are inferior. But alas for the Practical Man, and alas for us whom he so often governs! For the world is full of him, and our politics are a reflection of his practicality. He knows nothing of diplomacy, little enough (and that mistaken) of human nature, and he can neither tell a lie with conviction, nor with certainty detect one. But all women, save those who have become efficient in the modern way, are diplomats from childhood, and when they lie it is with the strength of truth, for they can turn truth round about and show its behind without embarrassment. They defer to the Practical Man for their own sufficient purpose. They meet him with their own weapons, and he, seeing no weapons at all, supposes them unarmed. Poor innocent!

Yet in one or two matters the Practical Man may be right; as when, for example, he disapproves of women candidates for Parliament. For indeed they will only waste their time there. But I wish there were some thirty or forty of them, handsome to look at, agreeable, and good natural liars, in the Diplomatic Service. The world would have a healthier prospect of peace.

Now, to clinch the matter, here is a proof of what I have said, that anyone may test for himself or herself. Go to a man, a man well known for exceptional ability in some art or profession, and say to him, "You have the most powerfully creative intelligence that has been granted to mankind since Shakespeare lived."

Watch, then, his pitiable confusion, his wretched simpering, his rank incredulity, or listen to his hoarse, unmeaning laughter. For he knows his littleness, and cannot forget it.

Then go to a woman, no matter whether she is beautiful or not, and say to her, "Since Helen died, and Deirdre, nothing has been seen on earth so lovely as you."

She will take it to her heart like roses, and her eyes will shine like dew on the roses. And why? Because you have merely spoken her own unspoken thoughts.

Inferiority complex? Tell it to the Marines.

IDEAL FAMILY TOWN APARTMENTS
In Europe's Largest Square of Self-contained Flats

Three Minutes West from Westminster along London's Riverside Drive

. . .

Bus No. 24 to Grosvenor Road

River-front Terraces

. . .

Three Acres of Charming Central Gardens

. . .

Children's Day and Boarding Centre

Practical attractions for true lovers of home have never been so well blended with the conveniences of a town residence as at Dolphin Square.

The generous spaciousness of its family flats at moderate, inclusive rentals; the abundant built-in storage and wardrobe accommodation; the sensibly fitted kitchens and attractive bathroom suites; the installed services of central heat, constant hot water, telephone, radio, refrigerators, gas and electrical appliances—these all bear evidence of an unusual effort to satisfy those who would make a permanent home in the Royal Borough, as well as those who want a convenient and complete town apartment for seasonal use.

Attractive amenities of life here include Squash Courts, Gymnasium, Swimming Pool, Restaurant, Domestic Service as required, 3-Acre Garden maintained by the Owners of Dolphin Square, Garage for 300 Cars underground, Laundry, Beauty Parlour, Library, etc.

Residents with children are fully catered for by the Children's Centre. This Matron-governed organisation offers hourly, daily, weekly or period boarding facilities and qualified guardianship of the highest order, for children from 10 days to 7 years of age. Occupying a charmingly appointed Suite of Bedrooms, Dining-rooms, Bathrooms, Day and Night Nurseries and Play-rooms, it is controlled by Matron Evelyn Pantin, R.S.C.N., S.C.M. (Photo. inset.)

GRATIS BROCHURE TO "GOOD HOUSEKEEPING" READERS

The beautifully illustrated book, "Dolphin Square," will be posted free to readers, mentioning this advertisement, who are interested in town apartments. Show Flats open daily until 8 p.m.

Dolphin Square
S.W.1.

RICHARD COSTAIN LTD., COSTAIN HOUSE, UPPER WOBURN PLACE, W.C.1
Builders and Owners

★ **"GOOD HOUSEKEEPING" EXHIBITION,** *under the direction of The Institute of Good Housekeeping, March 1st to 31st, will take place in Show Flat Suites at Dolphin Square, specially furnished and decorated by the Institute, and equipped with Approved products. Members of the Institute will be in attendance to welcome "Good Housekeeping" readers.*

4783

4624

4787

4866

4729

PARTY CLOTHES FOR THE YOUNGER SET

4624. *Nothing has ever been prettier than the Red-Riding-Hood cape for the small girl's party cloak. This one has a detachable hood, that forms a cowl at the back when not in use. Tootal's broad rib cord velvet (price 3s. 11d. a yard) is suggested, and as it is only 27 inches wide, four yards will be required to make size 10. In sizes 4 to 14 years. Price 9d.*

4783. *The older girl will feel very grand in this slim-fitting Empire dress, tied with a sash. A band of the same fabric is caught loosely round the neck in front and, as a soft frill, outlines the small V at the back. Most materials could be used, possibly a plaid Courtauld taffeta. For size 12, allow 5½ yds. of 36-in. material. Sizes 11 to 17 years. Price 1s.*

4787. *The young man of the party wears belted knickers of Tootal corduroy and a blouse in a toning shade of rough crêpe from Courtaulds. For the trousers allow 1¼ yds. 27-in. corduroy and for the blouse 1¼ yds. 36-in. crêpe, in size 4. Available for 2, 4 and 6 years. Price 9d.*

4866. *This gay little dress, with frilled neck and sleeves and gauging at the waist, is pretty in a soft or stiff fabric, and is here shown in printed Fergoneen (price 2s. 11d. a yard), with plain frills. Allow 2¾ yds. printed, and ¾ yd. plain for size 12. In sizes 8 to 15 years. Price 9d.*

4729. *Very demure is this fluttering frock in Tootal's crease-resisting printed chiffon, which costs 3s. 11d. a yard and is not as fragile as one might expect. Allow 3⅛ yds. for size 12. In sizes 8 to 16. Price 9d.*

What has happened to the "Femme Fatale"?

J.S.GOODALL

Godfrey Winn

looking back on Circe, Helen and Cleo-patra, deplores the uniformity and lack of mystery of the woman of to-day

A COUPLE of years or more ago I attended the Law Courts for the first time in my life—out of curiosity, not from compulsion, I was a spectator of the unfolding of a domestic drama that filled the newspapers at the time. For many and obvious reasons, I will not go into details now, but it was one more version of the eternal triangle.

That in itself would not have interested me sufficiently to leave my desk for days and sit squashed like a sardine in an atmosphere that was more characteristic of the Black Hole of Calcutta than a Court of Justice, and listen to famous K.C.s squabbling with each other like small children, had it not been that as a writer eternally in search of copy, I was immensely intrigued with the psychology of the case. Here was a woman, who in her photographs looked a "pretty little thing," nothing more, who yet had possessed the power to wreck two men's lives, to so overwhelm one man with passion that he cast professional honour to the winds, another with such an attack of possessive jealousy, such a determination to achieve revenge that he was ready to go to any lengths—far beyond his legal rights—to circumvent his rival's doom, to destroy not only his chances of love, but his means of livelihood, too.

The more I listened to the details of the case, which might have been the twentieth century version of a play by Sophocles, the more amazed I was every time I glanced across the sea of faces to where the cause of all the trouble sat smiling beside her solicitor. What could be the secret of her amazing attraction? She was pretty, yes—pretty in the way that hundreds of other women are pretty to-day who rely for their looks on make-up rather than natural features and colouring, and spend pounds every month on so-called beauty culture. Her taste in clothes was typical of a generation which prefers to wear a uniform rather than quarrel with fashion; her figure was attractive without being alluring; she walked with the grace of youth and self-confidence. Her voice, on the other hand, equally self-confident, was hardly an asset. Yet here was the civilised descendant of Circe, here was the newest edition of the *femme fatale,* phrase made memorable in history. . . .

Cleopatra, Helen, Mary Queen of Scots, Ninon de Lenclos . . . what did this "pretty little thing" possess in common with all the other figures in that procession which, through the ages, has caused such havoc in men's hearts?

Clearly the answer was —nothing. I could find no contacts other than that innate audacity, which fundamentally is a feminine rather than a masculine attribute, and which enabled Madame du Barry, at one moment the uncrowned queen of France, to smile at her executioner and remark, "*Un moment, monsieur le bourreau,*" as she patted her hair into place. . . . I could find no contacts, only contrasts. Even making allowances for fashions in clothes and modes of deportment, changes again of circumstance and situation, still the fact remained that the essential core of mystery that in the past has always surrounded such women, that overwhelming sense of being in the presence of a person apart, someone in whose eyes the light of Destiny shines like an everlasting lamp, was entirely absent. There was nothing, simply nothing to distinguish this girl from any other modern woman. You would not have turned your head to look at her in the street.

Indeed, emerging from the Law Courts at last, I did come face to face with her sister, and a few yards on, again her sister, and again. Here was the same type duplicated a dozen times, but never (*Continued on page 165*)

WHAT HAS HAPPENED TO THE "FEMME FATALE"?

(*Continued from page* 164)

a single face or personality, so different, so arresting, that one's curiosity was instantly aroused, one's thoughts went after her. Every face was a mirror of the age we live in—this standardised, everyday world, in which it is the ordinary in all things that meets with success, the extraordinary that is an embarrassing failure. As with things, so with people. The *femme fatale,* in all her glamorous glory, her exaggerated appeal, her elaborate technique, no longer exists as a type, unique or otherwise, except, of course, on the screen, where the creating of a hopelessly unreal atmosphere continues to be a profitable concern.

But in real life, this prosaic and practical post-war life of refrigerators and canned music and baby cars, her place has been usurped by a universal type, the physical epitome of our epoch. Men still lose their hearts and their heads just as extravagantly, just as helplessly, if indeed, not more so, than in previous centuries, but the cause of all the trouble no longer resembles in appearance the traditional picture of the *femme fatale,* and seldom, if ever, looks like a film star, but is far more likely to remind one, both in face, character and temperament, of what is known in the sphere of sport, as an "all-rounder."

I am not being facetious, but deadly serious. The modern woman, especially the modern vamp, seductress, call her what you like, is an all-rounder. She has to be. Once it was considered more than enough for a woman just to *be*. To-day she must be objective as well as subjective, if she wishes to meet with success. To be beautiful but dumb is no more the criterion of feminine perfection.

Of course, once, I know—and not so long ago either—men infinitely preferred the object of their emotions to look not only as lovely as the sort of study in porcelain that used to stand upon the drawing-room mantelpiece, but also equally as still and equally as silent. The two last qualifications were almost as important as the first. It helped the necessary harbouring of illusions on both sides. For what man would not be a god, and what woman would not remain an enchanted figure of mystery so long as the couple in question only addressed each other in the language of love?

So it went on for centuries, and might indeed have gone on for ever, despite the efforts of pioneers like Dame Millicent Fawcett, had not the War come and driven nail after nail into the coffin of this so carefully nurtured romantic approach of the sexes. Men were suddenly forced to realise that women were people as well as playthings; women found that men made charming friends and companions as well as husbands and lovers. The result was that both sexes automatically lost their lovely, impossible illusions about each other, and replaced them, little by little, after much shock and disillusionment, by a shrewd and sympathetic tolerance based on shared experience. To-day men and women have gone farther than sharing each other's life: they share the same life. They do the same work and play the same games with the same degree of success: and in addition they sow the same wild oats, and are faced with the same responsibilities and problems of behaviour.

Now men have always been all-rounders, not only by nature, but from environment and force of circumstances, whereas women have only become so recently, and not altogether, I feel, of their own free will in many cases. However, their constant presence in public life

(*Continued on page* 166)

FINE FEATHERS MAKE FINE BIRDS

—AND SO DOES 'BISTO' GRAVY

You will thoroughly enjoy all your roast dishes from the choicest game to the humblest sausage if you serve them with plenty of thick, rich Bisto gravy. It is easily made and gives *that rich effect* to all meat dishes.

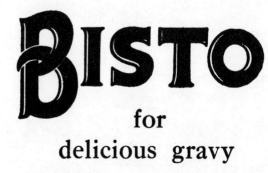

BISTO
for
delicious gravy

WHAT HAS HAPPENED TO THE "FEMME FATALE"?

(*Continued from page* 165)

has already come to be part of the fabric of modern civilisation. Further, the majority of men, so far from resenting this increasing encroachment on their own preserves, hasten to encourage the once-weaker sex along the road that leads to complete emancipation, and dare I add complete disillusionment, too. Who knows, it may even bring complete revulsion also one day in the future, when both sexes become mutually exhausted by each other's competition, sick of a world that is peopled with sexless robots.

Surely that must be the end of this giant "debunking act," for which this age will go down in history, a "debunking," not only of customs and institutions and traditions, but of people, too, and most of all, of the old-established relationship of the sexes. Let me add here, that I dare say in the past there was a great deal of humbug and deception on both sides, in consequence of which a man and woman did not always understand the secret places of each other's heart, even after half a century of eating meals at the same table, and sleeping in the same bedroom. Was that, after all, such a drawback to their happiness? Would they have been happier, if they had behaved like the principal characters in Noel Coward's *Private Lives?* Again, were men and women less attractive to each other physically, because their minds instead of being beautifully (or hideously) bare, were decorously clothed in the equivalent of flannel? I wonder. One always hears what happy, contented lives our grandparents lived together. Was that contentment merely pretence, the making the best of a bad job, that time has softened into a legend of peace and goodwill? I doubt it. I doubt it very much.

On the other hand, what *is* pretence, I have a shrewd suspicion, is that we modern men and women manage our relationships any better. Are we really any happier—and surely lasting happiness is the ultimate test—for this new kind of relationship, in which there are no barriers and no mystery, in which everything is shared and nothing is sacred? We are eternally swearing that we are, ignoring the evidence of the divorce courts and other contemporary signposts, but all the same, I can't help feeling that we protest too much, that we are like small children who the first day after the departure of their governess have made themselves sick on cheap sweets bought at the corner of the street, and whose pride won't admit their mistake.

Especially is this so, I feel, in the case of the modern woman with her everlasting, eulogistic references to her present "all-round" existence. The chameleon has nothing on her, as they would say so graphically across the water. The perfection of ordinariness, yes—but a perfection that has to include a dozen times as many different branches of living as were exploited, enjoyed or endured (it depends on one's point of view) by her ancestresses. Does she really enjoy being all things to all people so much as she so ardently asserts?

I should have imagined that it must be too exhausting for a contented frame of mind: a "pretty little thing" to this man, an amusing, gay companion to another, and to another a "good sport," who can hold her own on the tennis court and the golf course, to yet another, the perfect private secretary, and to even yet another, the efficient housekeeper and mother, who can run her house like clockwork and bring up her children in the approved modern way, and still have time left over to run around with her husband.

Surely, too much is expected of the modern woman. Urged on by my sex, she has set herself an impossibly high standard of all-round excellence. It is not surprising when she fails, and when she succeeds, her success runs along such stereotyped lines that its repercussions pass almost unnoticed until one morning you open your newspaper, and there on the centre page is a picture of a face that reminds you of someone you know, until you remind yourself in turn that the only reason it is familiar is because it is like every other face you pass in the street.

Here we are back at the beginning again, and with it the end approaches. For what more is there for me to say except that I can't help regretting the passing of the *femme fatale* in all her glory? I can't help feeling sorry that her place should have been taken by a type that is so familiar, so ordinary and everyday, that you would not look twice at it in the street, unless you happened to know from personal experience that behind that pretty mask—plucked eyebrows, pillar-box mouth, uniformly waved hair—lay the soul of a "good trooper," a "good mixer," a good "all-rounder"? Or at any rate, behind that mask lay *something*—something memorable, something worth-while—not visible to the naked eye.

Presumably it must be so, but all the same my sadness lingers, the same sense of helpless sadness that I experience when I am forced to note the passing of one more magnificent, stately mansion, full of character and personality, and the erection in its place of yet another enormous block of anonymous flats, slavishly true to the pattern of modern architecture, a nightmare of the multiplication table.

If men must continue to lose their hearts and their heads at the same time over the other sex—and presumably the law of nature decrees that some of us must—then I wish with all my own heart and head that the *grandes passions* of my fellows could continue to be played out in the grand manner, as once upon a time, instead of deteriorating into a bedroom farce that hasn't even the excuse of being funny, or else, into a poor imitation of a Greek drama that lacks the purging, purifying omniscience of the original.

Perhaps I am falling myself into the old, old trap of romanticising the past. After all, Helen of Troy is only a legend, while if we had to rely solely for our impressions of Cleopatra's charms upon Plutarch, instead of the descriptive and dramatic genius of Shakespeare, I don't know what we would think of her. This I do know that when the apotheosis of women as a sex ceased to be a popular practice, and instead woman left her pedestal where for centuries she had been an object of awe and reverence to men, and of her own free will, I admit, drew the veil of mystery from across her eyes, that day was far from being the gala it is always depicted, but, rather, was a day of mourning in the relationship of the sexes.

At least, that is my own opinion, and I can't help feeling that it is the right one. So in the future may the pendulum swing back again, and that sense of mystery, of being in the presence, not of an effeminate edition of oneself, but of a glamorous creature from another world, may return—and with it, the *femme fatale* in all her glory.

BRAINWAVES for Parties

The 1930's 1936

Mother gets hints on decorations and refreshments.

Bobby swots up the latest games and riddles.

Father practises some startling conjuring tricks.

48 Pages of Brand New Ideas in

STONE'S *FREE* PARTY BOOK

A truly original "Wizard's Corner" for conjuring Fathers; dozens of games, riddles, conundrums and jokes for the children; thrilling decoration, surprise and entertainment hints for Mother; all contained in STONE'S Free Party Book. STONE'S Ginger Wine, with its genial warmth, has always been the supreme brightener of festivities. Only STONE'S could produce so rollicking a book to accompany the cheeriest of cold weather beverages. Get your copy from the grocer or wine merchant who supplies you with STONE'S Ginger Wine. In case of difficulty write for your copy (enclosing 1d. stamp) to Stone's Ginger Wine, Moreland Street, Finsbury, E.C.1.

Stone's PARTY BOOK

STONE'S
Original GINGER WINE

"*Central Heating For All*"

A new and charming portrait of H.R.H.
Princess Elizabeth. (By Marcus Adams.)

A Second Queen

The parallel between our Princess Elizabeth

Decoration by

THERE is a Golden Age in the history of every country, and in ours it is the Elizabethan Age. "Ah, those were the days," Englishmen have sighed ever since, thinking of the time when Shakespeare and Ben Jonson were providing a steady succession of First Nights that were worth paying double prices for, and tough fellows such as Francis Drake and Raleigh had beaten the Spaniards at their own game and given cause to every youngster who was sick of an office stool to think he might run away to sea with nothing in his pockets and come back in his own ship, sailing up the Thames with sails of blue damask, and a gold chain round the neck of every man in his crew, to see, leaning from a balcony in Greenwich Palace, Queen Elizabeth

herself waving her hand to greet him home.

England was still Merrie England then, her Golden Age as pagan as that in the dawn of the world; the Reformation had meant politics far more as yet than religion; the Civil War had not yet split England into a self-conscious division between the Serious-and-Industrious classes and the Gay-and-Gentlemanly, from which it has never recovered (even now the clash of Highbrow and Lowbrow arouses sentiments as bitter as those between Roundhead

and Cavalier. Even some of the nicknames of opprobrium remain the same, for what were the "Steeple Hats" of the Puritans but the "High Hats" of to-day?).

But the Elizabethan, like the Golden Age, was before this division; men might kill each other more frequently then, but they had less reason to hate each other; men of different classes went to the same village school together; Sunday was still naturally, and not defiantly, a holiday as well as a holy day; and a man could write a sonnet to

Elizabeth, the English princess who became Queen of Bohemia. (From an old print.)

Elizabeth by Margaret Irwin

nd James I's daughter is full of interest

anley Herbert

s mistress's eyebrow or tinkle tunes the lute while waiting his turn at e barber's without being called a golo or even a bounder.

That there really was a time when nglishmen were gay, glorious, proud, nfident, poetical, musical, as well as ing good sportsmen and good at mes (especially at bowls and especi- y when the Spanish fleet was sighted) naturally a memory to arouse the stful longings of a nation.

Memory and longing—those are the sential ingredients of human life, for a man must have something to look both back and forward to, otherwise he is an isolated atom floating in meaningless space—and no man is going to stand that. We cannot bear to lose hope, to believe that Queen Elizabeth is dead, even as Queen Anne is dead; and she herself could not bear it, which was why she would not let go, would not go to bed and be ill and die like any other hard-working, tired-out old woman, but would sit on the floor, fully dressed, ill, dazed, barely conscious, but still holding tight on to those last precious moments of the Elizabethan Age that were slipping so fast through her fingers, spilling out their gold, never to return again.

"Little man, little man!" she exclaimed in rebuke to the minister who tried to make her go to bed—but he won. The Elizabethan Age had gone, and the little men had come to rule instead.

She had gone, but hope of her could not go. Like all great leaders, she had left the belief that she was too good not to last. King Arthur is not dead, but sleeps with his knights inside the Eildon hills until this island shall have need of him again; Roland was not killed at Roncesvalles; Charlemagne and Frederick Barbarossa did not die, but sleep out the time until they shall come and rule the (Continued on page 170)

---

world again as they did so long ago.

And when the painted hag, mean and magnificent, who gave England her greatest hour of greatness, had crumbled into dust, she left the belief that there would one day come "a Second Queen Elizabeth" in her own right, who would bring back that hour.

Since then there have been two Princess Elizabeths to inherit that hope. Three centuries separate these two little girls, on whom the romantic tenderness and wish-fulfilment dreams of this nation have been lavished to an extent unparalleled even by a film star or a flying ace. The "fan-mail" of the present Princess Elizabeth is, I am told, equal to that of Greta Garbo ; but the Princess is the more fortunate in being kept unaware of most of it, for it is the chief aim of those about her to treat her as much like an ordinary child and as little like an heir to the throne as possible. Letters and presents from women and children all over the world, who yearn to link themselves somehow to royalty, romance, something different from their own drab everyday ; loudly cheering crowds who have waited for hours to see her pass ; pictures of her everywhere ; a postage stamp of her somewhere—these are kept in the background as much as possible.

In the foreground are her daily regular lessons, her walks and rides and games with her little sister, her picture books and fairy tales, her Golden Retrievers and Yellow Labradors and Cocker Spaniels and Corgis, all sporting dogs, with the one exotic exception of the little Tibetan Lion dog. People throughout the empire want to make her presents of dogs of various rare and perfect breeds, but she remains faithful to the family's pets. Dogs are more important than toys, but they too loom large in the foreground, especially the smallest, a cabinet of tiny glass animals and infinitesimal objects of all kinds. The biggest toy is the smallest house in the world, perfect to its last detail of electric heating, lighting and wireless set, large enough for the Princess (but not for a grown-up) to walk about in and go upstairs to the bedroom and bathroom and cook with the tiny glittering pots and pans in the kitchen, for everything, from the telephone to the pattern on the curtains is reduced to the scale of a little girl's size—just such a house as the Seven Little Dwarfs, grown extremely up-to-date, might have provided for themselves.

Now it is just this recognition of the needs and tastes of ordinary childhood, however royal, which is supposed to mark our age as different from all preceding it. We no longer think it right to send the children of the poor to work down in the mines from the ages of three and four onwards, as did our pious and respectable forebears of a hundred years ago ; and no longer are the children of the educated classes as well educated as the child of Mr. Evelyn, who before his fifth year could "turn English into Latin and vice versa, had a wonderful disposition to mathematics and a strong disposition to Greek."

And when we come to royal children, we find the author of the classic work on the royal household of to-day writing, " In the 16th century it was perhaps scarcely fun to be a child at all, certainly to be a possible heir to the throne was a grim fate. . . . The Princess Elizabeth of four centuries ago was, never for one moment permitted to be childlike."

That might well be so, since that particular princess was the daughter of Henry VIII and Anne Boleyn, had had her mother beheaded by her father and herself declared illegitimate—enough to cloud any childhood, let alone the possible inheritance to a throne in rivalry with the very grim, distrustful elder half-sister who earned the singular distinction in the English monarchy of being nicknamed " Bloody."

But take the second Princess Elizabeth, the Stuart princess, daughter of James VI of Scotland, afterwards James I of England as well, who followed her father down into England at the age of seven.

She was so gay and pretty and adventurous that the whole country rapturously claimed her for their own in a way that outshone even their welcome for her gallant, popular elder brother Prince Henry, while as for her younger brother, Baby Charles, they never really claimed him at all, either then as a backward child or later as King Charles I.

But " our English Elizabeth," as they were to call her so often in later life, was instantly accepted as the joy and hope of the nation—to an extent that was distinctly inconvenient when it came to Mr. Guy Fawkes attempting to blow up all the rest of the Royal Family, as well as the Houses of Parliament, in order to place her on the throne at the age of ten and proclaim her as Queen Elizabeth II.

" What a queen should I have become by this means ! " she exclaimed in very properly expressed indignation, which was at once reported to her royal father by her tutor, who had probably inspired it, for it is her only recorded unchildlike remark.

But apart from the unfairly exceptional circumstance of the Gunpowder Plot, Elizabeth Stuart, daughter of James I, completely belies our conception of the grim fate of royal children in the past, for she had as free and happy an upbringing as any modern child could wish.

The present Princess Elizabeth's love of animals is matched in the former Elizabeth ; to the end of her life she was so devoted to her dogs and horses and dozens of strange pets that she was accused of preferring them to her baker's dozen of children. And as a child this passion was given full rein. The Little House of the present-day Princess seems as modern in its idea as in its mechanical magnificence. But Elizabeth Stuart, three hundred years ago, when childish pleasures were not supposed to be considered, had her own Fairy Farm, stocked with the most minute breeds of every species, Shetland ponies and tiny Highland cattle and dogs small enough to hide in her pockets, as well as the big jolly hounds that pulled down the buck for her when she went hunting. And every great traveller that visited or returned to England brought a present for the Princess in the shape of some new animal or bright, rare bird for her Fairy Farm.

Lessons too, instead of being the lengthy, laborious affair that is commonly believed to have driven many a child of the past into an early grave, were made into a game by her tutor, Lord Harrington. He showed her stars through the newly invented telescope, and insects and flowers through the microscope, taught her to put no faith in astrology, and that the earth moved round the sun.

But it is when we come to history that Lord Harrington fairly amazes us by the modernity of his methods, for he taught it with packs of pictures like cards, arranging them in separate groups to show Elizabeth what was happening all over Europe at the same time, so that there in France were the French and Spanish and English kings meeting on the Field of the

(Continued on page 172)

POPULAR FORD
(£6. Tax)

Saloon, £115.   Double-Entrance Saloon, £125

For years past, August and September

have been among the best of months, throughout the British Isles, more dependable than May and June, less scorchingly hot than July.

Why not a Popular FORD (£6. Tax) for your August and September journeyings?

Amply powered for four and holiday baggage, picnic impedimenta, and the like, surprisingly roomy, yet very compact in overall measurements, for ease of parking and garage away from home, the essence of simplicity to handle over strange roads, smart but not ostentatious, with its famous weather-proof finish, and

aboundingly economical to run and maintain, the Popular Ford will pay handsome dividends of service and pleasure.

Its gear-change, steering, brakes and suspension confound the sceptical, while delighting the expert. And the Popular Ford Double-Entrance Saloon is still Britain's lowest-priced saloon with four doors, remember!

The Local Ford Dealer will be glad to furnish an exhaustive demonstration, and explain Ford Facilities, everywhere, Britain's least costly service-organisation.

Literature on Request • All Prices at Works • Dealers Everywhere

FORD MOTOR COMPANY LIMITED, DAGENHAM, ESSEX. LONDON SHOWROOMS: 88 REGENT STREET, W.1

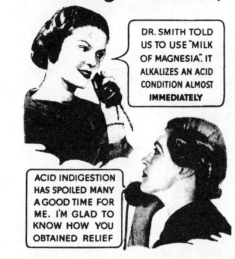
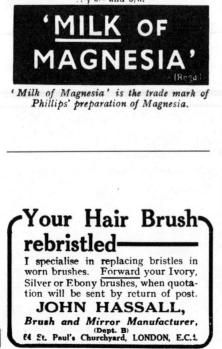
A SECOND QUEEN ELIZABETH
(*Continued on page* 170)

Cloth of Gold, while at the same moment Elizabeth's own great-grandfather, King James V of Scotland, was taking leave of his mother on the banks of the Tweed before her visit to England. As a child I always wanted to know what was happening in other countries at the same time as the monotonous procession of events in our own, but I never had the luck to have a teacher as advanced as Lord Harrington in his recognition that the best form of lessons is like play. For languages, Elizabeth and her brother Henry, Prince of Wales, wrote letters to each other in French and German and Latin, signing them fantastically with floss-silks entwined in sealing-wax, a gorgeously messy business over which they probably took more trouble than with the foreign words for their messages to each other, written while he was in his palace at Ham and she in hers at Kew.

They went on boating expeditions together, each visiting the other's river palace —it sounds more of a fairy tale than the Little House, but one with an unhappy ending, for Henry died of the river, swimming to Richmond one hot summer night.

It was not only in the schoolroom or on her Fairy Farm that Elizabeth was encouraged to be a child. The Court ceremonies of the time sound more like charades to our solemn modern ears. Elizabeth met her new governess, Lady Arabella Stuart, in a wood where a band of Arcadian shepherds and nymphs broke off their dance to lead her (together with stags whose horns were tipped with gold) up to the goddess Diana—her new governess. Lady Arabella indeed complained of always being expected " to play the child " at Court—probably she found dressing up in green gauze chilly in an English wood, or thought that dressing up at all was undignified. The Queen Mother had no such inhibitions; she insisted on blacking her face and neck and arms all over in order to dance as a negress in a Court masque. It was not only the children then

who were childlike, but the grown-ups too, in spite of the elderly courtiers who objected to so many children (Elizabeth had scores of little girl friends to come and visit her) scampering up and down the palace corridors " like little rabbit starters about their burrows."

But no one was allowed or wanted to quench Elizabeth's high spirits. They were indeed unquenchable. On her marriage at sixteen to the young Elector Palatine she was so much amused at everything—at the anti-masques of little boys dressed as monkeys, at the river pageants and the fireworks and the new play of *The Tempest* that Shakespeare had written for her, at her mother's chaff of her for becoming a German *Hausfrau*, at the German sausages of her husband's servants and the bad French of the interpreter—that she could not stop giggling all through the preliminary marriage service, and everybody caught the fever; they all giggled and giggled until the Archbishop had to close abruptly with a blessing.

Then she sailed away down the Thames in a glittering barge, and the shores were darkened all the way to the sea with the thousands of people come to cheer themselves hoarse at this last glimpse of their English princess, whose laughter and good looks and lovely courage had so bewitched them. They went on longing for her to be their queen, they went out in thousands to fight for her in foreign wars, then spoke of her as their " Queen of Hearts " and, still greater compliment, " a second Queen Elizabeth."

The bright promise of their hopes was belied. She did not return to England till the last year of her life as an elderly woman, to see once again the scenes where she had danced and sung and acted.

Whatever happened later in her stormy, disappointed, tragic life, no princess could have had a more dazzlingly happy and unhampered childhood, so much so that we have to wait three hundred years to find one that can even be compared with it.

(*Readers are reminded that Miss Irwin's last novel,* The Stranger Prince, *is all about the " Second Queen Elizabeth " of this article, and her son, Rupert of the Rhine.*)

OLYMPIA

DAILY MAIL IDEAL HOME EXHIBITION

OLYMPIA . . . W.

MARCH 30 – APRIL 24

10 A.M. TO 10 P.M.

ADMISSION

2/4 INC. TAX

After 6 p.m. 1/2

THE GOLDEN HALL OF HOMAGE—THE GARDENS OF THE LOVERS—THE ALL-IN HOME—ROOMS OF BRITISH MONARCHS—THE BRIDGE OF R.M.S. QUEEN MARY—THE CRYPT OF GLAMIS CASTLE—ROBERT BURNS' COTTAGE—BACKGROUNDS FOR BEAUTY—THE NAVY AT HOME—KITCHENS OF THE WORLD—PICCANINNY CIRCUS—THE CORONATION FASHION PAGEANT—ALFREDO AND HIS GIPSY ORCHESTRA—SYDNEY BAYNES' BROADCASTING ORCHESTRA

More than 600 original features and displays covering every aspect of home-making.

NEW SIX-FLOOR GARAGE FOR 1,200 CARS ADJOINS OLYMPIA

The 1930's
1937

Shopping
Service

Instructions for
ordering and Last-
minute Bargains
appear on page
222.

4. Smart frock for the house or
under a fur coat in wool and
angora, with large daisy pattern
of self material embroidered on
yoke at neckline. A row of
covered buttons runs from neck to
waist and is seen under the two
folds in the centre front. The
belt is of fine tucks, and the skirt
has a panel flare. Available in
navy, green and brown. Sizes
S.W. and W. Price 49s. 6d.
Post free U.K.

5. Unusual and pretty evening
coatee in black poult, patterned in
lacquered dancing flowers in every
imaginable colour so that it can be
worn with any coloured frock or
with black. Made with smart
collar revers and new sleeves.
Bust measurements 34, 36 and
38 ins. Price 52s. 6d. Post free
U.K.

1. Pretty house dress in wool, made with a coat-
frock effect. There are front panels of beige from the
high stand-up collar to the hem, and lady-bird studs
on the bow at neck. Available in brown, navy, wine
and green. Sizes S.W. and W. Price 18s. 11d.
Post free U.K.

2. Afternoon gown in a soft woollen material giving
warmth without weight. The style is becoming, with
broderie anglaise embroidery on the tucked revers,
which are crossed over. There is also tucking on the
skirt. The vest is in beige matt crêpe, and there are
buttons at one side of the bodice. Available in green,
wine, dark blue and black. Sizes 40, 42 and 44-in.
hips. Price 37s. 6d. Post free U.K.

3. In wool and angora mixture, this pretty frock,
made with a basque and giving the effect of a coat and
skirt, has a circular neck and contrasting wool scarf.
Self buttons open to the waist, and there is tucking on
the basque and at the neck. Available in heather,
blue and green. Sizes S.W. and W. Price 49s. 6d.
Post free U.K.

7-8

Editorial Notice

READERS of GOOD HOUSEKEEPING this month will find on the cover the words "incorporating Nash's—Pall Mall Magazine." They need have no fear that this incorporation will alter the special character of GOOD HOUSEKEEPING in the slightest degree. It will merely be strengthened by the addition of fiction by such famous writers as James Hilton, Alec Waugh, Francis Brett Young, Mazo de la Roche, and others whose work, in any case, we should have been proud to publish in GOOD HOUSEKEEPING ; and all the existing features will receive the same prominence as before.

Nash's Magazine has had an honourable career of more than twenty-five years. During that period it has published work by the world's most famous writers and artists. It is indeed true to say that many of Britain's greatest writers were introduced first through the pages of *Nash's Magazine*. Galsworthy, Locke, Hall Caine, Marie Corelli, Chesterton, Wells, Arnold Bennett, and Rudyard Kipling have all been regular contributors to the magazine, and coming to more recent years, we are proud to think that *Nash's* has published much of the work of Dr. A. J. Cronin, whose novel *The Citadel* has been the most outstanding book of the present publishing season.

But tradition, however great and honourable, has sometimes to bow before the financial exigencies of present-day life, and the continued heavy rises in the costs of production have made it advisable for us to amalgamate our two magazines. We felt it was better to adopt this course rather than lower our standard of production. GOOD HOUSEKEEPING readers will gain by the amalgamation, and we hope that women readers of *Nash's* who do not already take GOOD HOUSEKEEPING will find much to interest them in the present and subsequent issues.

And what about the men readers of *Nash's*, of whom there are a considerable number ? May we suggest to them that GOOD HOUSEKEEPING has already many male supporters, who are specially interested in the Housing articles; the features by St. John Ervine and Helena Normanton and in the financial article, which is written by the most reliable money expert of the day ?

The shilling that you spend for the combined magazine will be returned to you many times by the service you obtain through its regular features.

New lines for
the fuller figure

Special fashion houses, concentrating on the problem of dressing the fuller figure, have discovered that by clever cutting, a slim and becoming effect can be achieved by adapting the current fashions. On the extreme left, for instance, is a dark marocain dress, a misty blue shade, with a waistcoat front, smartly embroidered in gold thread and a dark maroon silk. The neckline is high, and up the front runs a dark red plastic Lightning fastener

The woollen two-piece is always useful, particularly for spanning the seasons between the soft coolness of autumn and the cold of winter. The dress in dark blue-green hopsack woollen carries on by itself when the graceful, three-quarter length jacket, trimmed with embroidery made from piping, is laid aside for a warmer coat. Also for the full figure

Below : a very sophisticated dress this, a heavy black marocain, embroidered with a large appliquéd motif design of black patent leather. The theory of shiny materials, as regards the fuller figure, is that they can be used exceedingly well when combined with a dull surface. The two together succeed in " breaking the width." All models from Netta

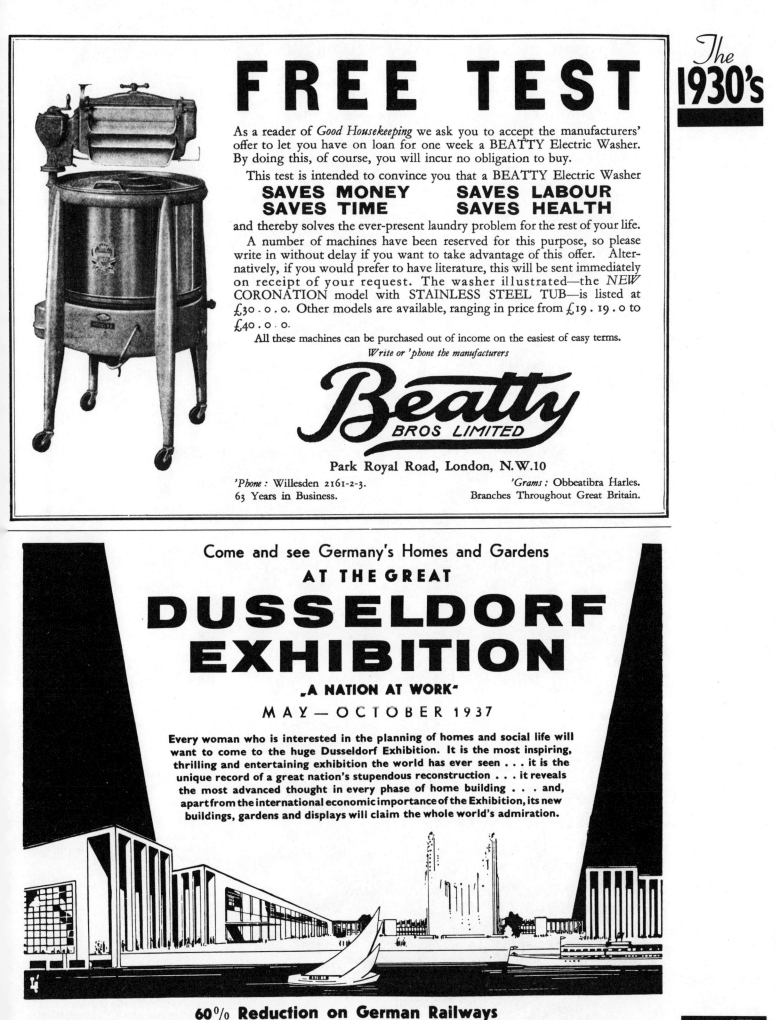

Charladies

by FRANK SWINNERTON

Illustrations by C. Clixby Watson

MOST of the charladies to be met with in novels and plays are comic characters. They talk ungrammatically and copiously about "me spasms," murders, child-birth, and such-like horrors. Some of them sport comic black eyes ("me ole man come 'ome drunk agin larce night"), suffer from palpitation of the heart or a love of something contained in little bottles, write letters which they formally sign "Mrs. Clapper" or "Mrs. Sniggs," and as a whole derive less from life than from that celebrated but imaginary creature Sairey Gamp.

On the stage they are often film-struck or anæmic, and make audiences laugh by creeping dismally from wing to wing, sniffing or wiping their noses with the back of their hands, leaving pails and mops to be tripped over, and uttering proverbial wisdom with ridiculous mispronunciations. They speak of their haricot veins, of their master's whereabouts having been sent to the wash, and, as if underclothes were so called from a habit of loitering, of their lingerie. They

are nearly always bedraggled creatures who look like last year's scarecrows.

This ridicule of a whole class does not mean that novelists and dramatists hate charladies, but only that the novelist and dramatist is never quite master of his own book or his own play. Just as—this is the oft-told tale which you have certainly heard—he must be funny when his heart is breaking, so, less sentimentally, when jokes and fancies and subtleties are mischievously thrusting themselves to the very tip of his pen, he has to repel them and subject himself, and others, to poignant distress because certain imaginary characters are in an irremediable pickle.

Now in real life the most appalling absurdities are visibly woven in with tragic events as a part of the same pattern; but in books and plays, by a paradox, the writer who reproduced this fantastic pattern would disgust his readers by apparently heartless flippancy, and he often has not the courage to take such a risk. Instead, unless in the modern fashion he despises everybody but himself and becomes a mere grammarian, he more and more strictly simplifies his pattern and deals with only one thing at a time.

He specialises. Like the shirt-makers, he has private designs. Black and white. Grim and gay. While ready to be woeful for whole scenes and chapters upon end, he tries to lighten the overwhelming solemnity of his art by a blessed thing called comic relief. And since all novelists and dramatists without genius, when not being grim about the bitter, tortured lives of the poor, are usually being mortally serious about middle-class people entangled by Fate, the only comic relief they can invoke depends less upon the invention of side-splitting situations than upon the manners and speech of recognisably comic characters. That is, upon characters who would not exist at all if they were not needed as foils to those more beautiful, sensitive, unhappy, harassed, and important than themselves.

It is the business of all such comic characters to say and do things so extravagant that the slowest-witted reader or theatre-goer can instantly see that they are *meant* to be funny. And nothing strikes a stupid person as more ridiculous than a way of life different from his own. A foreigner is always amusing; a yokel is a sure-fire laughter-maker; and in olden days domestic servants who aped their betters, carried and mixed private messages, used long wrong words, were vulgar, and generally made fools of themselves, were very popular indeed—almost inevitable. Now-

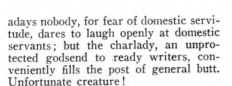

" Among the superior charladies there are some who clean with almost open derision, as if one's furniture were fit only for the local rummage sale "

adays nobody, for fear of domestic servitude, dares to laugh openly at domestic servants; but the charlady, an unprotected godsend to ready writers, conveniently fills the post of general butt. Unfortunate creature!

She has innumerable uses. She can appear in any room in any garb at any time of day. She can look at teatime as if she had just been sweeping the flues.

Her mop and pail can trip as easily before dinner as before lunch. She can make preposterous mistakes while waiting at table, or herself be mistaken for another guest by some purblind visitor and supplied with melancholy back-chat enough for any timely purpose. She can gossip, reveal secrets, pick letters from waste-paper baskets and read them aloud to herself.

A spirited defence by the famous novelist,
who finds these much-maligned
women neither comic nor cut to one pattern

Do you put Chickens into Soup?

—Heinz do!

Would you buy a plump young chicken just to make soup? Would you make soup with rich cream? Would you take new peas, choice asparagus, and expensive mushrooms and put them into soup? Perhaps—if you were a millionaire! But that's just what Heinz do. They have that old-fashioned notion that nothing but the best is good enough for their soups. That is why every one of Heinz 19 perfect soups tastes so good—so utterly fresh and delicious. The amazing thing is that they are so reasonable in price—but that's just because Heinz pass on to you all the economies that come from doing things in a big way.

CREAM SOUPS		MEAT SOUPS
TOMATO		SCOTCH BROTH
ASPARAGUS		BEEF BROTH
CELERY		VEGETABLE
GREEN PEA		JULIENNE
SPINACH		MULLIGATAWNY
MUSHROOM		KIDNEY
CHICKEN		OXTAIL
ONION		MOCK TURTLE
		CHICKEN NOODLE
		CHICKEN CONSOMMÉ
	5ᵈ & 7ᵈ	CLEAR CHICKEN BROTH WITH RICE

HEINZ
CREAM
OF
TOMATO
SOUP
H J HEINZ CO LTD
LONDON

HEINZ PERFECT SOUPS
COOKED AND SEALED IN 57 OUR LONDON KITCHENS

PORTRAIT OF A Lady

by RUTH MURRIN

SHE LIKES .... *To please the men.* So her aim is to look pretty. Her clothes, her coiffure, her make-up are chosen not to startle but to charm. She knows, however, that masculine eyes soon weary of monotony, so she never permits herself to settle lazily into a stereotyped pattern no matter how much *he* says he likes it.

.... *A fresh, rosy complexion.* She specialises in cleansers. She is pernickety about her soap, and she tries out creams and fresheners until she finds the ones that do the best cleansing job in the pleasantest way. When her skin is dry, she uses a rich night cream faithfully, for without it she knows her skin cannot have the depth and smoothness she admires.

.... *Rouge on her cheeks.* She is stingy with it, uses just enough to give her a beguiling blush, but that little makes her colourful hats more becoming. Besides, it gives her a cheerful air she likes, because her motto is " Brighten the corner where you are."

.... *Powder and make-up foundation with a rosy tinge.* They give her skin a healthy bloom, so she can wear a wider range of colours becomingly.

.... *Pastel make-up.* It harmonises with the soft greens, blues, lilac and pink she wears. It symbolises the new gentleness of her speech and manners. Her favourite lipstick is pinky-rose or light plum or dahlia. Occasionally, though, she changes to a dashing true red with belt, handbag or flower to match.

.... *Clear, candid eyes.* She knows all the tricks to make hers worth gazing into. She washes them with eye lotion, darkens her lashes, keeps her eyebrows neatly brushed into line and covers any scantiness in them with mascara. She is a master hand at applying eyeshadow delicately, and is experimenting now with a new one in stick form.

.... *A variety of hair styles.* In a twinkling she can change her personality by pinning her hair up or tying it with a ribbon, revealing her brow or concealing it with a fringe— and she adores change.

.... *Perfumes with character.* Not too sweet are the scents she chooses. Instead, she likes blends that are crisp and rather dry. On very hot days she uses no concentrated perfume at all, but cologne and toilet water in such fresh scents as rose geranium, clover and lotus lavender.

.... *A low-pitched, appealing voice.* She takes lessons, not because she wants to sing, but because she longs to have a voice as resonant and romantic as Claudette Colbert's.

SHE DOESN'T LIKE .... *Anything lugubrious.* She detests talk of diseases and disaster, and rigorously censors gloom out of her own conversation.

.... *A pudgy waistline.* She can't bear the idea of a tight corset, so she trims off the least thickening by diet and exercise. She rather likes the newly fashionable round-hipped figure, but plans to keep her circumference within strict limits.

.... *Her hair cut short.* She had it done and burst into tears when she first saw the result in the mirror. She felt shorn and lightheaded, and missed the handsome mane that she could do in a new way as often as she liked.

.... *Set, rigid curls and waves.* She hates that just-out-of-the-dryer look, and after a visit to the hairdresser she always brushes her hair until it is beautifully soft.

.... *Hair hanging down at the sides.* She used to think it framed her face more flatteringly than any other style, and can't explain her distaste for it now except to say that it makes her look " Blah."

.... *The Greta Garbo pallor.* There was a time when she thought that pale look of destiny was stunning, but now she prefers to personify a rosy future.

.... *A made-up look.* She especially dislikes beaded lashes or lashes that stick together. She thinks hectic spots of rouge and a heavily powdered face are provincial and not pretty. She rubs off all but a faint tone of rouge, brushes off excess powder and does her eyes with a light hand. But she is generous with lipstick.

.... *Broken nails.* Her hands are busy and capable, yet she likes them to look as if they never did a tap of work. So she drinks milk daily to get her quota of calcium. She lets her nails grow moderately long, but rounds them, and never files them down at the sides because that makes them too fragile. She oils them faithfully every night, and uses the gentlest methods in her manicure.

.... *Too many white touches.* White collar and white gloves she thinks look fresh and cool in summer, but gloves, collar, cuffs, belt and bag are too many white spots on a dark costume. They have a disorganising effect which spoils the ensemble.

.... *Too much jewellery.* A little is gay and charming, but she is wary of piling it on so that it looks cluttery.

Delicacy is the charm of her make-up. Her cheeks are flushed and her lips deepened with the pastel tone called sky-blue pink. Her powder is rosy.

SPRY CHANGED THE FAMILYS JEERS .. TO CHEERS

GOODBYE DARLING—ARE YOU SURE YOU'LL BE ABLE TO MANAGE TO COOK FOR THE FAMILY?

I'LL HAVE A GOOD TRY, DEAR, DON'T WORRY ABOUT ME

AFTER THIS EFFORT I'LL EAT IN TOWN TILL MOTHER GETS BACK

THIS PASTRY'S LIKE LEAD

AND THE FISH — UGH!

Mother hadn't been feeling well for some time, so we all decided she must go away for a long holiday. She was very anxious about leaving us to fend for ourselves, but I said that would be all right. Off she went, and I was left to do the cooking.

The first week I made an awful hash of it. The family complained about everything—and the way I'd worked to please them. I was weeping over the remains of a sad-looking pudding when dear old Mrs. S. came to my aid.

COME NOW, STOP CRYING USE THIS SPRY — IT'S A NEW FAT, ready-creamed AND GUARANTEED TO MAKE YOU A GOOD COOK

MM.. MM.. EVEN MOTHER COULDN'T MAKE CAKES AS LIGHT AS THIS

I listened wide-eyed while she told me how one can cook absolutely everything with Spry. It sounded marvellous — the idea of having only *one* fat for every *kind* of cooking. It's an all-vegetable fat, and it's ready-creamed to make mixing easier and quicker.

Of course I had to try it right away. I made some cakes; when I creamed Spry with the sugar it just seemed to mix at a touch. The cakes were ready for the oven in half the time; they turned out a lovely golden brown, and tasted delicious.

JOLLY FINE DINNER, SIS

MIND IF I BRING SOME FRIENDS TO DINNER TO-MORROW?

NOT A BIT, NOW I'VE GOT SPRY TO MAKE COOKING SO EASY

AN ALL-PURPOSE COOKING FAT! I CAN HARDLY BELIEVE IT

WELL, IT'S TRUE, MOTHER; AND DADDY SAYS HE NEVER GETS INDIGESTION SINCE HE'S BEEN EATING SPRY MEALS

1 lb. 10d
½ lb. 5½d

From then on all my cooking was a success —father even came home to lunch! Fish was delicious; all the goodness sealed in and the grease sealed out — and fried without a sign of smoke or splutter. Roasts done to a turn, puddings light as a feather, and pastry that really melted in one's mouth. With Spry I just couldn't go wrong.

When mother came back she was thrilled with my discovery. She said, " It looks so pure—and I do like the tin, it's so clean and handy." After cooking one meal with Spry mother was as enthusiastic as the rest of us! She said, " I thought I could cook. Why, I've never turned out such a perfect meal in my life ! "

The 'ready-creamed' FAT · ONE FAT for ALL cooking

DISAPPEARANCE
by Ogden Nash

Have you seen Linell?
She was three years old;
Her eyes were grey,
And her hair was gold.
She had three dolls,
They were all named Maggy;
She wore pyjamas,
And the knees were baggy.
She wore a dress,
It was sprinkled with flowers;
She left her blocks—
I can see the towers;
She wore a hat,
With an Indian feather,
And galoshes, in case
Of nasty weather;
And when she was sick,
She went to bed;
And when she was better
She got up instead.
Oh, where she is hiding
I can't tell.
Has anybody possibly
Seen Linell?

Has anybody seen
My absent child?
She seldom fussed,
And she often smiled.
She threw a penny
To the organ=grinder;
Wherever she is,
I want to find her.
I looked in the corner,
I looked on the stair;
I couldn't catch a glimpse of her
Anywhere.
Is she in the cupboard?
Or a bureau drawer?
I tried and I spied,
But I never saw her.
She had a bike
With a jingly bell.
Has anybody possibly
Seen Linell?
Did she tell the postman
She was his?
Why, who's that coming?
Here she is!

Miracle Workers
for a tired wardrobe

9566

These Pictorial Patterns are specially chosen and available from GOOD HOUSEKEEPING Pattern Dept., 28–30 Grosvenor Gardens, London, S.W.1. Prices include postage, but in the U.K. only. If readers abroad wish patterns to be sent to them by Airmail, they should send 6d. postage for each pattern.

Please note fabric prices cannot be guaranteed, as prices rise so rapidly : there may be difficulty with supplies, too.

(a)

(b)

(c)

9483-9584

9566. *Three grand blouses from this one pattern ! View (a) with the zipped front will look attractive, and be warm, for afternoon wear if you make it in a pastel-coloured angora and wool fabric. Make the monogrammed version (b) for wear with your evening skirt—with the addition of pearls or clips it looks really smart—while to go with slacks or skirt the crisp little shirt (c) is perfect, especially if you choose plain or patterned Viyella for it. Size 34 : view (a), 1½ yds. 54-in. ; view (b), 1¾ yds. 39-in. or 1⅜ yds. 54-in. ; view (c), 1⅝ yds. 35-in. Misses' and women's sizes, 30–40 bust. Price 1s.*

9483. *Good in all sizes, this blouse will prove particularly successful if you're a bit heavy-bosomed. Both the short version and the long-sleeved one (smaller sketch) are grand for " dress-up " wear, though in simpler materials they're adaptable for mornings too. Tootal's R700, a crease-resisting heavy crêpe with a " jersey " finish, approximately 4s. 6d. a yard, will make up attractively. In size 34 the long-sleeved blouse takes 2¼ yds. 35-in., and the short-sleeved one 1½ yds. In misses' and women's sizes, to fit 32–43-in. bust. Price 1s.*

9584. *The evening skirt shown with blouse 9483 is a special " easy to sew " pattern—it only takes 2⅞ yds. 54-in. material for the 28-in. waist size. Make it in a fine wool jersey or crêpe, it'll be warm but chic too. If you prefer a silky stuff, such as rayon poult made with Courtauld's tested quality rayon (approximately 3s. 3d.), you'll need about 4½ yds. The street-length version takes 2⅛ yds. 54-in. material. Sizes to fit 24–32 waist. Price 1s.*

9748. *The long-sleeved, high-necked, dinner or at-home dress that smart but practical women will wear this chilly winter ! Make it in Tootal's new cashmere-like crease-resisting rayon and wool mixture, " Lova " (approximately 3s. 6d.), which comes in lovely jewel-tones and a charming paisley print (size 34 takes 5½ yds.), or in Celanese semi-sheer (approximately 4s. 11d.), of which you need about 4¾ yds. Available in misses' and women's sizes, 30–40 bust. Price 2s.*

9517. *Treat yourself to a really luxurious housegown cut on easy-to-slip-into coat lines, with really full skirt. Size 34 takes 7⅛ yds. 35-in. velvet (Celanese dress velvet, approx. 4s. 11d., would be perfect). Sizes 30–36 bust. Price 1s. 6d.*

9586. *An odd jacket will prove more-than-ever a boon just now. This pattern gives day and evening versions. For the former, size 34 takes 1⅝ yds. 54-in. material ; for the latter you need 2⅛ yds. 39-in.—a soft lamé would be ideal to brighten up last year's dresses. Available in sizes 30–34 bust. Price 1s.*

9273. *About the house, for your war-work or for " shelter " wear, you can't beat a slacks suit. This one takes (size 34) 4¾ yds. 35-in. material (Marshall's Herringbone serge, made from Courtauld's " tested-quality " rayon, about 2s. 6d. would be economical). For separate slacks, 2⅝ yds. 36-in. material or 2¼ yds. 54-in. are required. In misses' and women's sizes, 32–40. Price 1s. 6d.*

The
1930's
1939

9586

9273

9748

9517

Paper patterns available for all these designs

Christmas
AS USUAL—

"IT is now Christmas and the cup must not pass without a Carroll; the Beasts, Fowle and Fish come to a general execution, and the Corne is ground to dust for the Bakehouse and the Pastry. . . . Now good cheer and welcome, and God be with you."

The spirit of Christmas in England was thus expressed over three hundred years ago, and to-day that essential spirit remains the same. Although this Christmas may not be quite so expansive as in the past, in most homes, especially where there are children, a great effort will be made to give an air of normality to this Christmas week-end, with entertaining more carefully organised so that it need not be extravagant.

It will indeed be a "home" Christmas, as perhaps never before in this generation, a time for the "Please stay the whole week-end" invitation, and entertainments so planned that rations, darkened roads and trains, and other restrictions need not spoil the fun of those who can be at home. And, of course, we are all hoping that our homes will be the lucky ones to have a husband, father or brother home on leave.

Outside amusements may be absent, but they can be replaced by the rolled-back carpet and dancing to wireless or gramophone. The annual visit to the theatre may have to be abandoned in favour of a programme of home ciné productions, and the treasure hunt give place to a bridge drive.

A word of warning to those who plan to augment their programme of private films—it is advisable to book the films you wish to hire in good time, otherwise you may have cause for disappointment. But whatever may be planned this year for the entertainment of guests and family, it will depend on the ingenuity and resourcefulness of the household to create its own amusements, rather than rely on outside attractions. Nothing amuses children—and not only children—more than "dressing up," and mothers should collect a trunk or chest full of anything that holds possibilities in this direction. Discarded evening-dresses, ribbons, scarves, laces, beads and baubles, pieces of fur and lengths of material—in fact the wider the choice the greater the fun, and lucky indeed is the home that can boast, beg or borrow some old military or other uniforms.

Decorating the home is always half the fun, and should not be neglected. Even if paper decorations are dispensed with, use can be made of natural sources of supply; oak apples and fir cones lacquered or touched with aluminium paint; little fir and spruce sprigs in tiny pots along the window-sills; or bare, shapely branches embedded in a bowl of earth and painted a ghostly white, whereon to hang glass icicles, blue birds and red luminous balls. Nothing is more effective and less costly than silvery-white Christmas trees or branches of fir or yew trees. The spraying on of white distemper quickly achieves a snow-like effect. This should, of course, be done out of doors or in a garage or shed. Those who do not possess a spray can obtain almost as professional a result by dipping an old brush into the distemper and sprinkling or brushing it on. Do not forget when spraying or sprinkling to turn the branches upside down as well, so that the underside is not all green.

A very good substitute for the real tree, and one that is easily obtained by those who live in the country, is a branch from a fir or spruce tree. It should be planted deep in a box or tub, and the soil well pressed down, so that it will support the weight of the loaded tree.

Even if for reasons of economy you are dissuaded from using festoons of electric fairy lights, do not be tempted to use candles—with the possible exception of one or two well out of the children's reach. A more generous use of tinsel and silver stars and crescents, and iridescent ornaments will make up for the loss of light.

Presents to Buy

For a stay-at-home Christmas, when times are difficult, the giving of presents should not be a haphazard affair, involving merely a stroll round the gift department of large stores, which is apt to result in the bearing away of an armful of pretty coat hangers, lavender sachets, purses, fancy brooches, etc., this armful then being scattered amongst friends and relations more or less indiscriminately.

This year the Christmas gifts should be essentially utilitarian, but not drab and uninspired.

Even with foodstuffs rationed we can enjoy the holiday season, provided we exercise a little forethought and ingenuity. For instance, in planning the decorations for the Christmas Cake we should remember to choose designs that will not use an undue amount of sugar, like the Mistletoe and the Christmas Tree ones illustrated. Home-made sweets and candies are delicious for home consumption or to give as presents. A large selection of recipes is given in the GOOD HOUSEKEEPING book of "Sweets and Candies"

number seven

beauty preparations by **Boots**

❛*Uniforms, yes, but not uniformity.   The girl in service kit preserves her own personality, her own charm.   True, life on service leaves less time for studied attention to beauty details.   So she turns, with even greater appreciation, to Number Seven Preparations, so easy to use, so economical, so natural in their effect.   Because fifty years of Boots' experience has gone to their perfecting they are effective to-day in the service of beauty.*❜

CLEANSING CREAM 3/-, 8/6.   LEMON CREAM 3/6.
COMPLEXION MILK 3/-,   SKIN TONIC 2/6, 4/6, 10/6.
ASTRINGENT LOTION 3/6.   SKIN FCOD 3/6, 10/6.
MUSCLE OIL 2/6.   HAND LOTION 2/6.   FOUNDATION
CREAM 3/-.   TISSUES 2/-.   FACE POWDER IN
NINE SHADES 3/- AND, OF COURSE, COSMETICS,
LIPSTICK, ROUGE CREAM, EYE SHADOW AND
EYELASH COSMETIQUE.   ALL IN MANY SHADES.

still
time
for
charm

ONCE again it is the season of holly berries, carols, panto- mimes and Christmas cards. It does not matter whether we are carefree young-youngs or young-olds with memories, we are sure to enjoy ourselves and be caught up by the festive spirit. For several weeks our thoughts will linger lovingly round the idea of a party. And why not? Every party is a success if you play amusing games, and here they are, waiting for you! You will find games to suit every type of party: the party with aunts, grandmas and the youngest grand- daughter; the party consisting of the oh-so-clevers; the party —well, after all, what does it matter? All your guests will enjoy themselves, if you choose the right types of games

Games for Parties

by MARY VIVIAN

Bed Time

ON a table at one end of the room put two boxes of matches, two candles in candlesticks and two old cushions to represent babies. The players divide into two equal teams at one end of the room. At the word "Go" the first players run to the table, light a candle, grab the baby and carry both back to their team, passing all the way round it and then pro- ceeding back to the table. Here they put down the baby, blow out the candle and run back to their places. The next player then follows on and does exactly the same. The first team back in its original place is the winner. Needless to say, any player whose candle blows out before it should must return to the table, light it up and begin the putting to bed all over again.

Stamp Hunters

BEFORE the party hide a number of used stamps of every value you can collect, including foreign ones. This collection will not be so difficult at Christmas-time, when parcels and cards are an everyday occurrence. No stamp should be absolutely covered by anything else, and if you have young visitors none should be placed too high to be reached easily.

All the guests are invited to make a collection of these stamps and allowed twenty minutes to find as many as possible. At the end of that time the numbers are counted up. Each halfpenny one counts one point, each penny one two, and so on. Foreign stamps count two if they are ordinary countries and three if they come from colonies, irrespective of value. The winner is the one with the highest number of points at the end of the game.

What's in the Shopping Basket?

THIS attractive competition needs only a little preparation beforehand. Before the party put a dozen things to eat (each one beginning with the same letter) into a shopping basket, each object being put into a paper, or better still, a material bag, and tied securely so that nothing may escape. Number each packet.

Each guest is provided with paper and pencil, and the shopping basket is brought in. In turn each object is taken out and passed round among the guests, who are allowed to feel it and then write down what they guess it to be. At the end of the time the correct list is read out, and the winner with the highest total is given a small prize.

The letter S is an excellent one to choose. Here are a dozen suggestions for this: (1) Sultanas, (2) Sugar, (3) Salts, (4) Salt, (5) Soda, (6) Sage, (7) Sago, (8) Semolina, (9) Suet, (10) Sausages, (11) Tin of Sar- dines, (12) Sherbet.

The players should, of course, be told in the first place the initial letter with which all the words begin.

I Resolve

EVERYONE is given paper and pencil and is asked to write the word RESOLUTION twice down the left-hand side of the paper, the letters arranged so that the R is on top, E below and so on. Everyone then begins to write down New Year resolutions, the first set being " I Resolve To Do So-and-so" and the second " I Resolve Not To Do So-and-so." In each case the first word of the resolution must begin with the given letter. Thus the first set might begin: " Read good books instead of rubbish," " En- tertain more friends," " Save as much money as possible," and so on to the end of the word. Every- one should be invited to make the resolutions as amusing as possible, as they are read out at the end of twenty minutes.

The Perfect Rose

THIS is a restful game which will be enjoyed by all. Into a bowl put a number of ordinary pins—sufficient for every guest to have one—and a packet of rose petals such as are sold for weddings.

The guests sit round in a circle, and while music is played the bowl is passed from hand to hand. As soon as the music stops whoever is holding the bowl takes out a pin, which repre- sents a stalk. The aim of every player is to collect in this way one pin and five rose-petals, but nobody may take more than one petal at a time. As soon as a player has a com- plete flower by putting the five petals on to the pin, he cries out " I have a rose," and is proclaimed the winner.

The music should be played as for Musical Chairs, but for very short periods of time only.

Cushion Circle

THIS is played on the lines of Musical Chairs, only cushions are used instead of chairs and placed in a circle, leaving spaces between them. There (Continued on page 189)

Games for Parties

(*Continued from page* 188)

should be one fewer cushions than there are guests.

While music plays the guests walk round, as soon as it stops each sits down on a cushion. This is never as easy as it sounds, for in the excitement of the moment one is apt to land on the floor. When this happens the player is out, just as much as if he had been without a cushion at all. One cushion is removed after each round, the winner being the one who succeeds in sitting accurately on the cushion in the final round.

Filling the Gap Backwards

ALL the players except one join hands in a circle and the one who is out goes round the outside of the circle touching any player he chooses on the shoulder. He then continues his way round the circle as before, but now backwards. The player who has been touched proceeds round the circle in the opposite direction to the other player, also travelling backwards. The player who first gets into the gap left by the first player remains there, while the other less fortunate one proceeds on his way in a forward direction until he chooses to touch another player.

Ham and Eggs

YOUR guests will thoroughly enjoy this novel competition. Before the party write out each of the following descriptions on a separate numbered card, putting them up in prominent positions round the room. When you are ready to play the game, provide all the guests with paper and pencil and invite them to guess the answers to the descriptions. Explain that the odd number solutions begin with HAM and the even with EG or EGG.

1. Ham that is an English county (Hampshire).
2. Egg that is a going out (Egress).
3. Ham that drives in nails (Hammer).
4. Egg that is conceited (Egotistic).
5. Ham we connect with the Pied Piper (Hamelin).
6. Egg that is a bird (Egret).
7. Ham which hangs from two trees in the garden (Hammock).
8. Egg that is sweet-briar (Eglantine).
9. Ham that is a famous Court (Hampton).
10. Egg that is a man's name (Egbert).
11. Ham that is found on the Continent (Hamburg).
12. Egg that is an old exclamation (Egad).
13. Ham that is a small village (Hamlet).
14. Egg that is self-conceit (Egotism).
15. Ham that is taken on picnics (Hamper).
16. Egg that is foolishly distinguished (Egregious).
17. Ham that was a friend of Nelson's (Lady Hamilton).
18. Egg that urges people on (Egg).
19. Ham that is found at the back of the knee (Hamstring).
20. Egg that is self (Ego).

Keep the answers handy, and award the prize to the player who first brings you a correctly completed list.

IMPORTANT

Owing to the paper restrictions during the War it will be necessary for readers to place a definite order in advance with their Newsagent or Bookstall for their regular monthly copy of GOOD HOUSEKEEPING

PRESENTS
at Christmas

Whatever the circumstances of our life may be, nothing can diminish the joy of receiving gifts

PERSONALLY, I am all in favour of Christmas presents. It seems to me that they are very nearly the only remaining signs that we dwellers in the modern nightmare love one another. And when I see the thought, the anxious care, and the charming kindness that take shape in the contents of a parcel, and the delight which those contents so generously give to the recipient, I believe the world is a good place and life is worth living.

These remarks may cause you to imagine me a greedy man, counting his own parcels with a miser's eye. Nothing could be more unjust. We are, as they say, three in family; and if you visited our home on Christmas morning before we were awake (if you wished to find us still asleep you would have to come very early), you would see one colossal pile of packages, one smaller but still respectable and appetising pile, and one little almost nothing lurking under the lee of these mightier assemblies. The last, the almost nothing, is mine.

Long after I have inspected the book, the ties, the box of Carlsbad plums which our cat, Daisy Buchanan, has bought with her pocket money (her gifts are always edible), the electric torch, the slippers, and the beautiful new pipe which is the best of all, I can hear the fevered tearing of brown paper, the impatient cries, the gasps, the ecstatic squeals of the youngest member of the family, and am called upon to admire the dazzling bounty of friends and well-wishers to both my companions.

I admire with rapture. Never have I seen toys and doilies, brooches, dolls, scarves, glass boxes, "knitwear" (horrible term!), china bowls, frocks, bed-jackets, and marron glacés as beautiful as they are nowadays. Never have friends been kinder or more generous. Never before have I realised as I do in these hate-filled times how the receipt of presents in flowing plenty can lift the heart and make it like a floating balloon of rapture. Indeed, indeed, I am in favour of them all.

Or no, not quite all. There are exceptions, few but vital.

I do not mean only the white elephants—Uncle James's great oil painting of a St. Bernard dog and a mackerel, or Aunt Matilda's monumental sideboard with the knobs and bow-legs—though these, obviously, present a problem. No, I mean smaller misconceptions and maladjustments of taste. Drums and trumpets, for example; concertinas, mouth-organs, and handbells. Anything that makes a noise quellable only by maddened protest. Anything that does not fit the people to whom it is given or the house in which it is expected to find a resting-place. All are exceptions.

There are others. I have a complete detestation of those implements of practical joking, the matches that will not strike, the sugar spoons that gather no sugar, the cigars that explode in the face. Certain ornaments and china dishes send one's spirits hurtling into darkness. There are indestructible monsters in wrought iron and hard wood and imitation brass, and worthless new books which have been sold cheap because at their original price nobody would have them, and mouldy Victorian relics suited only to small museums in country towns far from civilisation. There are bedspreads guaranteed to produce nightmares, and majolica bowls which need large, lofty rooms for their proper oblivion. There are —but I need not continue. What I hate, other men love. Already, in the moment of enumeration, my mood of Christmas benevolence is exasperated, and I cease to feel on behalf of the receivers that gratitude which the

donors, opulently giving, deserve. Nor do I wish to speak ill of any givers whatsoever. Far from it. Taken by and large, they are the salt of the earth.

They are the salt of the earth; and far too many of them suffer from those fixed ideas to which dwellers in our age seem especially prone. They pick up some notion, and ride it to death. Dogmatically, they say: "A present should always (or never) be useful." "A present should always be something the recipient would not dream of buying for himself (or herself)." "A present should be blue, for happiness." Or "A present should last for ever, as a perpetual reminder of my love."

They are quite wrong, of course. Presents are things you give to individuals, to please them. There is much more to be said, in some cases, for the gift of a piece of cheese than for a deplorable footstool that breaks one's shins or a modern painting that destroys one's eyesight. There is a whole encyclopædia to be written in favour of the dress which a diffident young woman would have liked to buy if she had felt sure—as the giver is sure—that it would suit her, or if she had been able to spend two pounds more than her outside limit. The one quality that makes a present perfect is its appropriateness. On a desert island a piece of string might be worth more than a pearl necklace in Mayfair.

by Frank Swinnerton

Illustrations by Clixby Watson

Editing Good Housekeeping
in Wales

★   ★

ABOUT half of this month's issue of GOOD HOUSEKEEPING has been assembled and passed for press from a perfectly peaceful and remote spot in Wales.   We are preparing layouts, reading proofs, sub-editing manuscripts and answering correspondence from trestle tables set up in all the window-recesses of a beautiful old Castle within sight and sound of the sea.   There is remarkably little to remind us of the turmoil of the outside world, and we are writing these words before the issue of Peace or War has been decided.   But to protect our staff, our business records, and our necessary equipment for bringing out the magazine, this move to the country was decided upon during the last days of August. Vans were loaded with manuscripts, drawings, photographs, stationery, and typewriters; the staff followed, and to-day we are working under singularly peaceful conditions.   The reaction from the last few days in London is so great that we seem to be living in another world entirely.   By the time these words are published we may be back in London again at our usual offices, but in the meantime the General Post Office officials have undertaken to forward all communications to us down here, from our London address.

EDITOR.

Good Housekeeping

SEPTEMBER 1931

ONE SHILLING NETT

Beginning GOOD-BYE, SUMMER
By Fanny Heaslip Lea

John Galsworthy ~ J.E. Buckrose ~ A. Duff Cooper, M.P.

Good Housekeeping

NOVEMBER 1931

ONE SHILLING NETT

SPECIAL FURNISHING SUPPLEMENT
EARLY XMAS PRESENTS FOR ABROAD

Good Housekeeping

DECEMBER 1931

1/- nett   Double Christmas Number
New Novel by O. Douglas
Virginia Woolf · Marguerite Steen · Coningsby Dawson

Good Housekeeping

FEBRUARY 1933
ONE SHILLING
NETT

MEMORIES OF A ROYAL FRIENDSHIP
by Clare Sheridan

Mariel Brady ~ L.A.G. Strong ~ Kathleen Norris
Mary Borden ~ William Armstrong ~ E.M. Delafield

Good Housekeeping

SEPTEMBER 1934   ONE SHILLING NETT

THE INSTITUTE'S TENTH BIRTHDAY
Beginning Mary Queen of Scots by Esmé Whittaker
Stella Gibbons · Marion Cran · Lorna Rea

Good Housekeeping

OCTOBER 1934   ONE SHILLING NETT

AUTUMN FURNISHING NUMBER

Rafael Sabatini · Marion Cran · Princess Troubetzkoy
Helena Normanton · St. John Ervine · Winifred Holtby
Ethel Smyth · Christine Jope-Slade · Lorna Rea

Good Housekeeping

MARCH 1935   ONE SHILLING NETT

SPRING CLEANING NUMBER

"I Wish I Had Been a Man" by
THE COUNTESS of OXFORD
AND ASQUITH

New Short Story Series
by
SHEILA KAYE-SMITH

Good Housekeeping

APRIL 1935   ONE SHILLING NETT

SPRING FASHIONS FOR EASTER

Sheila Kaye-Smith : Florence White : Dr. Maude Royden
Victoria Sackville-West : Countess of Oxford and Asquith

Good Housekeeping

In This Issue

Millicent
Duchess of Sutherland

F. Brett Young

The Countess of
Oxford and Asquith

Sheila Kaye-Smith

Kathleen Wallace

1/-

MAY 1935

SPECIAL JUBILEE NUMBER